The Pew and the Picket Line

THE WORKING CLASS IN AMERICAN HISTORY

Editorial Advisors
James R. Barrett, Julie Greene, William P. Jones,
Alice Kessler-Harris, and Nelson Lichtenstein

A list of books in the series appears at the end of this book.

The Pew and the Picket Line

Christianity and the American Working Class

Edited by
**CHRISTOPHER D. CANTWELL,
HEATH W. CARTER, AND
JANINE GIORDANO DRAKE**

UNIVERSITY OF ILLINOIS PRESS
Urbana, Chicago, and Springfield

Library of Congress Cataloging-in-Publication Data
Names: Cantwell, Christopher D., 1980– editor.
Title: The pew and the picket line: Christianity and the American
    working class / edited by Christopher D. Cantwell, Heath W.
    Carter, and Janine Giordano Drake.
Description: Urbana, Chicago : University of Illinois Press, 2016.
Series: The working class in American history
Includes bibliographical references and index.
Identifiers: LCCN 2015029049
ISBN 9780252081484 (pbk. : alk. paper)
ISBN 9780252098178 (ebook)
ISBN 9780252039997 (cloth : alk. paper)
Subjects: LCSH: United States—Church history. | Working
    class—Religious life. | Labor—Religious aspects—
    Christianity. | Work—Religious aspects—Christianity.
Classification: LCC BR517 .P49 2016 | DDC 277.3/08208623—dc23
    LC record available at http://lccn.loc.gov/2015029049

Contents

PART II: CHRISTIANIZING CAPITALISM

A Spiritual Turn?

It is a real delight to see the development of this volume and of the work of the young historians who make up the contributors. The range of their topics is exciting and the ease with which they blend working-class and religious history would have been unthinkable a generation ago, or a little bit longer in my own case. Equally important, the chapters in this volume explore a wide range of Christian expressions among varied segments of the working class without reducing the essence of their spirituality to simple dichotomies that either assist or impede class formation. This is a giant step forward. The excellent introduction to the volume by Chris, Heath, and Janine makes it unnecessary to rehash the reasons that most labor historians paid so little attention to Christian faith. Meanwhile, scholars of American Christianity were not doing much better at paying attention to the part that faith played in the consciousness and ideology of social movements led by working people, nor did they recognize the contributions of working people to religious transformations. The combination of these lacunae in both fields of historical inquiry perhaps accounts for the long life of Herbert Gutman's 1966 article as well as the passages on Methodism and dissenting religion in E. P. Thompson's *The Making of the English Working Class* that scholars, myself included, picked through for helpful ideas.[1]

This volume comes at just the right time. During the past decade, there has been a flood of exciting new work on the connections linking particular aspects of Christianity to the flourishing of modern capitalism and the rise of the New Right. Darren Dochuk, Bethany Moreton, Darren Grem, Kevin Kruse, and the late Sarah Hammond have unearthed the evangelical underpinnings of the free-enterprise ideology that spawned not only Billy Graham and Jerry Falwell, but also Reaganism and the Wal-Martization of the economy.[2] However, although these new historians of capitalism have demonstrated how business-backed evangelicals seized the pulpits of many Christian churches, their work leaves out the pews. Missing in this scholarship are the workers who ostensibly internalized Christian free enterprise and became the foot soldiers for the transformation of America's political economy. In other words, we now know about free-enterprise preachers and evangelically inspired entrepreneurs, but political scientists Byron Shafer and Richard Johnston alert us that we should be wary of assuming that the working people who attended the conservative churches and tuned in the broadcasts of *The PTL Club* uncritically followed the political directives of the Christian Right.[3]

The essays in this volume demonstrate the need to get under the surface of religious practices and sermons; only then can we understand how working people interpreted the messages they heard and how those interpretations affected their actions. One interesting example comes in the form of a memoir from Wilt Browning that I came across in my research. Growing up as the child of "lintheads" in Easley, South Carolina, Browning recalled the tense months in the late 1940s when his father and mother, a loom fixer and a spinner at the Easley Mill, talked quietly over Saturday and Sunday meals about the arrival of union organizers and "the pressure they felt to resist" their enticements. It was still a time when the majority of local disputes, even ones as minor as young men hitting a baseball onto another man's porch, might be settled by the superintendent of the cotton mill. The arrival of the union thus represented a considerable challenge to the world that mill management had carefully constructed. But it was also a "boom time" for local churches, which received new pews for the sanctuaries, new pianos, or fresh coatings of tar and gravel for the parking lot.

On a Sunday shortly before the looming union representation election, the mill superintendent attended the services of Wilt Browning's church to accept the gratitude of the congregation on behalf of the mill owners who lived elsewhere. The sermon that day at the Easley Church of God began with the Book of Revelation, chapter 14, which deals with worshipping the beast and receiving his mark. The preacher concluded by reading the nineteenth and twentieth verses of Revelation 19:

> And I saw the beast, and the kings of the earth, and their armies, gathered together to make war against Him who sat on the horse and against His army.

And the beast was taken, and with him the false prophet that wrought miracles before him, with which he deceived them that had received the mark of the beast, and them that worshipped his image. These both were cast alive into the lake of fire burning with brimstone.

With those words, the preacher closed the Bible with a thump and claimed that the "mark of the beast would most certainly be conferred first upon union members, people who through greed sought more than their fair share from their employers."

The impact on Browning was unnerving. After that sermon, the young boy feared that some people sitting in the nearby pews might show up for work in a few days with a hideous mark on their foreheads or in the palms of their hands. Fortunately for the youngster, the union lost by a one-sided margin. Thus, perhaps just a few of his neighbors had been "lost to the beast." Nearly forty years later, Browning recalled the incident with his mother. He learned that her foreman had actually asked her to be an informer against union sympathizers. Instead, despite the fear of the superintendent and the "fire and brimstone sermon," Browning's mother quietly decided to vote for the union. "Certainly, I heard the sermon," she told her son, "but I was and still am fully capable of thinking for myself and making my own decisions."[4] A "proud linthead," Browning called her. This tale speaks volumes about how little the words of ministers and church publications can tell us about working-class Christianity. After all, the sufferance of following one's own conscience about the meaning of the scriptures was the essence of popular evangelicalism in the postwar South.

The contributions to this volume cannot claim to predict how working people in other situations would navigate between the personal and political aspects of their spirituality. The mix of determining factors typically derives from localized conditions and individual inclinations. The impact of the sacred on the politics of working people may follow patterns, but it is rarely certain. For instance, much of my reading on twentieth-century Protestantism suggests that working people should have absorbed the dire prophecies on the dangers of a powerful state and of creeping socialism. These were signs of the end times, according to the new evangelicals who were generously funded by antiliberal entrepreneurs. Meanwhile, labor historians who have listened to the voices of southern white workers emphasize something quite different. They note that many devout Christian workers loved Franklin Delano Roosevelt and the New Deal. What are we to make of such incongruities? We have yet to adequately understand how evangelical workers reconciled these divergent feelings and came to grips with their admiration for a president whom radio preachers warned was the Antichrist?[5] Meanwhile, we are only beginning to discover the similar inconsistencies that characterized the outlooks of northern Catholics, black Baptists, or Latino Pentecostals. The maze between the pew and the picket line starts to look incredibly intricate.

Of course, the popular Christianity of the working classes is not only about such stark choices. We do an injustice to the sacred if we see it solely in such functional terms. It is, instead, about "the ways in which individuals take religious belief, interpret it in practical terms, and put it to work to do something that will give order and meaning to their lives," according to religious historian Charles H. Lippy. For Lippy, Americans have long operated within both sacred and secular realms, each with their own measure of power. For those without power in the material world, access to sacred power can nevertheless give "one a sense of control, of being able to chart one's own destiny. That control becomes the key to experiencing happiness and to seeing life as endowed with meaning."[6] Such notions of power and meaning lead us far away from the old idea of false consciousness that reflected how working-class historians at one time talked about religion.

Consequently, I am honored to say a few words in advance of this collection of outstanding young scholars who are introducing a new generation to working-class popular Christianity. I suspect that readers interested in religious history will rediscover the importance of considering social class and its dynamics when writing about the sacred. Likewise, I am certain that scholars of social class will see that religious symbols, rituals, values, and beliefs are essential to the ways that working people make sense of the world and their experiences in it. I am hopeful that this volume will be just the beginning of a renaissance in historical writing that includes the pew and the picket line and that murky area in between.

Ken Fones-Wolf

Notes

1. Herbert G. Gutman, "Protestantism and the American Labor Movement: The Christian Spirit in the Gilded Age," *American Historical Review* 72, no. 1 (1966): 74–101; E. P. Thompson, *The Making of the English Working Class* (New York: Vintage Books, 1966 [c. 1963]). For a critique of a similar emphasis in Gutman's essay, see Nick Salvatore, "Herbert Gutman's Narrative of the American Working Class: A Reevaluation," *International Journal of Politics* 12, no. 1 (1998): 62–66. The exception, of course, was the work that focused on the history of African Americans in slavery and freedom. One of the real mysteries in scholarship on class and faith revolves

around the segregation of two subsets of scholarship—"black religion" from religion and slaves and freedpeople from the working class.

2. Darren Dochuk, *From Bible Belt to Sunbelt: Plain-Folk Religion, Grassroots Politics, and the Rise of Evangelical Conservatism* (New York: Norton, 2011); Bethany Moreton, *To Serve God and Wal-Mart: The Making of Christian Free Enterprise* (Cambridge, MA: Harvard University Press, 2009); Darren E. Grem, *Corporate Revivals: A Business History of Born-Again America* (New York: Oxford University Press, forthcoming); Kevin Kruse, "Beyond the Southern Cross: The National Origins of the Religious Right," in *The Myth of Southern Exceptionalism*, ed. Matthew D. Lassiter and Joseph Crespino (New York: Oxford University Press, 2009), 286–307; and Sarah Ruth Hammond, "'God's Business Men': Entrepreneurial Evangelicals in Depression and War" (PhD diss., Yale University, 2010).

3. See, for example, Byron E. Shafer and Richard Johnston, *The End of Southern Exceptionalism: Class, Race, and Partisan Change in the Postwar South* (Cambridge, MA: Harvard University Press, 2006), 29–36. They argue that poorer whites were far less likely (from 10 to 26 percent, depending upon the decade) to vote Republican than were middle-class and wealthier whites.

4. Wilt Browning, *Linthead: Growing Up in a Carolina Cotton Mill Village* (Asheboro, NC: Down Home Press, 1990), 11–22.

5. In particular, I am thinking of the oral histories recorded as part of the Piedmont industrialization project of the Southern Oral History Program at the University of North Carolina. See also Matthew Avery Sutton, "Was FDR the Antichrist? The Birth of Fundamentalist Antiliberalism in a Global Age," *Journal of American History* 98, no. 4 (March 2012): 1052–74.

6. Charles H. Lippy, *Being Religious, American Style: A History of Popular Religiosity in the United States* (Westport, CT: Praeger, 1994), 2–3, 10.

Acknowledgments

In one sense, this volume emerged from a 2012 panel on "Class and the Transformation of American Protestantism," which we three editors put together for an American Society of Church History annual meeting. For their careful and formative commentary at this gathering we thank Joe Creech and Jacob Dorn, who acted as chair and commentator, respectively.

Yet in another sense, the focus of this collection emerged much earlier—out of a series of ongoing conversations we have had with mentors and colleagues. For this we are grateful to Jim Barrett, Mark Noll, Nick Salvatore, and Andrea Turpin, who introduced us not only to our topics, but also to each other. Ed Blum, Dave Burns, Suellen Hoy, Thomas Rzeznik, and the contributors to this volume also became important interlocutors in these conversations at several points. Leon Fink and Paul Harvey proved particularly vital and deserve special mention. Each read an early draft of our introduction and offered substantive feedback. We are grateful for their comments, and, more importantly, for their support and friendship. And no collection on this topic would be complete without some reference to Ken Fones-Wolf. He and his partner Elizabeth raised many of the questions we ask here much earlier. This alone is worthy of an acknowledgment. But when Ken found out about our own inquiries into this field, he took an interest, welcomed critiques of his earlier work, and repeatedly asked to hear more about our projects. His model of humility and scholarly collaboration both encouraged and inspired us. We are honored to have him open this volume.

To our contributors, we appreciate not only their willingness to author essays for this collection, but also their ability to challenge our presumptions about the book's scope and argument. We are also grateful for their good spirits and patience as we slogged through summer and winter deadlines, and especially when the critiques they received were threefold.

Laurie Matheson and her colleagues at the University of Illinois Press have supported the project from the start. We are grateful for their interest and thankful for their ongoing assistance.

Finally, between the time this book was conceived and its publication, all the editors went through a number of major life changes. In the span of about a year, each of us accepted at least one job, moved across at least one state line, and had at least one child. We appreciate the patience and support from one another that all these changes required. Cowriting a book is not easy—even with the wonders of Google Hangout. Yet, the training that cowriting provided is probably one of the best apprenticeships in historical scholarship we have had. We consider ourselves truly privileged for the opportunity to assemble and edit this volume.

The Pew and the Picket Line

Between the Pew and the Picket Line

CHRISTOPHER D. CANTWELL, HEATH W. CARTER,

AND JANINE GIORDANO DRAKE

Fully a half century has passed since the *American Historical Review* published Herbert Gutman's groundbreaking article, "Protestantism and the American Labor Movement: The Christian Spirit in the Gilded Age." In it Gutman argued that the standard interpretation—that with industrialization came waning working-class religiosity—had no basis in history. For him, the prominence of local churches in many working-class communities and the prevalence of Christian idioms in the language of labor leaders readily underscored religion's centrality to many working people. Yet Gutman found that few scholars had paid such realities any mind. Historians, he argued, had focused too much on either "academic economics" or the writings of "leading clergymen" and presumed that "wage earners, busy laboring, found little time to ponder existential questions." Such wrong-headed assumptions had rendered invisible the religious lives of late nineteenth-century American workers. Only by shifting the focus to "the varieties of working-class community life," Gutman argued, could historians begin to comprehend working people's lived experience, let alone the impact their faith had upon America's shift "to an industrial social order."[1]

In retrospect, Gutman's essay was well ahead of its time. His suggestion that working people's religious worlds have, in profound and complicated ways, shaped the larger stories of both American Christianity and American capitalism rings true. Yet for generations before him, and even in the generations that followed, the histories that scholars produced did not reflect this central insight. With some notable exceptions, labor and religious historians long pursued distinct lines of inquiry. Pioneering scholars of the "old" labor history focused almost single-mindedly on trade unions and industrial relations in their work, while even the "new" labor historians, with their heightened interest in communities, did not often stop to peer through the stained-glass windows of the churches that saturated working-class neighborhoods. Meanwhile, for generations the field of religious history revolved around the stories of Protestant ecclesiastical institutions and the clergy that led them. Working people's contributions to the life of American Christianity were often nowhere to be found.

Recently, however, scholars have begun to see that attention to working-class faith yields rich insight into the interrelated histories of Christianity and industrial capitalism in America. In the past decade the fields of working-class history and religious history have unexpectedly converged in a new generation of scholars whose work is situated in those moments where Christianity, wage labor, and industrial capitalism have intersected. Perhaps unsurprisingly, those moments have been legion. Exploring everything from workplace Bible studies to the coalitions between Christian assemblies and trade associations, this burgeoning subfield is inflecting and reframing venerable debates. It turns out, for example, that the intricacies of working people's beliefs and practices are more closely related to rates of unionization than we have previously thought. It turns out, furthermore, that it was often workers, rather than ministers, who provided the impetus for major ecclesiastical and theological innovations.[2]

This book incorporates many of the leading scholars and ideas in this emerging body of work. Gathering a number of deeply researched local histories, we suggest that although many Americans worshipped in churches and worked on shop floors, most lived in the space between the pew and the picket line. In this space, we find Pentecostal miners who had faith in prosperity and sought miracles at the mine. We find automobile workers and sympathetic ministers evangelizing one another on the shop floor. We find black sharecroppers and white Protestant liberals who saw the creation of a credit union as an investment in a more cooperative capitalism. This volume covers a vast chronological and geographic scope, and draws upon the diverse experiences of the American workforce—urban and rural, male and female, black, white, and Latino. Yet it is more than just a collection of disparate stories. Together, these essays underscore that the space between the pew and the picket line is not only where most Americans have lived, but where the contours of both American Christianity and American capitalism have been shaped and reshaped.

While American workers have identified with a variety of religious traditions, we have opted to focus especially on Christianity in this collection.

This decision stems from a number of factors, the first being that in industrial America, Christianity enjoyed a unique political, economic, and cultural purchase. This power derived in part from simple demographics. Christians have always comprised a majority of the United States' population and continue, even today, to account for just over 70 percent of those who identify a religious affiliation.[3] But Christianity's cultural import went beyond sheer numbers. To be sure, America's fractious Christian majority did not often agree about the meaning of faith for industrial modernity, a fact that is hardly surprising given the ways that class has shaped the experiences of American Christians.[4] Yet the stories and symbols that Christians shared were long at the heart of contests over the nation's political economy.[5] From nineteenth-century debates over Sunday closings to twentieth-first-century fights over the religious rights of corporations, America's industrial history has often been a history of contact and collision between Christianity and capitalism. Finally, we chose to focus on Christianity because we could not adequately capture its disproportionate influence while also doing justice to the vital contributions Jewish, Muslim, Hindu, Buddhist, and freethinking workers have made to American labor history—and the industrial era certainly saw all of them and more.[6]

In its focus on Christianity, this book enters into a conversation that began well before Gutman. Scholars and social theorists of all stripes have interrogated Christianity's relationship to industrial capitalism since the first factories opened their gates. These earliest scholars of labor and religion produced theories and frameworks that required the complete exclusion of working people's religious lives. By the time these fields professionalized at the turn of the twentieth century, this early omission had evolved into a discernible pattern of obfuscation. The remainder of this introduction traces this genealogy of absence. Set in this context, the essays that follow can be seen for what they are: intentional forays into spaces scholars have long circumnavigated. We conclude by previewing the contents of this collection, casting the vital questions they raise as pressing invitations for scholars to map more fully the terrains that lie between the pew and the picket line.

*   *   *

Working-class faith was written out of the story early. If one wanted to pinpoint an exact year, 1844 would be a standout choice. That year, a twenty-six-year-old Karl Marx published his widely known "Contribution to the Critique of Hegel's Philosophy of Right." Building on the avant-garde theology of his contemporary, Ludwig von Feuerbach, who had insisted that the Christian idea of God was deeply anthropomorphic, Marx elaborated an account of religion as a man-made illusion standing in the way of "real happiness." He believed faith was an effective salve for the woes of downtrodden workers—in fact, too effective. In his now-notorious turn of phrase, he said, "Religion is the sigh of the oppressed creature, the sentiment of a heartless world, and the soul of soulless conditions. It is the opium of the people."[7] Of course, for Marx, religion was more than just an opiate. It was an ideological tool that the bourgeoisie wielded to pernicious effect. Although Marx was deeply interested at a theoretical level in working-class faith, the religious experiences of actual workers remained completely obscure in his writings. So long as workers took solace in the compensatory promises of the afterlife, the revolution would remain permanently on hold.

The early 1840s proved momentous for other reasons as well. As Marx was first drafting his "Critique" in 1842, a Presbyterian divine on the other side of the Atlantic by the name of Robert Baird was publishing his own account of religion's social and political importance. The book's title, *Religion in America*, spoke to the ambitious scope of this first survey of American religious life. Yet his subtitle—*An Account of the Origin, Progress, Relation to the State, and Present Conditions of the Evangelical Churches in the United States, with Notices of the Unevangelical Denominations*—exposed the author's prejudices. Baird's tome inaugurated a scholarly tradition that persistently privileged Christianity's "evangelical" branches. Though nebulously defined, this category had clear boundaries. It always included Methodists, Presbyterians, and Baptists, as well as the many smaller denominations that rose upon the tide of nineteenth-century revivalism. Meanwhile, Unitarians, Mormons, Catholics, and most others were cast into outer (narrative) darkness as "unevangelical," "countervailing," and the like. But even when Baird did consider Christian communities beyond the Protestant mainstream, working people remained outside his view. *Religion in America* was also trendsetting in its focus on white, male clerics and the institutions they served. In Baird's estimation, ministers and denominational leaders were the ones with the power to effect change, not to mention the most accurate bellwethers of Christian belief, practice, and opinion. As such, they were the only figures of any consequence in American religious life. It may never have occurred to him that working people were important players in the unfolding drama of American religious history; if so, he was far from alone.[8]

The debates that Marx and Baird initiated developed in separate spheres and along separate tracks throughout the last half of the nineteenth century. Marx's material focus would go on to inform Western radicalism as well as the more moderate social sciences. His comrades in the International

Workingmen's Association and eventual Communist parties would follow him in claiming that the landholdings of ecclesiastical institutions and the self-interest of state-supported clergy were like priestly heels upon the throats of workingmen.[9] And while many social theorists would dispute Marx's reading of religion as an upper-class conspiracy, few sociologists and political scientists departed from his assumption that Christianity was fundamentally a tool of bourgeois advancement and consolidation. Indeed, the view had become so axiomatic that by the early twentieth century Max Weber could write almost nonchalantly that "there were no 'proletarian instincts' in the doctrine and teaching of Jesus."[10]

Baird, for his part, set the standard for the writing of American religious history. His immediate intellectual descendants were, like him, ministers established in Protestant seminaries who thus worked also as church historians. Although their theological commitments and denominational affiliations varied, their interpretations of American religious history were cut from a similar cloth. In his 1888 survey, Daniel Dorchester reported on the "nearly thirteen million emigrants infused into our population since 1845," though nary a one of these ended up as a central character in his story. Leonard Woolsey Bacon's 1897 study similarly omitted the nation's wage earners, though he was certainly aware of them. Anxious that an increasing proportion of the Catholic Church's ranks was drawn from this "illiterate and unskilled laboring class," Bacon saw America's growing working classes as one of the many "disadvantages" the Church faced.[11] As much as working people troubled historians of American Christianity, they were not integral to its history.

As the academic study of both American labor and American religion professionalized in the early twentieth century, it did so in this atmosphere of heightened anxieties. The economists, sociologists, and political scientists who first examined the history of industrial relations, for example, were motivated in part by the sustained industrial violence in their midst. Strikes, boycotts, uprisings, and riots had come to seem almost routine, and many of these early scholars hoped their work would provide a corrective. They understood themselves primarily as Progressive reformers, committed to bringing order and justice to the industrial world.[12] Yet even as academics such as John R. Commons and Richard T. Ely sympathized with and participated in the Social Gospel movement, they remained fully aware of Marx's dictum that organized religion was not the worker's friend. Instead, they saw their scholarship as a path to a more secular salvation in the gritty world of mandatory arbitration and industrial regulation. The same would be true for their allies in the field of history. The first generation of scholars in the "old" labor history, with its quest to uncover those institutions that could yield a broad solidarity among America's workers, never considered Christianity's role as a force shaping the American labor movement, let alone industrial capitalism. For scholars like Selig Perlman, Philip Taft, Philip Foner, and Norman Ware, the focus remained upon questions of organizing tactics, union structure, and action at the point of production.[13]

Meanwhile, the loose cohort of seminarians and social scientists who first approached "religion" as a category of analysis did so increasingly with the assumption that their subject was in crisis. The mass migration of southern and eastern European Catholics and Jews that Bacon had noted was continuing unabated, even as a startling number of lay Protestants were abandoning established denominations for upstart Holiness, Pentecostal, and Fundamentalist associations. The nation's religious landscape was once more being transformed—and in worrisome ways, or so it seemed to the white, native-born, liberal Protestant scholars who comprised the first generation of American religious studies. The supernatural beliefs and ecstatic devotional practices of these new religious communities represented a frightening return of the premodern in a self-consciously scientific age. That many of these religious "others" were often found in the crowds of labor demonstrations only underscored their threat to the Protestant civility that supposedly anchored America's vital institutions.[14] Much like their colleagues in economics and history, these early scholars of religion saw their scholarship as a necessary corrective. In his 1905 survey of the American religious landscape, sociologist and future U.S. representative Frederick Morgan Davenport wrote that all these groups exhibit "primitive traits which need elimination or modification in the interest of religious and social progress."[15]

The notion of the "primitive" is central here, for it became one of the most dominant tropes in the study of working people's religious lives throughout much of the twentieth century. Despite the remarkable diversity of working-class Christian communities, many scholars claimed that immigrant Catholics; black and white evangelicals, Fundamentalists, and Pentecostals; and countless religious others all shared a number of peculiar characteristics that stemmed from their low social standing. Purportedly among these were a widespread belief in miracles, a fatalistic obsession with the world's end, the worship of supernatural entities, and the literal reading of sacred texts. Each embodied, and then reinforced, working people's dislocation from the economic and social advancements of the modern age. Lacking economic stability, workers sought spiritual certainty; deprived of political authority, they sought religious efficacy. By mid-century, this loose association of presumptions had coalesced into what scholars called "deprivation theory," a school of thought that viewed religion as a compensatory vehicle of self-worth for those who failed to attain social advancement via "real" social action in labor unions or democratic politics. This view inflected scholarship throughout the academy for much of the twentieth century. It made unintended allies out of social scientists and seminarians, lurking behind everything from Richard Hofstadter's famed "paranoid style" to Robert Mapes Anderson's widely read portrayal of Pentecostalism as the "visions of the disinherited." Although these scholars disagreed on much, few seemed to dispute Anderson's assessment that working people's spiritual devotions "deflected social protest from effective expression, and channeled it into the harmless backwaters of religious ideology."[16]

Of course, there were alternative views. While negative assessments of working-class religious life predominated, a number of scholars began to suggest that religious beliefs and institutions were in fact sites of class conflict. In his 1929 classic *The Social Sources of Denominationalism*, theologian H. Richard Niebuhr saw poor people's faith not as a psychosocial capitulation to material conditions, but as a kind of ecclesiastical insurgency against them. Turning to the history of European Christianity, Niebuhr interpreted the rise of groups like the Mennonites, Methodists, and Quakers—all of which had plebeian origins—as "revolutions of the disinherited." The moral austerity, supernatural spirituality, and radical apocalypticism of these religious "sects," as Niebuhr enduringly labeled all such movements, were more than just anguish. They were also intentional and apt critiques of Europe's established churches. Indeed, in Niebuhr's view, "the rise of new sects to champion the uncompromising ethics of Jesus and 'to preach the gospel to the poor' has again and again been the effective means of recalling Christendom to its mission."[17]

Niebuhr's central insight—that ordinary people had deeply shaped the larger history of Christianity—anticipated later characterizations of religious life as a resource for working-class protest. Yet it took time for other scholars to recognize this possibility. Sociologists, for example, would go on to elaborate an intricate theory of "sect-church" development in which proletarian uprisings inevitably evolved back toward the bourgeois mean. When rooted in tightly honed community studies like Robert and Helen Lynd's classic *Middletown* or Liston Pope's analysis of a mill town's "class churches" *Millhands and Preachers*, this framework could yield remarkable stories of the class tensions that lay at the heart of American religious history. Yet it was just as often codified into wooden and deterministic models that presumed established religious institutions were always the domain of the middle class.[18] This same assumption informed histories of American Christianity well into the second half of the twentieth century, as a number of influential scholars came to see religion as a form of social control. This perspective received its clearest distillation in Paul Boyer's 1978 classic *Urban Masses and Moral Order*. But Boyer's footnotes reveal the much-wider prevalence of this social control thesis. Scholars read everything from urban evangelism, to the Social Gospel, to other forms of Christian benevolence, as manifestations of some vague Protestant undertaking to circumscribe the social lives and political expressions of the urban poor. Sunday schools, YMCA locals, settlement houses, and even cornflakes all became extensions of a widely shared, if never fully articulated, middle-class effort to enforce what Boyer called an "adherence to a general standard of right conduct" through "consciously planned and organized (but voluntarist and extra-legal) efforts."[19]

In the postwar era, as before, the developments of the present continued to shape perspectives on the past. As iconoclastic social movements gained momentum on the streets in the 1960s, American historians paid new attention to the many ways common people utilized a variety of spaces to resist social control. Whereas the earliest labor historians tended to focus almost solely on trade unions, a new generation of social historians led by scholars like Gutman sought to uncover the networks and experiences that informed working people's decisions to engage in grassroots activism. In deeply researched and richly detailed studies of specific communities, scholars uncovered working people's vibrant and complex social worlds. Workplaces, street corners, dance halls, fraternal organizations, saloons, amusement parks, and even churches all became sites where working people forged their communities and identities. Religious historians similarly became attuned to the devotional lives of ordinary people, documenting the many ways "popular" religion departed from the official doctrine of religious leaders. Yet the ghosts of Marx and Baird were not so easily vanquished. The presumption that the religious lives of working people had little impact upon American Christianity, or could be defined solely as ineffective in protesting industrial capitalism, remained woven into much of the "new" social history. As historian James R. Barrett claimed in his exemplary study of Chicago's meatpacking industry, "religion was not a unifying force in Packingtown."[20] Other historians concurred, seeing the mutualism of congregational life as inherently limited because it benefited only workers who shared a particular religious identity. Even Gutman was not immune to this limited purview, concluding his call to understand the complexity of working-class religious life by solely documenting the theologies of labor's most privileged leaders.[21]

Regardless of the intellectual baggage of previous debates, however, the widespread commitment among both social and religious historians to study American history "from the bottom up" transformed scholarly understandings of working people's religious lives. The increased attention to nonelite communities powerfully validated the social, cultural, and religious lives of working people. It not only exploded the hierarchies of American religious life that had rendered ordinary Christians somehow inferior to the Protestant elite, but also opened new interpretive possibilities for understanding the impact local religious worlds had upon broader political and economic landscapes. As Robert Orsi argued in his now-canonical study of the *festa* of Our Lady of Mount Carmel among working-class Catholics in Italian Harlem, the political consequences of working-class religious life were never predetermined. Expanding on the scholarly interest in popular religion by anchoring his study of a particular religious devotion directly in the material realities from which it emerged, his deeply local study showed that, on the one hand, the *festa* accommodated the residents of Italian Harlem to their lot as industrial workers. The prayers and processions to the Madonna of Mount Carmel provided emotional outlets that assuaged the traumas of industrial capitalism. Yet, as Orsi also went on to show, another profound consequence of the annual Catholic processions was that they transformed the streets of east Harlem into a sacred site of community, devotion, and fellowship. This sacralization helped inspire and justify the efforts by many Italian American women to demand city hall provide better services in keeping the neighborhood clean.[22]

Building off of such groundbreaking studies, scholars began to find other instances of resistance and protest emerging from the rhythms of working-class religious life. The rise in the study of "lived religion" encouraged scholars to focus, as Orsi had, not only on traditional sacred sites like the church pew, but also the streets and shop floors that religious communities occupied.[23] Social historians, meanwhile, began to reevaluate the relationship between local churches and working-class movements. Ken and Elizabeth Fones-Wolf, for example, pushed the new labor history's emphasis on community to its logical conclusion, noting that in particular times and places, local churches had often been working people's major allies. In the former's pathbreaking book on Philadelphia, Fones-Wolf noted how the interlocking directories of labor unions and working-class churches generated opportunities for mutual support. The city's Central Labor Union accepted clergymen as fraternal delegates and welcomed the intervention of Social Gospelers into labor disputes, while Protestant ministers cheered the involvement of leading craft unionists in evangelistic campaigns.[24] Similarly, Earl Lewis found in his study of the

African American community in Norfolk, Virginia, that local churches were crucial in turning "segregation" into "congregation," providing vital spaces for African Americans to organize political campaigns and even Congress of Industrial Organization locals.[25]

In addition to highlighting such institutional connections, historians uncovered the processes by which workers not only fashioned Christian idioms and ideas into tools of resistance, but also wielded them against their economic and religious betters. Going as far back as the early republic, scholars found white male artisans weaving republicanism and evangelical Protestantism together into a producerist tradition that took exception to leading clergymen's endorsement of laissez-faire economics.[26] Meanwhile, new studies increasingly emphasized that for women, African Americans, and other workers excluded from the early labor movement, Christianity was often the main resource at their disposal. Scholars of the antebellum era found slaves making their master's religion their own and mill girls rebuking their employers for the "heaps of shining gold" that stood between them "and a righteous God."[27] As much as earlier scholars and theorists had predicted such religious language would meet its demise in the modern age, research from the past decade has shown that working-class Christianities continued to suffuse working-class protest, dissent, and organizing throughout the industrial age. The rites, rituals, and recitation of scripture turned most Knights of Labor locals into "veritable workingmen's churches"; Populists considered themselves "Restorationists" hastening the moral economy's second coming; hymns transformed the Industrial Workers of the World's rallies into working-class revivals; "labor priests" made the Congress of Industrial Organizations' inroads into Catholic communities possible; Appalachia's network of independent Pentecostal churches became the organizational infrastructure of the United Mine Workers; an egalitarian evangelical theology turned the Southern Tenant Farmers Union's commitment to parity into a gospel of the working class; and Catholic imagery was essential in communicating the message of the United Farm Workers when language failed. In these and countless other instances, historians have collectively uncovered that working people have often resorted to the institutional, social, and spiritual dimensions of their faith in their quest to overcome the inequalities of industrial capitalism. Indeed, by the first decade of the twenty-first century, such instances had become so legion as to overturn the legacy of Marx and Baird entirely. As one historian concluded, Christianity had often fueled labor's "spirit of rebellion.[28]

*   *   *

The past decade has witnessed the emergence of a more balanced approach. Many scholars, including the editors of and contributors to this collection, have increasingly moved beyond the either-or framework first laid out by Marx and Baird, which suggested Christianity could only foment or assuage working-class dissent. In its place, scholars now attend to the complicated and often contradictory ways particular Christian communities, in specific times and places, drew upon the religious idioms available to them to engage, shape, critique, or even reinforce the industrial order. Alongside protest, scholars now consider the multifaceted consequences of even the most mundane religious practice; in place of delusion, scholars now trace the complexity, and sincerity, of working-class belief.

This more nuanced and comprehensive approach has in part been inspired by the "new" history of American capitalism, which has foregrounded the many Christian ideas, institutions, and individuals that have bolstered free enterprise. Bethany Moreton's religious history of Wal-Mart, for example, reveals how the company's success stemmed not only from management's portrayal of economic regulation as unchristian, but also from its characterization of work in its low-cost, family-friendly stores as a form of Christian service. Others have similarly discovered how management practices, public policy, and even entrepreneurial ambition have all emerged from a tangled web of self-interest and Christian concern. In all of these studies, Christianity is approached less as the presumed domain of an economic elite, and more as a vital force in American culture that managers and corporate executives could harness toward particular ends.[29]

This volume builds directly upon the contributions of this recent fiscal turn. But as the table of contents readily makes clear, our project remains rooted in Gutman's claim that in order to understand America's industrial order, one must attend to the religious lives of working people. Each essay seeks to map the worlds located in the space between the pew and the picket line. The contributions in part 1, for example, focus especially on the ways working people have often been major characters in the history of American Christianity. As Dan McKanan, Evelyn Sterne, Jarod Roll, Matthew Pehl, and Kerry Pimblott show, workers were a driving force in the creation of new theologies that powerfully shaped not only the American religious landscape, but also the industrial age. The miraculous wealth and supernatural healing that Roll's miners hoped to find both in the ground and in their churches, for example, steered Pentecostalism toward faith healing and what would later be called the prosperity gospel. Pehl's autoworkers, meanwhile, fashioned a faith that saw the assembly line's drudgery as an inescapable reality of a fallen world and scoffed at liberal ministers who claimed labor was something that should be dignified.

Yet, not every history was one of accommodation. As Sterne, McKanan, and Pimblott highlight, workers also forged Christianities that demanded churches advance their cause. For Sterne, these emerged from the demographic realities of Providence's Catholic churches, where wage-earning parishioners made sodality halls as much working-class strongholds as any trade union. Meanwhile, McKanan's and Pimblott's essays underscore that theologians need not be seminary trained. In recovering the devotional imaginations of George Lippard and Ignatius Donnelly and the political theologies of community organizers in Cairo, Illinois, their essays highlight the rich theological contributions of the American working class.

If the essays in part 1 attempt to reclaim working people as important agents in the history of Christianity, the essays in part 2 explore ways that working-class believers shaped the contours of industrial capitalism. Arlene Sánchez-Walsh's essay shows how Emma Tenayuca's devotional eclecticism helped her navigate the diverse religions of San Antonio's pecan shellers. Erik Gellman and Alison Collis Greene, meanwhile, chart the complicated relationships between white, middle-class Christian reformers and the black, working-class believers they attempted to help. Whereas Greene's southern sharecroppers drew upon the resources that middle-class Christian activists brought while simultaneously rejecting the expansive theologies that girded them, the black churches on Chicago's West Side in Gellman's essay proved to be difficult allies to the progressive white ministers who attempted to make the causes of black Chicago their own. Finally, Brett Hendrickson highlights how the Catholic Church's charge to care for its flock emboldened some priests in the Southwest to demand that ecclesiastical institutions fight alongside Mexican migrants.

While each essay tells its own story, the collection as a whole argues for an integration of scholarly fields. The work collected here suggests, on the one hand, that there is not a history of religion in America that is not also a history of labor. Working people have been overwhelmingly present, not absent, in the history of American Christianity. Their participation has deeply shaped religious life. On the other hand, there is no history of labor in America that is not also a history of religion. Working people have often been people of faith, and their willingness to challenge or consent to the conditions under which they work has often been shaped by that faith.

When we integrate these fields, new avenues of historical inquiry emerge. Consider, for example, the matter of religious labor. As these essays highlight, it takes work to sustain churches, denominations, and theological movements. And from Cairo's Black Power prophets to Providence's working-class deacons, working people have shouldered much of this load. How might the history of American Christianity change if we studied its ecclesiastical institutions less as denominational infrastructure and more as workplaces? What might the labor history of religious book publishing, church construction, or even the ministry reveal about the growth of particular Christian communities?[30] Similarly, consider how the American workplace itself has been a site of religious construction. We find in these essays that the monotony of Detroit's assembly lines prompted autoworkers to jettison long-standing religious valorizations of work, while the dangers of Joplin's mines yielded new fascinations with faith healing. What other religious forms emerged out of the American industrial workplace? And how did these religious forms not only shape the history of a specific cotton field or shop floor, but also of entire industries?[31]

Finally, this collection points to the continued importance of the local, the specific, and the particular conditions of working-class religious life. As we have seen throughout this introduction, scholars have often sought to make sweeping generalizations about both Christianity and working people in order to understand the relationship between the two. Was Christianity primarily a tool of the elite? Did the Bible's prophetic messages ordain it as the primary weapon of the weak? Was there such a thing as "working-class Christianity"? The stories in this volume represent, collectively, a rebuttal to all sorts of overdetermined analyses of the historical relationship between Christianity and capitalism. The only true answer to such questions is, "it depends." It depends upon the workers and workplaces in question, as well as wider political, economic, and religious realities. As this collection begins to show, the religious history of American workers is one of breathtaking diversity. At particular times and in particular places, working people have found in faith, ritual, and practice the elements of reform and even revolution, though when viewed in wider context, these moments can hardly be said to be the rule.

Future attention to the spaces between the pew and the picket line may only confirm what this collection suggests: that when it comes to religion and capitalism, there is in fact no set rule, but rather a series of unfolding conflicts and contingencies. Yet the story is no less important because it is unpredictable. On the contrary, if our histories of Christianity and the working class are punctuated by both rupture and stasis, by moments of overcoming and long seasons of being overcome, then they will no doubt better reflect the messy realities of history. At that point, perhaps, we might conclude that the work Herbert Gutman began some fifty years ago is finally done.

Notes

1. Herbert G. Gutman, "Protestantism and the American Labor Movement: The Christian Spirit in the Gilded Age," *American Historical Review* 72, no. 1 (1966): 76–77, 94, and 95.

2. On religious commitments and unionization, see Kenneth Fones-Wolf, *Trade Union Gospel: Christianity and Labor in Industrial Philadelphia, 1865–1915* (Philadelphia: Temple University Press, 1989); Matthew Pehl, "'Apostles of Fascism,' 'Communist Clergy,' and the UAW: Political Ideology and Working-Class Religion in Detroit, 1919–1945," *Journal of American History* 99, no. 2 (2012): 440–65; and James P. McCartin and Joseph A. McCartin, "Working-Class Catholicism: A Call for New Investigations, Dialogue, and Reappraisal," *LABOR: Studies in Working Class History of the Americas* 4, no. 1 (2007): 99–110. On the social origins of Christian theologies, see Robert A. Orsi, *The Madonna of 115th Street: Faith and Community in Italian Harlem, 1880–1950* (New Haven, CT: Yale University Press, 1985); Darren Dochuk, *From Bible Belt to Sunbelt: Plain-Folk Religion, Grassroots Politics, and the Rise of Evangelical Conservatism* (New York: W. W. Norton, 2012); and Heath W. Carter, *Union Made: Working People and the Rise of Social Christianity in Chicago* (New York: Oxford University Press, 2015).

3. On contemporary religious affiliation in America, see Pew Research Center, "America's Changing Religious Landscape," 12 May 2015, http://www.pewforum.org/files/2015/05/RLS-05-08-full-report.pdf, accessed 9 June 2015.

4. In terms of disparate class experiences, immigrant Catholics and rural evangelicals long formed a significant portion of the industrial workforce, while moneyed and often mainline Protestants exercised tremendous influence as managers, financiers, and politicians. The classic exploration of American Christianity's social hierarchies remains E. Digby Baltzell, *The Protestant Establishment: Aristocracy and Caste in America* (New Haven, CT: Yale University Press, 1987). See also Herbert G. Gutman and Ira Berlin, "Class Composition and the Development of the American Working Class, 1840–1890," in Herbert G. Gutman, *Power and Culture: Essays on the American Working Class*, ed. Ira Berlin (New York: Pantheon Books, 1987), 380–94; and Wade Clark Roof and William McKinney, *American Mainline Religion: Its Changing Shape and Future* (New Brunswick, NJ: Rutgers University Press, 1987), 106–47.

5. As Catherine Brekus and W. Clark Gilpin write, "Christians have infused American society with an extensive repertoire of stories, symbols, and ethical ideals that have been among the defining terms of American cultural debate." See Catherine A. Brekus and W. Clark Gilpin, eds., *American Christianities: A History of Dominance*

and Diversity (Raleigh: University of North Carolina Press, 2011), 2. For other works on Christianity, and in particular Protestantism's cultural and demographic prominence in American life, see Paul Boyer, *Urban Masses and Moral Order in America, 1820–1920* (Cambridge, MA: Harvard University Press, 1978); Robert T. Handy, *A Christian America: Protestant Hopes and Historical Realities* (New York: Oxford University Press, 1984); Mark A. Noll, *America's God: From Jonathan Edwards to Abraham Lincoln* (New York: Oxford University Press, 2005); Jackson Lears, *Rebirth of a Nation: The Making of Modern America, 1877–1920* (New York: Harper Perennial, 2010); David Sehat, *The Myth of American Religious Freedom* (New York: Oxford University Press, 2011); and Tracy Fessenden, *Culture and Redemption: Religion, the Secular, and American Literature* (Princeton, NJ: Princeton University Press, 2013).

6. The literature here is immense, but see, for example, Gauiutra Bahadur, *Coolie Woman: The Odyssey of Indenture* (Chicago: University of Chicago Press, 2013); Derek Chang, *Citizens of a Christian Nation: Evangelical Missions and the Problem of Race in the Nineteenth Century* (Philadelphia: University of Pennsylvania Press, 2010); Kristofer Allerfeldt, *Race, Radicalism, Religion, and Restriction: Immigration in the Pacific Northwest, 1890–1924* (Santa Barbara, CA: Praeger, 2003); Lisa Lowe, *Immigrant Acts: On Asian American Cultural Politics* (Durham, NC: Duke University Press, 1994); Lucie Cheng and Edna Bonacich, eds., *Labor Immigration under Capitalism: Asian Workers in the United States before World War II* (Berkeley: University of California Press, 1984); Haisa R. Diner, *Roads Taken: The Great Jewish Migrations to the New World and the Peddlers Who Forged the Way* (New Haven, CT: Yale University Press, 2014); Rebecca Kobrin, ed., *Chosen Capital: The Jewish Encounter with American Capitalism* (New Brunswick, NJ: Rutgers University Press, 2012); Marni Davis, *Jews and Booze: Becoming American in the Age of Prohibition* (New York: New York University Press, 2012); Tony Michels, *A Fire in Their Hearts: Yiddish Socialists in New York* (Cambridge, MA: Harvard University Press, 2009); Susan Glenn, *Daughters of the Shtetl: Life and Labor in the Immigrant Generation* (Ithaca, NY: Cornell University Press, 1991); and Bruce C. Nelson, *Beyond the Martyrs: A Social History of Chicago Anarchism, 1870–1900* (New Brunswick, NJ: Rutgers University Press, 1988).

7. Karl Marx, "A Contribution to the Critique of Hegel's Philosophy of Right," *Deutsch-Französische Jahrbücher*, February 7, 1844, reprinted in *The Marx-Engels Reader*, ed. Robert C. Tucker (New York: W. W. Norton, 1978), 54.

8. Robert Baird, *Religion in America; or, An Account of the Origins, Progress, Relation to the State, and Present Conditions of the Evangelical Churches in the United States, with Notices of the Unevangelical Denominations* (Glasgow: Blackie and Son, 1842).

9. For Marx, Engels, and other early Communist assessments of Christianity's contribution to the proletariat's oppression, see Karl Marx and Friedrich Engels, *The Communist Manifesto* (New York: Washington Square Press, 1964 [1848]), 91–92; Karl Marx, *A Contribution to the Critique of Political Economy*, ed. Maurice Dobb

(New York: International, 1970 [1859]), 130, 210–11; *Friedrich* Engels, *The Origin of the Family, Private Property, and the State* (New York: International, 1972 [1884]), 209–13; and Sean McCloud and William A. Mirola, "Introduction," in *Religion and Class in America: Culture, History, and Politics*, ed. Sean McCloud and William A. Mirola (Boston: Brill, 2009), 3–6.

10. Max Weber, *The Sociology of Religion* (Boston: Beacon Press, 1991 [1926]), 116.

11. Daniel Dorchester, *Christianity in the United States: From the First Settlement down to the Present Time* (New York: Hunt and Eaton, 1888), 585; Leonard Woolsey Bacon, *A History of American Christianity* (New York: Christian Literature, 1897), 320.

12. On the relationship between the origins of labor history and Progressive reform, see Robert H. Wiebe, *The Search for Order, 1877–1920* (New York: Hill and Wang, 1967), 145–55; Lears, *Rebirth of a Nation*, 195–200; Leon Fink, *Progressive Intellectuals and the Dilemmas of Democratic Commitment* (Cambridge, MA: Harvard University Press, 1999); and Philip Taft, "A Rereading of Selig Perlman's 'A Theory of the Labor Movement,'" *Industrial and Labor Relations Review* 4, no. 1 (1 October 1950): 70–77.

13. John R. Commons et al., *History of Labor in the United States*, 4 vols. (New York: Macmillan, 1918); Richard T. Ely, *The Labor Movement in America* (New York: T. Y. Crowell, 1886); Selig Perlman, *A Theory of the Labor Movement* (New York: Augustus M. Kelley, 1949); Philip Taft, *The A.F. of L. in the Time of Gompers* (New York: Harper, 1957); Philip Foner, *History of the Labor Movement in the United States*, 10 vols. (New York: International, 1947); and Norman Ware, *The Labor Movement in the United States, 1860–1895* (New York: D. Appleton, 1929).

14. On fear as an impulse behind the first scholarly treatments of American religion, see Ann Taves, *Fits, Trances, and Visions: Experiencing Religion and Explaining Experience from Wesley to James* (Princeton, NJ: Princeton University Press, 1999), 328–47; Robert A. Orsi, *Between Heaven and Earth: The Religious Worlds People Make and the Scholars Who Study Them* (Princeton, NJ: Princeton University Press, 2005), 182–99; Sean McCloud, *Divine Hierarchies: Class in American Religion and Religious Studies* (Chapel Hill: University of North Carolina Press, 2007), 35–42; and Tomoko Masuzawa, *The Invention of World Religions; or, How European Universalism Was Preserved in the Language of Pluralism* (Chicago: University of Chicago Press, 2005).

15. Davenport would go on to proclaim that he had written his book "to contribute, if possible, to the better ordering of religious method, that the tide, if it comes, may be rationally guided into reservoirs and channels and ditches, and may irrigate a thirsty land and not overwhelm it, and receding, leave far too much of wreck behind." Frederick Morgan Davenport, *Primitive Traits in Religious Revivals: A Study in Mental and Social Evolution* (New York: Macmillan, 1910), viii–ix; first cited in Orsi, *Between Heaven and Earth*, 186.

16. Robert Mapes Anderson, *Vision of the Disinherited: The Making of American Pentecostalism* (Peabody, MA: Hendrickson, 1979), 239; Richard Hofstadter, *The Paranoid Style in American Politics* (New York: Vintage Books, 1952), 67–79; and Hofstadter, *Anti-Intellectualism in American Life* (New York: Vintage Books, 1962),

117–36, 140–41. For a comprehensive survey of "deprivation theory" in the study of religion, see McCloud, *Divine Hierarchies*, 77–97; Charles Y. Glock, "The Role of Deprivation in the Origin and Evolution of Religious Groups," in *Religion and Social Conflict*, ed. Robert Lee and Martin E. Marty (New York: Oxford University Press, 1964), 24–36; and Anderson, *Vision of the Disinherited*, 239. For an important response and critique of Anderson's analysis, see Grant Wacker, *Heaven Below: Early Pentecostals and American Culture* (Cambridge, MA: Harvard University Press, 2001), 199–201.

17. H. Richard Niebuhr, *The Social Sources of Denominationalism* (New York: Living Age Books, 1929), 21. For a concise summary of Niebuhr's broader arguments, see McCloud, *Divine Hierarchies*, 60–64.

18. Robert Lynd and Helen Lynd, *Middletown: A Study in American Culture* (New York: Harcourt, Brace, and Jovanovich, 1956); Liston Pope, *Millhands and Preachers: A Study of Gastonia* (New Haven, CT: Yale University Press, 1962 [1942]). For the more formulaic usages of Niebuhr's thesis, see Paul E. Johnson, *A Shopkeeper's Millennium: Society and Revivals in Rochester, New York, 1815–1837* (New York: Hill and Wang, 1978); and Roger Finke and Rodney Stark, *The Churching of America, 1776–1990: Winners and Losers in Our Religious Economy* (New Brunswick, NJ: Rutgers University Press, 1992).

19. Boyer, *Urban Masses and Moral Order*, viii–ix. Boyer's analysis connects to a broader argument within American religious history on the intent of Christian benevolence, which indirectly touched upon the history of working people in that they were so often the objects of social reform and control. See, for example, Leonard I. Sweet, "The Evangelical Tradition in America," in *The Evangelical Tradition in America*, ed. Leonard I. Sweet (Macon, GA: Mercer University Press, 1984), 32–43; George Marsden, "The Gospel of Wealth, the Social Gospel, and the Salvation of Souls in Nineteenth-Century America," *Fides et Historia* 5 (1973): 10–21; Robert A. Orsi, "Crossing the City Line," in *Gods of the City*, ed. Robert A. Orsi (Bloomington: Indiana University Press, 1999), 15–16, 67; Clifford S. Griffin, "Religious Benevolence as Social Control, 1815–1860," *Mississippi Valley Historical Review* 44, no. 3 (1957): 423–44; and Lois W. Banner, "Religious Benevolence as Social Control: A Critique of an Interpretation," *Journal of American History* 60, no. 1 (1973): 23–41.

20. James R. Barrett, *Work and Community in the Jungle: Chicago's Packinghouse Workers, 1894–1922* (Urbana: University of Illinois Press, 1987), 75. Other examples of this framework include Alan Dawley, *Class and Community: The Industrial Revolution in Lynn* (Cambridge, MA: Harvard University Press, 2000 [1976]); Daniel J. Walkowitz, *Worker City, Company Town: Iron and Cotton-Worker Protest in Troy and Cohoes, New York, 1855–84* (Urbana: University of Illinois Press, 1978); John T. Cumbler, *Working-Class Community in Industrial America: Work, Leisure, and Struggle in Two Industrial Cities, 1880–1930* (Westport, CT: Greenwood Press, 1979); Roy Rosenzweig, *Eight Hours for What We Will: Workers and Leisure in an Industrial City, 1870–1920* (Cambridge: Cambridge University Press, 1983); Francis G. Couvares,

The Remaking of Pittsburgh: Class and Culture in an Industrializing City, 1877–1919 (Albany: State University of New York Press, 1984); Richard Oestreicher, *Solidarity and Fragmentation: Working People and Class Consciousness in Detroit, 1875–1900* (Urbana: University of Illinois Press, 1986); Jacquelyn Dowd Hall et al., *Like a Family: The Making of a Southern Cotton Mill World* (Chapel Hill: University of North Carolina Press, 1987); John J. Bukowczyk, "The Transforming Power of the Machine: Popular Religion, Ideology, and Secularization among Polish Immigrant Workers in the United States, 1880–1940," *International Labor and Working-Class History* 34 (1988): 22–38; and Kimberley L. Phillips, *AlabamaNorth: African-American Migrants, Community, and Working-Class Activism in Cleveland, 1915–45* (Urbana: University of Illinois Press, 1999).

21. For the debate over Gutman's own handling of religion, see Nick Salvatore, "Herbert Gutman's Narrative of the American Working Class: A Reevaluation," *International Journal of Politics, Culture, and Society* 12, no. 1 (1998): 43–80; Leon Fink, "On Nick Salvatore, 'Herbert Gutman's Narrative of the American Working Class: A Reevaluation'" and Salvatore's response, *International Journal of Politics, Culture, and Society* 12, no. 4 (1999): 662–70; and Ira Berlin, "Introduction: Herbert G. Gutman and the American Working Class," in Gutman, *Power and Culture*, 3–69.

22. Orsi, *Madonna of 115th Street*, 45.

23. On the study of "lived religion," see David D. Hall, ed., *Lived Religion in America: Toward a History of Practice* (Princeton, NJ: Princeton University Press, 1997). For examples that take seriously the question of social class, see Karen McCarthy Brown, *Mama Lola: A Vodou Priestess in Brooklyn* (Berkeley: University of California Press, 1991); Robert A. Orsi, *Thank You, St. Jude: Women's Devotion to the Patron Saint of Hopeless Causes* (New Haven, CT: Yale University Press, 1996); Timothy Matovina, *Guadalupe and Her Faithful: Latino Catholics in San Antonio, from Colonial Origins to the Present* (Baltimore: Johns Hopkins University Press, 2005); and Randall J. Stephens, *The Fire Spreads: Holiness and Pentecostalism in the American South* (Cambridge, MA: Harvard University Press, 2008).

24. Fones-Wolf, *Trade Union Gospel*.

25. Earl Lewis, *In Their Own Interests: Race, Class and Power in Twentieth-Century Norfolk, Virginia* (Berkeley: University of California Press, 1993), 90.

26. See, for example, Stewart Davenport, *Friends of the Unrighteous Mammon: Northern Christians and Market Capitalism, 1815–1860* (Chicago: University of Chicago Press, 2008); William Sutton, "Tied to the Whipping Post: New Labor Historians and Evangelical Artisans in the Early Republic," *Labor History* 36 (Spring 1995): 23–47; Mark Schantz, *Piety in Providence: Class Dimensions of Religious Experience in Antebellum Rhode Island* (Ithaca, NY: Cornell University Press, 2000); William Sutton, *Journeymen for Jesus: Evangelical Artisans Confront Capitalism in Jacksonian Baltimore* (State College: Pennsylvania State University Press, 1998); and Jama Lazerow, *Religion and the Working Class in Antebellum America* (Washington, DC: Smithsonian Institution Press, 1995).

27. Albert J. Raboteau, *Slave Religion: The "Invisible Institution" in the Antebellum South* (New York: Oxford University Press, 1978); and Teresa Anne Murphy, *Ten Hours' Labor: Religion, Reform, and Gender in Early New England* (Ithaca, NY: Cornell University Press, 1992), 209.

28. This list is culled from Robert Weir, *Beyond Labor's Veil: The Culture of the Knights of Labor* (State College: Pennsylvania State University Press, 1996), 69–73; Joe Creech, *Righteous Indignation: Religion and the Populist Revolution* (Urbana: University of Illinois Press, 2006); Kimball Baker, *Go to the Worker: America's Labor Apostles* (Milwaukee, WI: Marquette University Press, 2010); Richard J. Callahan Jr., *Work and Faith in the Kentucky Coal Fields: Subject to Dust* (Bloomington: Indiana University Press, 2008); Jarod Roll, *Spirit of Rebellion: Labor and Religion in the New Cotton South* (Urbana: University of Illinois Press, 2010); Erik Gellman and Jarod Roll, *The Gospel of the Working Class: Labor's Southern Prophets in New Deal America* (Urbana: University of Illinois Press, 2011), 48, 70–72, 120; Donald E. Winters, *The Soul of the Wobblies: The I.W.W., Religion, and American Culture in the Progressive Era, 1905–1917* (New York: Praeger, 1985); and Luis D. León, *The Political Spirituality of Cesar Chavez: Crossing Religious Borders* (Berkeley: University of California Press, 2015).

29. Bethany Moreton, *To Serve God and Wal-Mart: The Making of Christian Free Enterprise* (Cambridge, MA: Harvard University Press, 2010). See also Dochuk, *From Bible Belt to Sunbelt*; Kathryn Lofton, *Oprah: The Gospel of an Icon* (Berkeley: University of California Press, 2011); Sarah R. Hammond, "'God Is My Partner': An Evangelical Business Man Confronts Depression and War," *Church History* 80, no. 3 (2011): 498 519; Kevin Kruse, *One Nation Under God: How Corporate America Invented Christian America* (New York: Basic Books, 2015); Timothy E. W. Gloege, *Guaranteed Pure: The Moody Bible Institute, Business, and the Making of Modern Evangelicalism* (Chapel Hill: University of North Carolina Press, 2015); and Darren Grem, *Corporate Revivals: Big Business and the Making of the Evangelical Right* (New York: Oxford University Press, forthcoming). This turn to explore how particular Christians and Christian communities shaped American capitalism, it should be noted, has been accompanied, and in many ways preceded, by a similar turn within the study of religion that uncovered how the growth or decline of America's Christian communities has often been determined by their ability to successfully engage the market economy. See R. Laurence Moore, *Selling God: American Religion in the Marketplace of Culture* (New York: Oxford University Press, 1995); Colleen McDannell, *Material Christianity: Religion and Popular Culture in America* (New Haven, CT: Yale University Press, 1995); Leigh Eric Schmidt, *Consumer Rites: The Buying and Selling of American Holidays* (Princeton, NJ: Princeton University Press, 1997); Fritz Umbach, "Learning to Shop in Zion: The Consumer Revolution in Great Basin Mormon Culture, 1847–1910," *Journal of Social History* 38, no. 1 (2004): 29–61; Kate Bowler, *Blessed: A History of the American Prosperity Gospel* (New York: Oxford University Press, 2013); and Lerone Martin, *Preaching on Wax: The Phonograph and*

the Shaping of Modern African American Religion (New York: New York University Press, 2014).

30. For more on religion as a form of labor, see Callahan, *Work and Faith in the Kentucky Coal Fields,* 1–16; Shari Lisa Rabin, "Manifest Jews: Mobility and the Making of American Judaism, 1820–1877" (PhD diss., Yale University, 2015); and William A. Mirola, *Redeeming Time: Protestantism and Chicago's Eight-Hour Movement, 1866–1912* (Urbana: University of Illinois Press, 2015), 168–76.

31. For studies in this vein, see John Corrigan, *Business of the Heart: Religion and Emotion in the Nineteenth Century* (Berkeley: University of California Press, 2002); Kathryn Lofton, "The Spirit in the Cubicle: A Religious History of the American Office," in *Sensational Religion: Sense and Contention in Material Practice,* ed. Sally Promey (New Haven, CT: Yale University Press, 2014), 135–58; and Darren Dochuk's forthcoming *Anointed with Oil: God and Black Gold in Modern America.*

PART I

Manufacturing Christianity

1

George Lippard, Ignatius Donnelly, and the Esoteric Theology of American Labor

DAN MCKANAN

The American labor movement has always had a theology—indeed, many theologies. But it has not always had professional theologians who are credentialed by both academic and ecclesiastical authorities. The Social Gospel movement that began around 1880 has been rightly celebrated for forging an enduring link between American labor and the guild of professional theologians. Washington Gladden, Walter Rauschenbusch, George Herron, Clarence Skinner, Harry Ward, John Ryan, and Reinhold Niebuhr were genuine allies of labor, and they marshaled the intellectual resources of the Christian tradition on behalf of campaigns for living wages, the eight-hour day, safe working conditions, and an end to child labor.[1] Their efforts in mobilizing both Protestant and Catholic churches helped bring the American labor movement to its pinnacle of influence in the postwar period, and the alliance continues in the work of contemporary theologians who work in solidarity with Interfaith Worker Justice or congregation-based community organizing projects.[2] The Social Gospel, as traditionally defined, was an authentic theology of labor, but it was not the first or only such theology.[3] Nor was it a direct expression of the theological vision of the workers themselves. Social Gospel theology was always a theology of allyship; it expressed the convictions (sometimes moderate, sometimes radical) of middle-class intellectuals whose consciences had been pricked, who wanted to prick the consciences of their middle-class students and parishioners, and who had the power to transform educational and ecclesial institutions. Decades before the Social Creed of the Churches gave definitive expression to Social Gospel theology, another theology of labor—sometimes more militant and often much stranger—could be found on the pages of popular fiction.

In this essay, I explore the works of two labor novelists, George Lippard (1822–54) and Ignatius Donnelly (1831–1901).[4] I focus especially on their use of esoteric Christianity as a source of worker empowerment. By *esotericism* I mean that strand of belief and practice that finds hidden significance beneath the surface of religious traditions. Esotericists view all nature as alive and posit elaborate correspondences between heaven and earth, or the self and God. They use various "magical" practices, such as alchemy, to transmute earthly realities into heavenly ones.[5] In the West, most esotericists see themselves as bearers of an ancient tradition—traceable back to ancient Egypt, and sometimes behind that to Atlantis—that has been transmitted through initiations by secret brotherhoods. For some Western esotericists, this secret tradition is outside of and antithetical to Christianity; for others—certainly including Lippard and Donnelly—it is the vital heart of Christianity itself, albeit a heart that has often been suppressed by ecclesiastical institutions. Indeed, both Lippard and Donnelly built complex theologies—by which I mean religious reflection in general, not exclusively reflection on the doctrine of God[6]—on the foundation of their belief that Jesus of Nazareth had been a class-conscious worker with a revolutionary social blueprint. For them, this was the esoteric secret par excellence.

Both Lippard and Donnelly developed this idea by drawing heavily on such submerged spiritual traditions as ancient Hermeticism and Neoplatonism, and early modern alchemy and Rosicrucianism. Lippard was fascinated by the Rosicrucians and by the radical Pietists who had settled in Pennsylvania in the eighteenth century; indeed, he regarded his own labor union as the "exoteric" work of the Rosicrucian order. Donnelly was his generation's leading exponent of the Atlantis myth, and he imagined that economic change might involve the same sort of cataclysmic changes that had ended the Atlantean civilization. In telling their stories and retelling their fictions, I do not mean to suggest that they articulated a more "authentic" theology of labor than the Social Gospelers, or even that theirs was the most important alternative to the Social Gospel. Recent scholars have suggested that freethinkers, revivalists, Catholics, African American Protestants, and many others all made distinctive contributions to the theology of labor.[7] In lifting up the distinct contributions of esoteric Christianity, I hope simply to join this diverse chorus of scholarship. More specifically, I hope to show that Lippard and Donnelly articulated an esoteric understanding of social sin that was earlier and, in some ways, more profound than the articulations of the Social Gospelers.[8]

In their own time, George Lippard and Ignatius Donnelly were enormously influential spokesmen for the cause of the workers. Lippard's first novel, *The Quaker City, or, The Monks of Monk Hall*, published when he was just twenty-two years old, was a runaway best seller and the most influential exposé of urban injustice to appear prior to the Civil War.[9] Just four years (and twelve books!) later, he organized the Brotherhood of the Union, a labor organization that provided the organizational blueprint for the Knights of Labor, which would become the largest union federation prior to the American Federation of Labor. He cooperated closely with the German immigrants who planted the first seeds of Marxism in the United States. He was so sufficiently well regarded by labor activists that he was invited to give the valedictory address to the Industrial Congress of 1848, promising the gathered socialists and land reformers a coming day "when the regeneration of the workers, from the anguish of physical suffering, shall prepare the way for the spiritual redemption of all mankind."[10] Donnelly penned the founding manifesto of the Populist Party in 1892, galvanizing urban workers and rebellious farmers with a sweeping critique of the "vast conspiracy against mankind" that included mainstream politicians as well as plutocrats.[11]

Neither is well remembered today, in part because of the seemingly bizarre eclecticism of their interests. Lippard was utterly sincere in his radical commitments, but he was also addicted to salacious tales of rape and seduction, replete with gory deaths and heaving bosoms. At the same time, he published dozens of fanciful "legends" about George Washington and other Revolutionary heroes. Donnelly, for his part, espoused multiple ideologies over the course of his career, and he also introduced the rather questionable theory that Francis Bacon was the true author of Shakespeare's plays. In addition, both men harbored prejudices that sometimes obscured their radical intentions. Lippard was infuriated by both rape and slavery, but most of his female and African American characters are disturbingly two-dimensional. Donnelly trafficked in anti-Semitic stereotypes even as he professed to see Jews as a "noble race" who had long been victimized by "bigoted" Christians. The two writers, finally, have been victims of academic specialization. As novelists, they are of more interest to literary scholars than to historians of labor or of religion. But on purely aesthetic grounds, the novels are of only minor significance: the importance of Lippard and Donnelly is visible only to those who look simultaneously at the literary, radical, and religious dimensions of their work. A multidisciplinary approach to Lippard and Donnelly also has the potential to unlock aspects of the labor movement that have been obscured by the scholarly boundaries separating labor history from religious and literary scholarship.

Fortunately, scholarship on esoteric spirituality has a long-standing commitment to multidisciplinary approaches. At different historical moments, Gnosticism, Rosicrucianism, Freemasonry, Transcendentalism, Theosophy, and the New Age movement have all been important carriers of esotericism, but esoteric practice is not easily contained within obviously "religious" organizational structures. Esoteric practices are as likely to appear within artistic, medical, or conventionally religious organizations as within explicitly esoteric contexts.[12] For this reason, Wouter Hanegraaff and Catherine Albanese have argued persuasively that esoteric or metaphysical spiritualities are not a sideshow but "a neglected dimension of the general culture" of the West and "a *major* player in the evolution of the national religiosity" of the United States.[13] It was precisely the eclecticism of Lippard's and Donnelly's interests, and the liminality of their vocational identities, that allowed them to make esoteric resources accessible to labor activists and working-class readers who might not have understood themselves as esoteric practitioners.

Lippard's and Donnelly's access to labor activists was also enhanced by the fact that their primary commitment was to the esoteric dimension of Christianity. From the Middle Ages to the early modern period, Western esotericists generally worked within the broader cultural context of Christianity, exploring the hidden meaning of Christian texts and rituals.[14] This was changing in Lippard's and Donnelly's lifetimes, as Andrew Jackson Davis and other spiritualists explicitly rejected Christianity and the Theosophical Society turned to Buddhism and other Eastern alternatives. But Lippard and Donnelly largely followed the path charted by their early modern predecessors. They could be harshly critical of mainstream churches and ministers, but insisted that their alternative was actually more faithful to Jesus's original teaching. Indeed, their esoteric Christianity had porous boundaries with many other strands of Christian tradition: they shared an interest in the hidden meaning of prophetic texts with evangelical millennialists; an affirmation of humanity's essential goodness with liberal Protestants; and both were well aware of the strands of Roman Catholicism that were sympathetic to labor. (Although Donnelly's family roots were Irish Catholic, he did not practice the faith in his adulthood.[15]) Though they also drew on popular freethought's critique of Christian institutions, on the whole their spirituality did not pose as sharp a challenge to lay Christian culture as did such freethinkers as Thomas Paine, Robert Owen, and Robert Ingersoll.

Esoteric Christian resources are most clearly on display in Lippard's and Donnelly's novels. Lippard's first and by far most successful novel, *The Quaker City*, already contained most of the political and spiritual themes he would develop over the course of his brief and intense career. Centered on "Monk Hall," a brothel and gambling den controlled by wealthy Philadelphians who masquerade as monastics, the novel features multiple plotlines of rape, murder, and seduction. Borrowing tropes from anti-Catholic and anti-Masonic literature, Lippard suggested that the truly dangerous and secretive power was capitalism itself, buttressed by scheming and rapacious bankers, lawyers, politicians, merchants, and Protestant clergy. He also suggested that spiritual resources were available to combat capitalism, with an astrologer predicting the course of the plot early on, and a charismatic wizard offering an ambiguously utopian vision of the national future near the end.

Lippard was just twenty-two years old when he began publishing *The Quaker City* in serial form, and the early chapters are shaped more by his tragic family history than by a broader sociopolitical critique. Both of Lippard's parents and most of his siblings died during his youth, and the once-middle-class family sold off most of its property to pay debts. When the great depression of 1837 to 1844 hit Philadelphia, Lippard was a homeless teenaged orphan who turned to writing for survival. Concerned for the virtue of his one surviving sister, Lippard initially designed *The Quaker City* as a manifesto against seduction. But he was radicalized by the public response to his work: working-class readers bought up thousands of copies, while respectable editors blasted him for immorality. Lippard incorporated more pointed criticisms of capitalism into the novel's later chapters, and began making contacts with Philadelphia's community of labor radicals.[16]

In his subsequent writing, Lippard often built a novel's plot around just one of the interwoven themes in *The Quaker City*. *The Memoirs of a Preacher* (1849) is a scathing indictment of clerical hypocrisy and of attempts to merge church and state; *The Nazarene* (1846) takes aim at popular anti-Catholicism and nativism by portraying a series of Catholic, poor, and nonwhite characters who are victimized by a banker named Calvin Wolfe and his "Holy Protestant League."[17] Lippard's critique of capitalism is front and center in *New York: Its Upper Ten and Lower Million* (1853), the plot of which centers on a New York City fortune that is held in trust from 1823 to 1844, at which point it is to fall either to the rightful heir or to seven members of the extended family. Lippard uses the fortune itself, which grows from two million to one hundred million dollars, to illustrate the inhuman and irresponsible power of capital: "Has this wealth no duties to mankind? Is there not something horrible in the thought of an entire generation, for mere subsistence, spending their lives, in order to make this man, this estate, or this corporation, the possessor of incredible wealth?"[18] He uses the rival claimants to illustrate the complicity of the various professions with capitalism, as well as the righteous and violent anger of enslaved persons and the white working class.

References to Rosicrucianism, alchemy, Freemasonry, and other esoteric traditions are scattered through these novels, but appear in especially concentrated form in *Paul Ardenheim*, published in 1848 and set during the American Revolution. The title character of this book is a young man who gradually discovers that his father was the last surviving member of the Rosicrucian order—*and* that his grandfather many times removed was a Renaissance magician who murdered his father and wife and was condemned to live forever. In the novel's central scene, Paul discovers a cache of manuscripts that place Rosicrucianism within a long history of social radicalism. The manuscripts tell of a tenth-century heretic who was imprisoned for calling "the Lord Jesus a Carpenter's Son" and for promising the serfs that God would eventually give them "the land on which they spent their sweat and blood." They claim that the fifteenth-century Hussites shared a communion of bread and water—"emblematic, not of blood but of the tears of Christ" over the sufferings of the workers. And they describe a seventeenth-century "Parliament of the World" that celebrates Jesus's identity as a "mechanic" and prepares the way for William Penn, George Washington, and even Robespierre. In order to continue this work, Paul must navigate between two other secret societies: a network of wealthy capitalists on the one hand, and a quasi-Masonic order of bloodthirsty pirates on the other. As part of this task, Paul and his father initiate George Washington for his work as liberator of the nation. The contemporary task of the Rosicrucians, he makes clear, is to vindicate Washington's work by purging the United States of slavery and capitalism.[19]

All of this is set against the backdrop of the American Revolution, and the narrator suggests that Paul's inner spiritual struggle to choose his destiny is shaping the external course of the Revolution. In the conclusion, the narrator promises a sequel that will depict Paul "gliding like a Ghost—like an embodied Fate—through the incredible horrors and gloomy triumphs of the French Revolution."[20] The effect of this is to blend patriotism with radicalism: because Lippard portrays the secret message of the Rosicrucians as worker's revolution, the implication is that the true American destiny is socialism as well as democracy. Another effect is to posit a sharp choice between alternate American destinies: the nation can fulfill the sacred mission handed to George Washington or betray itself by tolerating slavery and capitalism. Lippard repeated this theme in visionary form in *The Entranced; or, The Wanderer of Eighteen Centuries*. Here an early Christian named Adonai guides the "Arisen Washington" on a tour through antebellum America, where they are equally horrified by Northern factories and Southern slave auctions.[21]

Increasingly, Lippard coupled his literary activity with more practical contributions to the cause of labor. Invited to give a valedictory address to the 1848 Industrial Congress, Lippard modeled his speech on Jesus's early sermon in Nazareth, calling for an "acceptable year of the Lord," "when there shall be left on the surface of this Union no Capitalist to grind dollars from the sweat and blood of the workers, no Speculator to juggle free land from the grasp of unborn generations. When every Man who toils shall dwell on his own ground, and when Factories, Almshouses, Jails, and the pestilential nooks of great cities, shall be displaced by the Homesteads of a Free People."[22] This formulation accents the agrarian vision of the Congress, which wanted the federal government to distribute western farmland to urban workers. But Lippard's anticapitalist vision was in fact quite eclectic. The pages of his *Quaker City Weekly* were filled with praise for such diverse exponents of socialism as Charles Fourier, Louis Blanc, and Etienne Cabet.[23] He designed his Brotherhood of the Union to function simultaneously as a labor union, mutual-aid society, workers' cooperative, and esoteric secret society; its goal was to achieve "the Union of the Workers against the Idlers who do not work, but who do steal the fruits of Labor's toil—the Union of Labor until Labor ripens into Capital."[24]

In introducing the brotherhood, he was also explicit about why the labor movement needed to borrow organizational models from the Freemasons and other secret societies. The Freemasons, he claimed, had originally been an order of workers: "Despised, oppressed, and crushed in the outer world, the Workman retreated to the shadows of his Lodge, and there became the equal of the Priest and King who had ground him to the dust."[25] Freemasonry's success in laying the foundation for democratic revolutions in the eighteenth century suggested that it could become a model for labor organizing in the nineteenth. Secret societies offered workers both the power of "combination" and secrecy's protection against capitalist retribution. And their "ceremonial rites" would give "degraded" workers the confidence they needed to confront capital directly.[26]

Lippard's brand of esoteric radicalism persisted throughout the nineteenth century. The Brotherhood of the Union itself survived for more than a century and did not reach its peak membership (of thirty thousand) until 1914, although by that time it had eschewed much of its early radicalism.[27] More significantly, Uriah Stephens borrowed much of Lippard's ritual when he organized the Knights of Labor in 1870, and dozens of smaller unions also used ceremonial ritual and secrecy to foster labor solidarity. Post-Christian strands of esotericism also contributed to radical movements, from the 1872 presidential campaign of spiritualist Victoria Woodhull to the Theosophical utopias formed at the turn of the century. So it was no accident that several of Lippard's literary devices reappeared in the novels of Populist Party activist Ignatius Donnelly, who published *Caesar's Column* in 1889, *Doctor Huguet* in 1891, and *The Golden Bottle* in 1892.[28] Like Lippard's books, these novels seek to provoke outrage in their readers by featuring graphic depictions of physical and sexual violence perpetrated by the rich against the poor. They castigate conventional churches for their support of the plutocracy. And they are replete with esoteric elements.

Although Donnelly did not acknowledge Lippard as a literary or political influence, he could not have failed to be aware of the older man's literary activism. Just nine years younger than Lippard, Donnelly was raised in Philadelphia and was a high school student at the height of Lippard's fame. The two men had a few other things in common: both came from middle-class families but lost their fathers early in childhood; both took pride in their immigrant heritage (German for Lippard, Irish for Donnelly); both were disillusioned by teenage experiences as law clerks. Donnelly's earliest publications demonstrated that he shared Lippard's opposition to Know-Nothingism and enthusiasm for the European revolutions of 1848, though his literary style was more highbrow and his political affiliation more conventional. Donnelly was a Democratic party operative through 1856, after which he moved to Minnesota and shifted his allegiance to the Republicans. During the Civil War he served two terms as Minnesota's lieutenant governor, in part because of his success in persuading working-class immigrants that they could escape the "degradation of bondage" only by making common cause with Southern slaves.[29] As a three-term Republican congressman, Donnelly fought for black suffrage and open immigration, then drifted toward economic radicalism as the Republicans became more conservative. Convinced that western farmers were victimized by eastern monopolies, the protective tariff, and the gold standard, Donnelly supported a series of third parties, culminating in his role in the founding of the People's Party in 1892.[30]

In short, while Lippard was a novelist first and an activist second, Donnelly was a career politician who used both fiction and nonfiction as strategies for publicizing his social and spiritual vision. By far his most successful published work was *Atlantis: The Antediluvian World* (1882), an exhaustive case for the historicity of Plato's account of Atlantis. This was followed up by *Ragnarok: The Age of Fire and Gravel* (1883), which argued—against the uniformitarian presuppositions that informed Darwinism—that catastrophic events occurring within human history (and recalled in the mythologies of most cultures) could account for observed geological phenomena. Finally,

The Great Cryptogram sought to demonstrate that Francis Bacon had written Shakespeare's plays.[31] These three works of popular nonfiction were not as explicitly radical as the novels that followed them, but they were equally indebted to esotericism, especially in their eagerness to find hidden meanings in ancient texts.

Donnelly's novels coincided with the height of his Populist activism, and they reflect both his solidarity with the cause of labor and his competitive antagonism toward other strands of radicalism, especially the revolutionary traditions of Marxism and anarchism. While *Paul Ardenheim* is set during the American Revolution, *Caesar's Column* is a futuristic dystopia set one hundred years after the time of its writing. In Donnelly's vision, the United States is secretly controlled by a cabal of plutocrats with the power to make and unmake presidents and politicians. They are opposed by an anarchistic "Brotherhood of Destruction" with one hundred million members, both white workers and black sharecroppers. As you might expect, this brotherhood begins its revolution by occupying Wall Street, "bursting open the great moneyed institutions and blow[ing] up the safes with giant powder and Hecla powder." Donnelly is clear about his distaste for both brotherhoods. By the novel's end, the leader of the Brotherhood of Destruction, a farmer named Caesar, is literally drunk with power, and "Caesar's Column" is a massive tower formed from the bodies of the millions slaughtered in the rebellion. Donnelly compares the outcome to the destruction of Atlantis, having his narrator muse that his record of the events would someday be "treasured as we now treasure the glimpses of the world before the Deluge, contained in the Book of Genesis."[32]

In *Caesar's Column*, Donnelly suggests that a more redemptive "Brotherhood of Justice" is needed as an alternative to the Brotherhood of Destruction, but it is only in *The Golden Bottle* that he spells out what this might look like. In this novel, the hero magically receives a bottle with an alchemical substance that turns iron to gold. This is an ironic device given Donnelly's opposition to the gold standard, but that's the point: by vastly expanding the supply of gold, his hero makes credit more widely available to the workers and farmers burdened by debt. As the plutocracy mobilizes against him, he mobilizes his supporters into a Brotherhood of Justice in order to forestall the forces of reaction. Fearful of reprisal, each member secretly designates three successors to carry on their work in case of assassination. The brotherhood is also an empowering self-help organization; it cheaply republishes "all the greatest books of antiquity and of modern times" to raise the intellectual culture of the workers. Soon, the brotherhood revolutionizes both the United

States and Europe, and eventually creates a sort of United Nations based in the Azores—chosen because of their proximity to ancient Atlantis.[33]

Despite the thematic continuity of *Caesar's Column* and *The Golden Bottle*, Donnelly wrote another novel in between, one that demonstrated his ongoing adherence to the racial egalitarianism of his days as a radical Republican. *Doctor Huguet* tells the story of a liberal white physician in the South who mysteriously switches bodies with a black chicken thief. Initially distressed by his new identity, Huguet ultimately rallies his black neighbors to join white farmers in "a vast army, with principles for banners and ballots for weapons." Although the novel draws heavily on stereotypes of black violence and debasement, and fails to imagine ways in which African Americans might become the agents of their own redemption, it is notable as a rare example of white Northern opposition to lynching and disfranchisement at a time when many white radicals ignored the horrors of Jim Crow. It also demonstrates an interesting theological parallel with Lippard's work. Just as Lippard delighted in spectral images of Jesus's "FACE" as an inspiration for social activists, Donnelly incorporated two dream scenes in which his hero sees "that unutterable, that indescribable face" of Christ, which then "resolve[s] itself . . . into millions of faces—faces brown, yellow, pale, black, but none of them white."[34]

The significance of Lippard's and Donnelly's novels lies partly in their chronology. Lippard wrote long before the emergence of the Social Gospel movement, and slightly before the early Christian socialist novels of Church of England minister Charles Kingsley. Donnelly published *Caesar's Column* and *The Golden Bottle* near the beginning of the Social Gospel movement— *after* Washington Gladden had called on Protestant ministers to pay more attention to workers' movements but *before* he had coined the term *social salvation*. Donnelly's novels appeared well before the most famous Social Gospel novel, *In His Steps* by Charles Sheldon.[35] (Sheldon's plot, in which a Christ-like visitor exposes the complacency of a bourgeois congregation, echoes that of Lippard's "Jesus and the Poor."[36]) Donnelly proposed his "Brotherhood of Justice" just a few years before Protestant ministers began organizing themselves in small brotherhoods, such as Walter Rauschenbusch's Brotherhood of the Kingdom and the Kingdom Movement of George Herron, like Donnelly a Minnesotan. This is not to suggest that Donnelly was the sole inspiration for such movements; indeed, his own vision may have been shaped by the "Nationalist Clubs" organized to promote the utopian vision of Edward Bellamy's 1888 novel, *Looking Backward.* As it happened, the Nationalist Clubs were organized by members of the Theosophical Society, and soon attracted many Protestant ministers.[37] So this is another case that supports the point I am making about Lippard and Donnelly: a great many laypeople with esoteric interests were thinking theologically about labor even before the ministers and professional theologians joined the conversation.

That is not the way the Social Gospel is usually understood. The conventional narrative views it as the response of Protestant ministers and theologians to the challenge of labor militancy and socialist agitation in the second half of the nineteenth century. The model of "challenge and response" implies that the labor and socialist movements had no religious or theological content of their own, and this is in fact the way some Social Gospel ministers talked about them. In many cases, they were radicalized by their realization that many working men were reluctant to attend church.

The cases of Lippard and Donnelly—and to the list I might add journalist Henry George and novelist Edward Bellamy—demonstrate that laypeople were already doing their own theologizing within radical movements, prior to the emergence of the Social Gospel. Donnelly, for example, opened *Caesar's Column* by promising to show the churches "why they have lost their hold upon the poor" and to teach them to regain it by becoming "the champion and defender of mankind against all its oppressors."[38] Lippard's and Donnelly's popularity as novelists gave them a bully pulpit for their lay preaching, and both were eagerly sought out as spokesmen by labor movements. Like Walt Whitman and Upton Sinclair, they were organic intellectuals of the labor movement, using their literary cachet to promote social change.

Their significance goes beyond chronological priority, however. In many ways Lippard's and Donnelly's religious vision is more complex and challenging than that of Charles Sheldon, Washington Gladden, or other professional theologians. In part this was because they did a better job of writing from the perspective of the workers themselves, rather than that of clerical allies. In part it was because they presented their theology as part of a continuous, hidden tradition, rather than a mere response to challenges coming from outside the Christian tradition. Most important, Lippard and Donnelly offered a more inclusive model of social sin and salvation. Whereas most Social Gospelers focused narrowly on economic issues, Lippard and Donnelly believed that capitalism was inseparable from the sexual exploitation of women by men, and from the hypocrisy of mainstream clergy. They also offered a more nuanced vision of how people who are complicit in social sin might nevertheless join the struggle to overcome it—as well as a prophetic warning of how efforts to overcome oppression might reconstitute that oppression in a new form.

Although Lippard and Donnelly were not themselves wage workers, they were more successful than the Social Gospelers at writing books that ordinary workers might want to read. Lippard, in particular, typically privileged the gaze of ordinary workers like Arthur Dermoyne (in *New York*), a brawny shoemaker who comes to New York in pursuit of the clergyman who has seduced his beloved. Dermoyne is a self-taught orphan who has remained within the working class because he "cannot separate myself from that nine-tenths of the human family, who seem to have been born only to work and die." When he confronts the seducer, he threatens him with his "almost super-human strength," but also waxes poetic about his desire to found "a community . . . where every one will have a place to work, and every one will receive the fruits of his work . . . [and where] will we, without priest, or monopolist, or slaveholder, establish in the midst of a band of brothers, the worship of that Christ who was himself a workman."[39] By contrast, the Social Gospel fictions of Charles Sheldon centered on middle-class professionals who used their power as ministers, employers, and editors to transform society from above.

Lippard's authorial gaze is insistently white and male as well as working class. His white, male, working-class characters are consistently three-dimensional; whether they are heroes or villains, they must struggle between virtuous and vicious impulses. Lippard's African American characters, by contrast, have either been reduced to sheer bestiality by their enslavement (as is the case for Mosquito and Glow Worm, the bodyguards of Monk Hall) or are incapable of reining in their murderous rage against slave masters—though Lippard clearly sympathizes with the righteous violence of Randolph Royalton in *New York* and Black Andy in *The Killers*, the latter an exposé of a Philadelphia race riot. Native Americans are virtuous but enigmatic, and usually the last remnant of a noble lineage. Lippard's women are a bit more complex, but for the most part they are either virgins or whores. Lippard professed the "doctrine" that "no angel around God's throne is purer than Woman when her intellectual nature alone is stirred into development, [and] that no devil crouching in the flames of hell is fouler than Woman, when her animal nature alone is roused into action."[40]

These features of Lippard's writing, coupled with his semipornographic fascination with women's bodies, have led leading Lippard scholar David Reynolds to characterize his work as a case of "immoral reform" that "deemphasized the remedies for vice while probing the grisly, sometimes perverse results of vice, such as shattered homes, sadomasochistic violence, eroticism, nightmare visions, and the disillusioning collapse of romantic ideals."[41] Reynolds intends this partly as praise; one of his arguments is that immoral reform prepared the way for Melville's and Hawthorne's canonical grapplings with moral ambiguity. But Dawn Coleman has rightly responded that the notion of immoral reform cannot account for the "animating force" of Lippard's moral and religious ideals, while Timothy Helwig has argued that Lippard's writings "are distinguished among nineteenth-century American literature for their racial sympathy."[42] Indeed, even in his stereotypical depictions of blacks and women, Lippard was struggling to articulate what we would now call a theory of interlocking oppressions. While many Social Gospelers simply did not address the concerns of women or of people of color, Lippard was convinced that seduction and slavery (as well as religious hypocrisy) were inextricably linked to capitalism. Nevertheless—perhaps because he was a young white man who had directly experienced economic privation but not other forms of oppression—Lippard failed to enter convincingly into the subjectivities of people other than white men. This failure had tragic consequences, for most of Lippard's imitators freely borrowed his images of black and female depravity (and his racially loaded invocation of "white slavery") without absorbing his radical critique. And, as Shelley Streeby has demonstrated, Lippard's enthusiasm for land redistribution as a solution to urban poverty led him to apologize for American empire in his two books on the Mexican War, *Legends of Mexico* and *'Bel of Prairie Eden.*[43] Similarly, Donnelly's choice to explore Southern racism through the experience of a white man in a black body reflected an incapacity to depict black agency, much as he personally deplored the effects of racial inequality.

Even though Lippard and Donnelly were not themselves wage workers, they displayed a keen sense of the ambiguous agency of white working-class men, and I suspect that was the key to their appeal. Their leading characters are not in control of their own destinies, but neither are they under the visible control of others in the way that enslaved persons or abused wives are. Instead, they are subject to shadowy social and economic forces, as well as to the wayward impulses of their own hearts. Ambiguous agency, of course, was the common experience of "free labor" in a rapidly industrializing and urbanizing nation. In the nineteenth century, artisans, industrial workers, and farmers all had to contend with impersonal and invisible forces that significantly constrained their life choices, whether by restricting credit, by reducing the chances for journeymen to become masters, or by causing widespread unemployment during times of economic contraction. These invisible forces were doubly vexing because most nineteenth-century Americans could still remember the ethos of the village, in which neighbors could shape their lives through face-to-face interactions. Indeed, ambiguous agency was felt with special intensity by migrants from the country to the city. These people enjoyed new economic, social, religious, and sexual freedoms—but these freedoms were coupled with new and frightening vulnerabilities.

Lippard, who was born in rural Pennsylvania and raised in a suburban area that was rapidly being incorporated into the Philadelphia metropolis, was fascinated by ambiguous agency even before he fully identified himself with the cause of the working class. In the early installations of *The Quaker City*, the most fully developed characters are not working class, but they most certainly *do* experience ambiguous agency. One of them, Luke Harvey, has risen from poverty to become the junior partner in a mercantile firm, but he has also seen his sweetheart married to his boss—and he has seen that same boss face both bankruptcy and the infidelity of his wife. In the face of such vicissitudes, he can only conclude that "if a prize were offered somewhere by somebody, for the queerest world a-going, this world of ours might be rigged up nice, and sent in like a bit of show beef, as the premium queer world." The other, Byrnewood Arlington, is a wealthy young man who has impregnated and callously abandoned a family servant—but is horrified to learn his drinking buddy plans to do the same to his sister: "And yet I, I, wronged an innocent girl, because she was my father's servant! Great God! Can she, have a brother to feel for her ruin?"[44] Unlike the seduction victims in sentimental novels or the enslaved persons in antislavery fiction, Luke and Byrnewood feel neither innocent nor powerless in the face of injustice. Instead, their righteous anger propels them to acts of violence that exacerbate the ambiguity to the point of madness.

As *The Quaker City* was serialized, Lippard realized that such plot devices divided his readership: middle-class critics denounced them as immoral, while working-class readers eagerly embraced them.[45] Lippard repaid the favor by incorporating more and more working-class characters into his fiction. Because he and Donnelly saw the world from a working-class perspective, they were more preoccupied with the question of how ordinary workers can gain power than that of how privileged persons can use their power more ethically. This marks a sharp contrast with the Social Gospel ethos: Charles Sheldon's main characters, for example, include an editor, an employer, and a minister, all of whom seek to infuse Jesus's idealism into those social roles. Lippard's and Donnelly's preoccupation with power makes their work relatively impervious to the charge of sentimentalism that Reinhold Niebuhr hurled at the Social Gospelers.

Niebuhr thought the antidote to sentimentality was a vaguely Marxist "realism." Lippard's and Donnelly's approach to power, by contrast, was rooted in magical traditions. Both used alchemical images—Donnelly's golden bottle and, in *Paul Ardenheim*, a leaden statue of a downtrodden Jesus with a golden statue of Jesus the worker hidden within—to suggest that workers might gain courage from magical talismans. Because these images appear in works of fiction, it is not immediately obvious whether they are to be taken literally or as symbols of more mundane ways of gaining power, such as union organizing or consciousness raising. But that distinction collapses when one considers that the book itself might be the magical talisman that inspires the workers to unite.

Lippard and Donnelly believed that empowering magic had a long history, and that the resources needed to resist capitalism were as old as Atlantis or the Gospels. This also set them apart from the progressive orientation of many Social Gospelers, who assumed that the problems of industrialism were new problems that demanded new theologies, but not necessarily a wholesale rejection of mainstream doctrines. By contrast, Lippard and Donnelly presented their ancient tradition as a hidden one, long suppressed but handed down by such valiant groups as the Rosicrucians. One key component of this vision was the idea that Jesus was himself a working-class radical. Prior to Lippard, labor radicals typically contrasted the prolabor "gospel of Jesus" with the false Christianity of the churches, but Lippard may have been the first to root Jesus's radicalism in his personal experience.[46] In a remarkable scene that appears both in *Paul Ardenheim* and in *Washington and His Generals* (as part of a section describing the prehistory of the Declaration of Independence), Lippard suggested that Jesus became fully divine only by virtue of his working-class solidarity. Young Jesus, he suggested, was a carpenter's apprentice "with a saw in one hand" when he began meditating on "his brothers—the Brotherhood of Toil! That vast family, who now swelter in dark mines, bend in the fields, under the hot sun, or toil, toil, toil on, forever in the Workshops of the World." And at that very moment "he felt the Godhead fill his veins—at that moment, he stood there a God."[47] The trope would soon be echoed by labor activists Terence Powderly, Mother Jones, Eugene Debs, and Bouck White; radical historian Cyrenus Osborne Ward; and novelists Eugène Sue and Upton Sinclair, as well as by Ignatius Donnelly, who declared that "Jesus was only possible in a barefoot world, and he was crucified by the few who wore shoes."[48]

There is little evidence to suggest that Lippard's writings directly influenced every subsequent radical depiction of Jesus as a class-conscious worker.

Some, perhaps, were indirectly inspired by the Jesus-centered rituals of the Brotherhood of the Union. Some, as David Burns has suggested, were indebted to the freethinking historical scholarship of Ernest Renan, whose *Life of Jesus* was published in French fifteen years after Lippard's writings on Jesus.[49] Since freethought and esoteric Christianity had a common critique of the institutional church, it is likely that their influences flowed together within working-class and activist communities that felt betrayed by wealthy churches. What is clear is that the image of Jesus as a working-class radical was not created by professional theologians; with the exception of ministers who were fully committed to the Socialist Party, Social Gospelers either ignored this image or sought directly to refute it.[50]

Unlike many subsequent authors, Lippard did not present his image of a radical Jesus as the fruit of historical critical scholarship, nor as a recovery of a historical truth that had been forgotten for centuries. It was, instead, a narrative that had been preserved by a continuous lineage of secret societies. Moreover, he assumed that it would be no easy matter for the workers to recognize Jesus as their brother. Only an alchemical process of personal transformation would allow them to discover the smiling, golden Jesus beneath the sneering, leaden Jesus of the church.[51] The same point was implied in Donnelly's appeals to Atlantean precedent. Although David Reynolds has suggested that Lippard's fascination with history introduced a "reactionary" element into his radicalism, such appeals allowed radicals to place themselves on an even playing field with the "historic" church.[52]

The most persistent magical images in Lippard's and Donnelly's novels were those of the individual magician and the secret brotherhood. The former possessed a mesmeric influence on other people and an intuitive capacity to intervene subtly in moments of crisis, changing the course of history while avoiding the notice of historians. Thus, one of Lippard's favorite plot devices was to have a mysterious stranger hold back the hand of someone who is about to commit violence. Sometimes this character is someone who might easily be the perpetrator of violence in the next scene; thus, Luke holds back the hand of his employer before the latter can murder his unfaithful wife. Such incidents underscore the notion that magic is potentially available to anyone. But certain characters clearly possess an unusually large share of magic. This is the case for Paul Ardenheim and for the quite similar Paul Mount-Laurel in *The Nazarene*. Even these characters, however, experience ambiguous agency. Paul Ardenheim continually wrestles with the choice between his Rosicrucian vocation and his desire for sexual fulfillment. After rescuing a woman from sexual violence, Paul Mount-Laurel compulsively tests her purity by offering to facilitate her liaison with a wealthy man, all the while preoccupied with his own attraction to her.[53]

The real task of the individual magician is to call the secret brotherhood into existence. Paul Ardenheim's vocation—the one that he has not quite fulfilled by the novel's end—is to reconstruct the Rosicrucian Order that he has inherited from his father. Lippard styled himself as an individual magician, complete with a mysterious cape, but he devoted the final years of his life to building up an actual organization that might outlive him. Similarly, the hero of *The Golden Bottle* uses his own magical talisman primarily for the purpose of creating the Brotherhood of Justice.

These benevolent magicians and brotherhoods square off against equally powerful but malevolent wizards and brotherhoods. True Rosicrucianism, Lippard contended, had descended from an ancient, antediluvian order, but it had always had to contend with more visible rivals. Its mystic symbols were first stolen by the exploitative religion of "Altars and Thrones," then turned into "childish mummeries" by modern-day Freemasons.[54] Donnelly also situated his true brotherhood between violent rivals. "Vast combinations," he explained, "depress the price of labor," while "great communistic organizations" oppose them, and "no white flags pass from the one to the other."[55] In many cases, the evil magicians and brotherhoods began with high ideals but were corrupted by their own pursuit of power. In Lippard's novel, the cursed ancestor of Paul Ardenheim, who had once dreamed of "rais[ing] mankind to godlike power," laments that he is "doomed to live with impulses of good always struggling in my heart, and yet always forced to do evil." The narrator asks rhetorically, "Can any-thing in the Universe be more appalling than this?" and then points out that the "Creed of a Church" posits just this about millions of human souls predestined to hell.[56] The title character of *Caesar's Column*, similarly, begins as an idealistic farmer who loses both his farm to a moneylender and his daughter's honor to the moneylender's lawyer. By the time he seizes power from the plutocracy, though, his only goal is to pile the bodies of the slaughtered into a gigantic column.[57]

The esoteric image of rival brotherhoods secretly competing to shape human destiny performed the same theological work as the Social Gospelers' notion of "social sin" and "social salvation." It allowed Lippard and Donnelly to present social evil as widespread, even pervasive, without implying that it was divinely ordained or unchangeable. Human history, for them, was not the straightforward outcome of the overarching will of divine providence; neither was it the contingent result of individual choices. Rather, it was the product of continuous conflict between shadowy organizations, both good and evil, operating just beyond the range of mundane sight. As was the case for the Social Gospelers, structural analysis allowed Lippard and Donnelly to denounce social evil while displaying some compassion for its perpetrators. In *Caesar's Column*, Donnelly's hero observes that the privileged inhabitants of New York City—the folks we would now call the "1 percent"—were physically and spiritually deformed by their privilege: "I could not but think how universal and irresistible must have been the influences of the age that could mold all these men and women into the same soulless likeness. I pitied them." Even observing the inner circle of plutocrats, his pity does not fade: "They were the victims of a pernicious system, as fully as were the poor, shambling, ragged wretches of the streets and slums." And when he gains access to the governing council of the Brotherhood of Destruction, he makes the same point: the "large heads" of both groups were similar, because "high and low were alike victims—unconscious victims—of a system. The crime was not theirs: it lay at the door of the shallow, indifferent, silly generations of the past."[58]

Such analyses placed Lippard and Donnelly within a larger theological conversation that was by no means limited to professional theologians. At the turn of the nineteenth century, utopian socialist Charles Fourier—a theorist much admired by Lippard—taught that social inequality was not divinely ordained, but simply resulted from humanity's failure to unlock the "Divine Social Code" that would make cooperation possible.[59] Similarly, Henry George's 1879 *Progress and Poverty*—the most influential work of radical economics in nineteenth-century America—framed the problem of inequality as one of theodicy. Malthusian pessimism about the inevitability of poverty in the midst of increasing wealth was, for George, "a gratuitous attribution to the laws of God of results . . . which really spring from the mal-adjustments of men."[60] Donnelly made a virtually identical point in *Caesar's Column*, declaring that "God is not at fault. Nature is not to blame" for the "hell of injustice, ending in a holocaust of slaughter."[61]

Lippard's and Donnelly's esoteric theology thus had much in common with the liberal anti-Calvinism that informed the Social Gospelers' critique of orthodox economics. Capitalist economists held that the invisible forces shaping society were, in fact, natural laws: an "iron law of wages" made it impossible for employers to pay employees more than the market rate; survival of the fittest ensured that there would always be both economic winners and economic losers. From the Social Gospel perspective, such claims put a scientific veneer on the old Augustinian and Calvinist theology of original sin and predestination: social injustice might be ultimately traceable to the

Fall, but the resulting structures of inequality had become so much "second nature" that there was no point in fighting against them.[62]

To varying degrees, the Social Gospel alternative built on the mainstream liberal tradition of William Ellery Channing and Ralph Waldo Emerson. These liberals flatly denied the doctrine of original sin, insisting that every person is free to renounce sin and grow in likeness to the divine. In the economic sphere, this meant taking the Golden Rule, rather than the iron law of wages, as one's guide to action. The problem with this theology was that it simply denied the existence of invisible, oppressive forces, rather than providing practical tools for overcoming them. It appealed to professionals and intellectuals who retained a lively sense of their own agency, and it inspired many of them to become allies of working-class movements. But it could not speak to the existential crisis of the workers and farmers themselves.

Lippard and Donnelly shared many of these liberal presuppositions. They, too, called for "deeds, not creeds," and "bread, not dogma." In ascribing social evils to secret brotherhoods, they hoped to vindicate both God and human nature, showing that the "hell of injustice" could coexist with people "fitted to sing among the angels."[63] They differed from other liberals in their willingness to acknowledge that impersonal forces could deprive individuals of free agency. As a consequence, their understanding of social sin and salvation went deeper than that of the Social Gospelers in three ways: in its inclusion of religious and sexual elements in its model of structural evil; in its insistence that people who were themselves entangled in social sin might nevertheless contribute to social salvation; and in its acknowledgment of the possibility that agencies of social salvation might themselves be twisted into expressions of social sin.

For Lippard and Donnelly, virtually every capitalist was also a rapacious seducer and a religious hypocrite. From one perspective, this was sensationalist overkill that undermined the seriousness of their analysis. But they were also pointing out some undeniable interconnections. Poor women *were* vulnerable to the sexual advances of their employers. Unmarried women who became pregnant were often forced into prostitution to feed themselves and their children. The daughters of wealthy men often agreed to loveless marriages in order to preserve a comfortable lifestyle. Fashionable ministers often turned a blind eye to the economic and sexual behavior of the men who paid their salaries, and sometimes used their own personal charisma for purposes of sexual exploitation. These were not merely add-ons to their critique of capitalism; at least for Lippard, concern with seduction and ministerial hypocrisy actually predated a thoroughgoing anticapitalism. By incorporating all these story lines into their fiction, Lippard and Donnelly implicitly called for a broad radical coalition, open to those whose first experience of injustice might have been sexual or religious rather than economic. They did so, moreover, with an evenhandedness that is lacking in the work of Marx and Engels, who certainly incorporated sexual and religious oppression into their model, but presented it as derivative of fundamentally economic realities. Yet, like Marx and Engels, they persisted in assuming that white men would lead the movement.

In addition to giving their view of structural sin a sexual and religious dimension, Lippard and Donnelly looked at structural sin from the inside—from the perspective of people who do not experience themselves as agents of their own destiny. Lippard in particular took addiction and compulsion seriously and compassionately in his description of Paul Ardenheim's emotional turmoil and in his willingness to ascribe benevolent impulses to his most depraved villains. By this means, he offers a path to radical commitment for people who experience themselves as radically flawed. Here we can make a fruitful contrast between Lippard's sensational radicalism and the sentimental radicalism expressed by many liberal women novelists of his day.

Sentimental heroines, at their best, are plucky, self-possessed paragons of protofeminist virtue. They stand up to their own lovers, and to men of power—Catharine Sedgwick's Hope Leslie tells John Winthrop that she must be faithful to "my own conscience and heart" rather than to the authority of "anybody that happened to be a little older than myself."[64] They honor their own desires by learning to channel those desires in socially appropriate ways, making sure they are not personally endangered along the way. They have what it takes to stand up to external adversity, whether in the form of evil stepmothers, religious persecution, or social injustice. As such, they are great models—for some people. But for some, their capacity to resist temptation is just too daunting—and those people seem to be the ones for whom Lippard writes.

Lippard's counterpart to Hope Leslie might thus be Long-Haired Bess, the prostitute and opium addict who helps ensnare the first seduction victim in *The Quaker City*—but subsequently intervenes to save her and several others. Bess is a "mass of contradictions," Lippard notes, but she is simply an example of the "self-warring heart" of every human being.[65] In keeping with this principle, a Lippardean hero like Paul Ardenheim is beset with compulsive desires; throughout the novel, he teeters on the brink of temptation. And Lippard's villains all possess benevolent impulses that they cannot smother. He describes one villain as still open to "some pure Spirit," and scolds believers in "Total Depravity" for doubting the plausibility of this. Echoing liberal polemics, he notes, "If there exists such a thing as Total Depravity on the face of the earth, you will find it in the heart of the man, who has so brutalized his nature, as to be able to believe the Dogma."[66]

Lippard wrote for those who had already succumbed to temptation; those who were beset with addictive, self-destructive desires; those whose adversities are more internal than external—those who have been mistreated not by an evil stepmother but by a father whom they are growing to resemble, those who are not only poor but deeply ashamed of their poverty. To all these people, Lippard says, "You, too, can be part of something larger than yourself; you too can join the cosmic struggle to right the world's injustices."

Donnelly's approach is much the same. One sympathetic character in *Caesar's Column* is simultaneously a member of the Brotherhood of Destruction and a trusted steward to the top plutocrat. Explaining his choice to do work that he loathes, he muses, "What are we? The creatures of fate; the victims of circumstances. We look upon the Medusa-head of destiny, with its serpent curls, and our wills, if not our souls, are turned into stone." Of course, this man's will is *not* entirely petrified: he has made the choice to support the brotherhood, despite its "terrible" methods, because "its grand conception" is "charitable and just."[67]

For Lippard and Donnelly, human nature is inherently good—indeed, in keeping with the esoteric perspective, all are inherently divine. "That in me which speaks, and that in you which listens," says one of Donnelly's heroes, "are alike part and parcel of the eternal Maker of all things. . . . Thought, love, conscience and consciousness are parts of God himself." But this divinity is visible only when people navigate between the shoals of tyranny and destruction. "Mankind is so capable of good," muses another character, "and yet all above is cruelty, craft and destruction, and all below is suffering, wretchedness, sin and shame."[68] Successful navigation relies not only on individual agency, but on the alchemical magic of Lippard's Rosicrucian initiation or Donnelly's golden bottle.

Both Lippard and Donnelly offered the workers of the world a rallying cry and an important caution. The rallying cry is that the cause of freedom is a cosmic one; the caution is that even the highest idealism can readily turn into its opposite. Because Paul is a symbol of the United States, the same double message can be directed to the United States: the United States has a sacred mission to bring freedom to the world, but its twin evils of slavery and capitalism can readily betray that mission. Lippard promised to elaborate on this in a sequel devoted to the violence of the French Revolution. Though he never wrote that novel, one of his last published novels, *Adonai,* made the vision explicit. Donnelly's warning was even more explicit in *Caesar's Column,* where he portrayed the anarchistic Brotherhood of Destruction as every bit as dangerous as the plutocracy itself.

Salutary as these warnings were, Lippard and Donnelly were playing with fire. If negative images of the secret brotherhood could be applied not only to the plutocracy, but also to radical organizations that have gone astray, so too could they be used to promote conspiracy theories about relatively uncorrupted radical organizations, or about government agencies, or about religious or ethnic minorities. Although Lippard was generous to virtually all stripes of radicalism in his own day, Donnelly's image of the Brotherhood of Destruction undoubtedly fed into late nineteenth-century stereotypes of all Marxists and anarchists as terroristic bomb throwers. Most twenty-first-century readers of Lippard and Donnelly will, I suspect, immediately notice the parallels between their rhetoric and that of right-wing conspiracy theorists—and these parallels are not entirely accidental. By borrowing anti-Catholic tropes and applying them to capitalism instead, Lippard vividly expressed his disgust with nativism—but many of his imitators turned the same tropes back to nativist purposes, or drained the moral purpose out of sensationalism altogether. (On the other hand, his European counterpart Eugène Sue evolved in tandem with Lippard, identifying ever more fully with the nascent socialist movement. And Lippard's analysis of class, sex, and religion appears in equally radical but somewhat less sensational form in the late nineteenth-century novels of Lois Waisbrooker.)

Donnelly came even closer to anticipating the xenophobic, semifascist populism of Charles Coughlin. He chose to cast Jews as leaders of *both* the plutocracy and the Brotherhood of Destruction, emphasizing the "Hebraic cast of countenance" that made the top banker's face appear to be "all angles." Donnelly's portrait of "the nameless Russian Jew who was accounted 'the brains of the Brotherhood'" was even more racialized: his "face was mean and sinister; two fangs alone remained in his mouth; his nose was hooked; the eyes were small, sharp, penetrating and restless; but the expanse of brow above them was grand and noble." The last detail reveals the perverse confusion underlying Donnelly's view of Judaism: he acknowledged that Christians had oppressed Jews for centuries, claimed that this had turned some Jews into monsters, and concluded that Christians deserved to suffer at the hands of these monsters. "Now the Christian world is paying, in tears and blood, for the sufferings inflicted by their bigoted and ignorant ancestors upon a noble race." Donnelly seems to have imagined that simply acknowledging that Jews had survived "infinite depths of persecution" gave him permission to portray Jewish bankers as occupying a position "higher than the thrones of Europe" in a "Semitized" world.[69] Obviously, this assessment ignored both ongoing pogroms in Eastern Europe and the precarious privileges of Western Jews in the era of the Dreyfus affair. In the utopian vision of *The Golden Bottle*, Donnelly made awkward amends by restoring the Jewish people to Palestine, and to an honored place in the Congress of the Universal Republic.[70] Still, his stereotypes surely made some contribution to the horrors of the next century. Both Lippard and Donnelly, I am convinced, intended to undermine the dualism inherent in lurid images of cosmic battle—yet they consistently made the lurid images more memorable than their subtle undermining of them. And so they fed into the dualistic currents of fascism and nativism.

By the same token, they avoided the corresponding danger of the Social Gospel, which (at least in its ecclesiastical manifestations) was perhaps too willing to embrace the liberal consensus of the middle of the twentieth century, with its ameliorative rather than socialist response to the evils of capitalism.[71] And the challenging vision of their fiction has lost little of its relevance today. If early twenty-first-century America is not quite as dystopian as Donnelly imagined, we certainly suffer from inequalities as sharp as those of 1890. Some of us today might lament, as he did then, that "the land is covered with a filthy scab, an eczema of mortgages, under which vermin swarm and fatten."[72] As the battle lines sharpen between the 1 percent and the 99 percent, it will be interesting to see which esoteric resources are brought into the struggle, and to what ends.

Notes

1. Excellent recent interpretations of this legacy include Gary Dorrien, *Soul in Society: The Making and Renewal of Social Christianity* (Minneapolis: Fortress, 1995); Gary Dorrien, *Social Ethics in the Making: Interpreting an American Tradition* (Malden, MA: Wiley-Blackwell, 2009), Christopher H. Evans, *Liberalism without Illusions: Renewing an American Christian Tradition* (Waco, TX: Baylor University Press, 2010).

2. C. Melissa Snarr, *All You That Labor: Religion and Ethics in the Living Wage Movement* (New York: New York University Press, 2011); Tex Sample, *Blue-Collar Resistance and the Politics of Jesus: Doing Ministry with Working-Class Whites* (Nashville, TN: Abingdon, 2006); and Jeffrey Stout, *Blessed Are the Organized: Grassroots Democracy in America* (Princeton, NJ: Princeton University Press, 2010)

3. By limiting my definition of the *Social Gospel* to the work of ministers and academics affiliated with mainline religious institutions, I am following a historiographical convention that dates back to the pioneering work of Charles Howard Hopkins, *The Rise of the Social Gospel in American Protestantism, 1865–1915* (New Haven, CT:

Yale University Press, 1940), and Henry F. May, *Protestant Churches and Industrial America* (New York: Harper, 1949). Many other people, of course, understood the gospel to have a social dimension, but for the sake of clarity I will use *Social Gospel* in a narrow sense and *theology of labor* as a more capacious term for the multiple theologies related to the cause of working people.

4. The standard biographies of these two authors are David S. Reynolds, *George Lippard* (Boston: Twayne, 1982); Martin Ridge, *Ignatius Donnelly: Portrait of a Politician* (Chicago: University of Chicago Press, 1962); and David D. Anderson, *Ignatius Donnelly* (Boston: Twayne, 1980). Insightful analyses of Lippard's religious vision can also be found in David S. Reynolds, *Beneath the American Renaissance: The Subversive Imagination in the Age of Emerson and Melville* (Cambridge, MA: Harvard University Press, 1988), and Dawn Coleman, *Preaching and the Rise of the American Novel* (Columbus: Ohio State University Press, 2013).

5. For more systematic accounts of the defining features of Western esotericism, see Antoine Faivre, "Introduction I," in *Modern Esoteric Spirituality,* ed. Antoine Faivre and Jacob Needleman (New York: Crossroad, 1992), xi–xxii; Arthur Versluis, *Magic and Mysticism: An Introduction to Western Esotericism* (Lanham, MD: Rowman and Littlefield, 2007); Nicholas Goodrick-Clarke, *The Western Esoteric Traditions: A Historical Introduction* (Oxford: Oxford University Press, 2008); and Wouter J. Hanegraaff, *Western Esotericism: A Guide for the Perplexed* (London: Bloomsbury Academic, 2013).

6. David Reynolds has described Lippard as fundamentally opposed to theology, but he uses *theology* interchangeably with *doctrine,* while my own sense of the term is broader. See Reynolds, *Lippard,* 73.

7. Robert H. Craig, *Religion and Radical Politics: An Alternative Christian Tradition* (Philadelphia: Temple University Press, 1995); David Burns, *The Life and Death of the Radical Historical Jesus* (New York: Oxford University Press, 2013); Jarod Roll, *Spirit of Rebellion: Labor and Religion in the New Cotton South* (Urbana: University of Illinois Press, 2010); Erik S. Gellman and Jarod Roll, *The Gospel of the Working Class: Labor's Southern Prophets in New Deal America* (Urbana: University of Illinois Press, 2011); William R. Sutton, *Journeymen for Jesus: Evangelical Artisans Confront Capitalism in Jacksonian Baltimore* (University Park: Pennsylvania State University Press, 1998); Robin D. G. Kelley, *Hammer and Hoe: Alabama Communists during the Great Depression* (Chapel Hill: University of North Carolina Press, 1990); Cynthia Taylor, *A. Philip Randolph: The Religious Journey of an African American Labor Leader* (New York: New York University Press, 2006); Edward J. Blum, *W. E. B. DuBois, American Prophet* (Philadelphia: University of Pennsylvania Press, 2007).

8. In stressing the esoteric dimension of Lippard's thought, I depart somewhat from the interpretations of David Reynolds and Dawn Coleman, both of whom have given thoughtful attention to Lippard's religious views. Reynolds, in my view, is too quick to dismiss Lippard's esoteric interests as "periodic infatuations" with "various faiths and fads," and as a consequence, he regards Lippard's essential religiosity as humanistic and skeptical. See Reynolds, *George Lippard,* 73. Coleman rightly stresses

Lippard's ties to the Universalism of his friend Charles Chauncy Burr, but fails to trace the connections between nineteenth-century Universalism and the seventeenth- and eighteenth-century strands of esoteric Pietism that so fascinated Lippard—despite the fact that one of the first proponents of Universalism was George de Benneville, a Pietist who lived in Lippard's hometown of Germantown, Pennsylvania. Significantly, the only extensive analysis of Lippard's relationship to Pietism was published forty-four years ago: Carsten E. Seecamp, "The Chapter of Perfection: A Neglected Influence on George Lippard," *Pennsylvania History* (April 1970): 192–212.

9. George Lippard, *The Quaker City; or, The Monks of Monk Hall*, edited with introduction and notes by David S. Reynolds (Amherst: University of Massachusetts Press, 1995).

10. George Lippard, "Valedictory of the Industrial Congress," in "Editor's Department," *Nineteenth Century* 2 (1848): 187.

11. "The Omaha Platform," in *A Populist Reader: Selections from the Works of American Populist Leaders,* ed. George Brown Tindall (New York: Harper and Row, 1966), 90–96.

12. Courtney Bender, *The New Metaphysicals: Spirituality and the American Religious Imagination* (Chicago: University of Chicago Press, 2010).

13. Wouter J. Hanegraaff, "Beyond the Yates Paradigm: The Study of Western Esotericism between Counterculture and New Complexity," *Aries* 1 (2001): 30; and Catherine L. Albanese, *A Republic of Mind and Spirit: A Cultural History of American Metaphysical Religion* (New Haven, CT: Yale University Press, 2007), 4.

14. For an overview of these traditions, see Arthur Versluis, *Theosophia: Hidden Dimensions of Christianity* (Hudson, NY: Lindisfarne Press, 1994), and Arthur Versluis, *Wisdom's Children: A Christian Esoteric Tradition* (Albany: State University of New York Press, 1999).

15. Anderson, *Ignatius Donnelly,* 22.

16. Reynolds, "Introduction," *George Lippard,* ix–xiv.

17. George Lippard, *The Memoirs of a Preacher, a Revelation of the Church and the Home* (Philadelphia: Joseph Severns, 1849); George Lippard, *The Nazarene; or, The Last of the Washingtons* (Philadelphia: Lippard, 1846).

18. George Lippard, *New York: Its Upper Ten and Lower Million* (Cincinnati: H. M. Rulison, 1853), ix.

19. George Lippard, *Paul Ardenheim, the Monk of Wissahikon* (Philadelphia: T. B. Peterson, 1848). Lippard's understanding of Rosicrucianism is considerably more socially radical than earlier Rosicrucian texts might suggest, and also more radical than the views of today's Fraternitas Rosae Crucis, which claims Lippard as part of its lineage. It is not entirely clear how Lippard reached the conclusions he did: Carsten Seecamp has demonstrated that many details in *Paul Ardenheim* can be traced to Johannes Kelpius's Chapter of Perfection, but finds little evidence that Kelpius was either a social radical or a Rosicrucian; see Seecamp, "The Chapter of Perfection," 201–2, 205–6. For more on the Fraternitas, see www.soul.org.

20. Lippard, *Paul Ardenheim*, 532.

21. George Lippard, *The Entranced; or, The Wanderer of Eighteen Centuries* (Philadelphia: Joseph Severns, 1849).

22. Lippard, "Valedictory."

23. David S. Reynolds, ed., *George Lippard, Prophet of Protest: Writings of an American Radical, 1822–1854* (New York: Peter Lang, 1986), 181–83.

24. George Lippard, "Platform of the Brotherhood of the Union," in Reynolds, *Prophet of Protest*, 209.

25. Lippard, "Secret Societies," *Quaker City Weekly*, August 18, 1849, in Reynolds, *Prophet of Protest*, 204.

26. Lippard, "The Great Secret Society," *Quaker City Weekly*, June 30, 1848, in Reynolds, *Prophet of Protest*, 205; and *Quaker City Weekly*, June 2, 1849, in Reynolds, *Prophet of Protest*, 210.

27. Reynolds, *George Lippard*, 25.

28. Ignatius Donnelly, *Caesar's Column: A Story of the Twentieth Century*, edited and introduction by Nicholas Ruddick (Middletown, CT: Wesleyan University Press, 2003); Ignatius Donnelly, *Doctor Huguet* (Chicago: F. J. Schulte, 1891); and Ignatius Donnelly, *The Golden Bottle*, with a new introduction by David D. Noble (New York: Johnson Reprint, 1968).

29. Ridge, *Ignatius Donnelly: Portrait*, 32–33.

30. Anderson, *Ignatius Donnelly*, 15–32.

31. Ibid., 33–54.

32. Donnelly, *Caesar's Column*, 191, 230.

33. Donnelly, *Golden Bottle*, 290.

34. George Lippard, *Adonai, the Pilgrim of Eternity* (Philadelphia: Published by the author, 1851), 98; and Donnelly, *Doctor Huguet*, 289, 283–84.

35. Charles Sheldon, *In His Steps: "What Would Jesus Do?,"* rev. ed. (Chicago: Advance, 1899).

36. Lippard, "Jesus and the Poor," *Nineteenth Century* 1 (1848): 57–81. I am grateful to Dawn Coleman for calling my attention to this parallel.

37. Edward Bellamy, *Looking Backward, 2000–1887* (Boston: Ticknor, 1888); J. Gordon Melton, "The Theosophical Communities and Their Idea of Universal Brotherhood," in *America's Communal Utopias*, ed. Donald E. Pitzer (Chapel Hill: University of North Carolina Press, 1997), 397–400.

38. Donnelly, *Caesar's Column*, 3.

39. Lippard, *New York*, 108–11.

40. Lippard, *Quaker City*, 85.

41. Reynolds, *Beneath the American Renaissance*, 59, 82–84.

42. Coleman, *Preaching*, 68–69; and Timothy Helwig, "Denying the Wages of Whiteness: The Racial Politics of George Lippard's Working-Class Protest," *American Studies* 47 (Fall/Winter 2006): 88. Michael Denning similarly concludes that Lippard was able "to work through, and to some degree transcend, these contradictions

within the ideology of artisan republicanism surrounding race and slavery"; Denning, *Mechanic Accents: Dime Novels and Working-Class Culture in America*, rev. ed. (London: Verso, 1998), 116.

43. Shelley Streeby, *American Sensations: Class, Empire, and the Production of Popular Culture* (Berkeley: University of California Press, 2002), 38–77.

44. Lippard, *Quaker City*, 34, 117.

45. Reynolds, *George Lippard*, 10–11.

46. Orestes Brownson's essay on "The Laboring Classes," for example, contends that "no man can be a Christian who does not begin his career by making war on the mischievous social arrangements from which his brethren suffer," and distinguishes the "Gospel of Jesus" from the "gospel of the priests." But at no point does Brownson suggest that Jesus's radicalism was shaped by his *personal* experience of class oppression. Orestes Brownson, *The Laboring Classes: An Article from the Boston Quarterly Review* (Boston: Benjamin Greene, 1840), 15, 21.

47. George Lippard, *Washington and His Generals; or, Legends of the Revolution* (Philadelphia: G. B. Zieber, 1847), 405–6.

48. Powderly cited in Robert E. Weir, *Beyond Labor's Veil: The Culture of the Knights of Labor* (University Park: Pennsylvania State University Press, 1996), 74; Mary Harris Jones, *Autobiography of Mother Jones* (Chicago: C. H. Kerr, 1925), 219; Debs cited in Upton Sinclair, *The Cry for Justice: An Anthology of the Literature of Social Protest* (self-published, 1921), 345; Bouck White, *The Call of the Carpenter* (Garden City, NY: Doubleday, 1914); C. Osborne Ward, *The Ancient Lowly: A History of the Ancient Working People from the Earliest Known Period to the Adoption of Christianity by Constantine* (Washington, DC: Press of the Craftsman, 1889); Upton Sinclair, *They Call Me Carpenter: A Tale of the Second Coming* (New York: Boni and Liveright, 1922); and Donnelly cited in Michael Kazin, *The Populist Persuasion: An American History*, rev. ed. (New York: Basic Books, 1995), 27. With the exception of Sue, all of the other individuals mentioned wrote at least twenty years after Lippard. In Sue's case, the relevant text (*The Mysteries of the People*) appeared in French just a few years after Lippard's work, but was not translated into English for several decades. Moreover, Sue did not link Jesus quite as emphatically to working-class identity, presenting him instead primarily as an opponent of slavery. But given the influence that Sue's *Mysteries of Paris* probably had on *The Quaker City*, the connection is intriguing. See Eugène Sue, *Les Mystères du people, ou, Histoire d'une famille de prolétaires à travers les ages, Tome second* (Lausanne: Société Editrice l'Union, 1850); Eugène Sue, *The Silver Cross; or, The Carpenter of Nazareth*, trans. Daniel DeLeon (New York: International, 1899).

49. David Burns, *The Life and Death of the Radical Historical Jesus* (New York: Oxford University Press, 2013), 47–60, 164, 254 n. 5.

50. The most systematic refutation was Francis Greenwood Peabody, *Jesus Christ and the Social Question* (New York: Macmillan, 1900).

51. Lippard, *Paul Ardenheim*, 188–89.

52. Reynolds, *George Lippard*, 49–72.

53. Lippard, *Nazarene*, 175.

54. Lippard, *Paul Ardenheim*, 132.

55. Donnelly, *Caesar's Column*, 4.

56. Lippard, *Paul Ardenheim*, 203, 156.

57. Donnelly, *Caesar's Column*, 99, 217.

58. Ibid., 15, 102, 115.

59. On Fourier's esoteric radicalism, see Dan McKanan, "Faith in the Phalanx: Esotericism, Socialism, and the American Fourierist Movement," in *Esotericism, Religion, and Politics*, ed. Arthur Versluis, Lee Irwin, and Melinda Phillips (Minneapolis: North American Academic Press, 2012), 199–214.

60. Henry George, *Progress and Poverty* (New York: Appleton, 1879), 134.

61. Donnelly, *Caesar's Column*, 57.

62. See, for example, Walter Rauschenbusch, *A Theology for the Social Gospel* (New York: Macmillan, 1919), 57–68.

63. Donnelly, *Caesar's Column*, 3, 57.

64. Catharine Sedgwick, *Hope Leslie; or, Early Times in Massachusetts* (New York: Harper, 1842), 255, 262.

65. Lippard, *Quaker City*, 82.

66. Lippard, *Paul Ardenheim*, 387–88.

67. Donnelly, *Caesar's Column*, 61.

68. Ibid., 130, 226, 29.

69. Ibid., 92, 116, 27–28, 78.

70. Donnelly, *Golden Bottle*, 280–81.

71. This criticism of the Social Gospel is made most sweepingly in Susan Curtis, *A Consuming Faith: The Social Gospel and Modern American Culture* (Baltimore: Johns Hopkins University Press, 1991), but Curtis overstates her case. Both individual Social Gospelers such as Harry Ward and Social Gospel organizations such as the Fellowship of Reconciliation maintained a consistently anticapitalist stance as others softened their critiques.

72. Donnelly, *Golden Bottle*, 150.

2

Catholicism and Working-Class Activism in Providence

EVELYN STERNE

On May 3, 1842, the narrow streets of Providence were filled with excitement.[1] Thousands of Rhode Islanders had flocked to the capital city to celebrate the inauguration of Governor Thomas Wilson Dorr. Artisans, shopkeepers, mechanics, and armed militia companies marched through the downtown streets to the festive accompaniment of the Providence Brass Band. The procession ended at the State House on Benefit Street, but the marchers did not enter. Instead they assembled in an unfinished foundry building where they sat on crossbeams and rafters, dodging the raindrops that leaked in as their new leader assembled his government.[2]

The humble setting for Dorr's inaugural was testimony to the unconventional nature of his position, for he was one of two governors claiming leadership of the nation's smallest state. By the spring of 1842, Rhode Island had divided into two camps, with suffrage reformers battling those who believed only landowners should vote. Frustrated in their attempts to achieve change through traditional means, suffragists had taken matters into their own hands by writing a more liberal constitution and forming a separate government. Dorr and his followers (a coalition of native-born workers, Irish immigrants, Democratic reformers, and Protestant ministers) had to form their administration in the shadow of the State House, which had been locked to keep the rebels out.[3]

Class, Religion, and the Limits of Electoral Politics

The drama of 1842 followed decades of agitation over the state's antiquated voting rules. Rhode Island had been the first state to industrialize, when

British immigrant Samuel Slater built a mechanized textile mill just north of Providence in 1793, yet it clung to the outlines of a royal charter designed for an agricultural society. The rule that only landowners could vote had been fairly equitable when most people worked the land, but by 1840 only 43 percent of men could vote statewide and the number was closer to 30 percent in Providence.[4] By this time, most other state legislatures had eliminated their land requirements for voting. Their goal was to enfranchise the "intermediate class" of artisans and professionals who did not make their living from the land, and few worried about the votes of an urban proletariat that might develop in the future. Such concerns resonated in Rhode Island, however, where Irish Catholics were immigrating to take jobs as construction or textile workers. Worries were especially pronounced in Providence, the state's industrial center. By 1845, almost 20 percent of the city's residents were immigrants, and that proportion would increase considerably in subsequent years as a result of the Irish famine.[5]

Native-born Rhode Islanders raised a host of arguments for why Irish immigrants should not vote. The Irish were dismissed as paupers, illiterates, and criminals, unfamiliar with democratic institutions and "bound to the State by ties which may, at any moment, be severed." If they did vote, warned Brown professor William Goddard, they would cast their ballots with the state's new industrial elite and "the centre of political power" would shift "from the country to the town; from the farm to the workshop; from the plough to the spinning-jenny."[6] Worse still, the Irish might use their votes to advance a Catholic agenda. Nineteenth-century Protestants believed Catholics simply could not be good citizens because they were unfamiliar with democratic traditions and beholden to the pope. One broadside circulated during the Dorr Rebellion warned that a franchise extension would "place your government, your civil and political institutions, your PUBLIC SCHOOLS, and perhaps your RELIGIOUS PRIVILEGES under the control of the POPE of ROME through the medium of thousands of NATURALIZED FOREIGN CATHOLICS." Unless natives took action, the writer warned, they would see "a Catholic Bishop, at the head of a posse of Catholic Priests, and a band of their servile dependents, take the field to subvert your institutions."[7]

Stymied by fears like these, Dorr's crusade ended in a disappointing compromise that would limit access to electoral politics for decades and, as this essay demonstrates, prompt immigrants to use their parishes as alternative political spaces. Under a new constitution approved in 1843, native-born men (black and white) could vote if they paid one dollar in taxes or served in the state militia, but immigrants had to own real estate worth at least $134. Because few foreign-born workers could afford to buy land, this rule amounted to a virtual ban on immigrant voting.[8] The two-tiered voting system remained in place until 1888, when a coalition of reformers finally convinced voters to repeal the land requirement. The Bourn Amendment was heralded as a significant victory for the ethnic electorate, now expanding as Italians and French Canadians arrived to work in the state's textile, jewelry, silverware, and tool factories.[9] Yet even as the amendment ended special restrictions on immigrant voting, it imposed a new rule that no one (regardless of birth) could vote in city elections unless he owned real or personal property worth $134. This class-based restriction disqualified two-thirds of voters from participating in local elections for decades, and complicated new registration rules made it even more difficult for workers and immigrants to cast ballots.[10]

The antidemocratic tenor of the Bourn Amendment echoed across the nation as other states rewrote their voting rules. In response to changes wrought by emancipation, immigration, and industrialization, other states were disenfranchising citizens who were not white, native born, or middle class. Poll taxes, literacy tests, residency requirements, and Asian exclusions affirmed the Rhode Island tradition of limiting the suffrage, as did new mandates that municipal voters own property. This pattern reflected a desire to weaken political machines, labor unions, and socialist parties and betrayed the social prejudices so rampant in Rhode Island.[11]

Alternative Politics and the Catholic Church

In this context, Americans who lacked access to the ballot had to find other ways to engage with public life. Some acted through unions, mutual-aid societies, women's clubs, or neighborhood networks. Others looked to places of worship. In Providence as in many industrial communities, the parish was the institution most accessible to an ethnic population overwhelmingly Catholic, working class, and underrepresented elsewhere. By 1905, almost 70 percent of Providence residents were first- or second-generation immigrants (the majority from Ireland, French Canada, and Italy), and just over half were Catholic. In that year, Rhode Island earned the distinction of being the first state with a Catholic majority.[12] Yet many of these Rhode Islanders could not participate in electoral politics because of citizenship status, language barriers, or suffrage restrictions. Without the vote they could not elect prolabor candidates or lobby effectively for worker-friendly laws; as a result, the city's unions were relatively weak and only a minority of workers were members. Some new Americans organized less formally at saloons or in mutual-aid societies, but these institutions rarely welcomed women. In short, the places traditionally recognized as ethnic organizational spaces—unions, political machines, taverns, and mutual-aid associations—were, while valuable to their members, limited in their scope. The Church was the only institution where every Catholic could, theoretically, be a member.[13]

This essay argues that Catholic parishes were the most accessible and important institutions in the city's ethnic, working-class neighborhoods in the late nineteenth and early twentieth centuries, and that as such they played critical roles in politicizing new Americans. It was at church that the largest proportion of immigrants congregated on a regular basis. Parishes functioned not only as sources of spiritual solace but also as dispensers of charity, promoters of upward mobility, and centers of neighborhood life. Parishioners had access to a vast array of recreational activities, and many joined the lay societies that organized them. Priests initially promoted these societies to foster congregational loyalties, but over time the groups also served as political organizing spaces for Catholic women (who generally lacked other formal means of self-assertion) and men. It was through lay societies that many Catholics learned to be leaders, fund-raisers, and public speakers, and that they forged alliances, traded information, and devised solutions to their problems. Some turned parish societies into activist groups, launching lobbying campaigns, organizing voter-registration drives, and using religious rhetoric to argue for social justice. Others drew on church networks to build political careers. It would be misleading to suggest that all or even most new Americans became practicing Catholics; certainly many rejected the Church for personal or political reasons. Yet many others—even some who arrived with a hostile relationship to the Church—learned to welcome the parish as a spiritual home, a community anchor and an alternative political space. For many it served as a space between the pew and the polls or the picket line, a place where new Americans organized for change. For the most part they organized with the blessing of their priests, who wanted Catholics to promote their own interests and those of their Church; yet as this essay demonstrates, sometimes parishioners used the skills learned at church to form unsanctioned movements that defied their clerics.

By no means was Providence unique as a city where parishes served as organizing centers and religion informed public debate; yet as the introduction to this volume argues, too often religion remains on the margins of modern American social history. Scholars have long acknowledged that African Americans used religion for inspiration and churches as mobilizing sites, but studies of white workers tend to ignore religion or dismiss it as a negative influence that distracted from more "radical" or "political" forms of activism. Labor historians have argued, justifiably, that employers used religion to promote discipline, that faith could encourage an otherworldly focus, and that clerics often discouraged strikes and radical unions. It is only recently that American labor historians have seriously considered that religion could inspire as well as detract from working-class protest. A rich scholarship explores the effects of Protestantism on antebellum labor protest. Disagreeing that religion was no more than a tool to discipline workers and instill bourgeois values, these studies prove that religion also inspired workers and legitimated their struggles.[14]

Twentieth-century American labor history, as a whole, still lacks the nuanced treatment of religion devoted to the earlier era. To be sure, scholars such as Gary Gerstle, Ken Fones-Wolf, Jon Gjerde, and John McGreevy (to name only a few) have made important steps in this direction by exploring alliances between unionists and ministers, the formation of Catholic worker movements, and the influence of faith on workplace activism and political strategies.[15] A younger generation of historians that includes Richard Callahan, Matthew Pehl, Jarod Roll, and the other contributors to this volume is exploring connections between class and Christianity in new contexts and taking this research in exciting new directions.[16] For the most part, however, historians have not considered the multifaceted roles that places of worship played in the daily lives and politics of working-class immigrants. Generally absent from their accounts is the Catholic Church, at least nominally the religious home of a majority of immigrants during the industrial era. If the Church enters the story at all, it usually does so as a negative influence that discouraged parishioners from joining the Socialist or Communist parties. Religion generally remains on the margins of the story. Disapproval of priests' antiradical politics have prompted most labor historians to forget that parishes were community centers and organizing spaces where working people spent a great deal of time. As such, they deserve more attention.

"Leadership-Training" Centers

In Providence as in other Catholic cities, the parish was the nucleus of neighborhood life. No institution could match it as a source of service and sociability, relief and recreation. At a time when immigrants had serious problems and few sources of public assistance, the Church played an indispensable role as a provider of charity. The Diocese of Providence ran hospitals, orphanages, and working girls' homes. Parishes such as St. Ann's and St. Bartholomew's operated day nurseries for their Italian American congregations and provided individual assistance in less formal ways. Father Joseph Bourgeois of St. John's in Arctic gave away coal to his poorest parishioners. Father Cooney of St. Edward's in Providence, for his part, helped his Irish American congregants deal with difficult employers or drunken spouses.[17]

Whereas the neediest Catholics looked to the Church for charity, others took advantage of programs that facilitated upward mobility. Parochial schools educated young Catholics; the St. Ann's Industrial School provided classes in composition, conversation, and gender-specific work skills; and the School of Domestic Arts at St. Mary's in Pawtucket trained women of all ages in cooking, nursing, and dressmaking. Many such programs encouraged immigrants to assimilate while preserving aspects of their Old World identities.[18] The Church also served as a critical source of information. The *Providence Visitor*, the weekly diocesan newspaper, printed government news, offered health and household tips, and took stands on everyday problems such as street repairs and the rising price of trolley tickets. Parishes such as St. Mary's and St. Bartholomew's published their own bulletins that carried both city and congregational news.[19]

These periodicals encouraged readers not only to go to Mass but also to avail themselves of a truly impressive parish-based recreational life. In any given year, the typical ethnic parish sponsored a packed social calendar of fairs, plays, concerts, bingo games, costume parties, and dances. Many events took place in parish halls that offered billiard rooms and bowling allies, libraries and reading rooms, and gymnasiums and bathing facilities. Completed in 1917, the St. Edward's hall was open every evening and all day Sunday to parishioners bearing membership cards. It boasted a bowling alley and poolroom, hosted dances and lectures, and offered sewing classes and weekly basketball games. It was little wonder, according to parish historian Rev. Richard Walsh, that the hall "soon became a beehive of activity and the center of the social life of the community."[20]

Parish halls also hosted meetings for the lay societies that abounded in this era. Parishioners had access to a stunning variety of organizations: rosary societies and altar guilds; temperance and Holy Name societies; sewing circles and St. Vincent de Paul societies; debating clubs, lecture series, and study groups; bands, sports teams, drama societies, glee clubs, and Scout troops. In 1910, Father Antonio Bove of St. Ann's boasted, "In my parish there is a religious society suitable for every person in the congregation."[21] He was not exaggerating, and many other priests could have made the same claim. In all these ways, the parish provided members with a social and spiritual center in an urban setting that could be alienating and unstructured. The parish, as historian Paula Kane puts it, functioned "both as a mini-city and as a macro-family."[22]

The parish also served quite naturally as a political organizing site. As Leslie Woodcock Tentler has argued, for many new Americans the very act of building a church was their "first New World experience of large-scale collective action."[23] Once the church was constructed, it provided an extensive associational life that quite naturally fostered political skills. Priests may have directed the spiritual affairs, but they relied on laypeople to raise the funds, teach the Sunday schools, run the societies, and organize the entertainments.[24] The Catholic Club at Holy Trinity in Central Falls, which formed in 1910 for men ages eighteen to thirty-five, shouldered enormous responsibilities: organizing lectures, dramas, and dances as well as an annual communion breakfast and moonlight sail; participating in statewide tournaments and debates; publishing a monthly newsletter; raising money for a new club building; and using that facility to show films, host sports competitions, and run classes in gymnastics, language, and domestic science. A St. Edward's history spoke truly when it described clubs like these as "leadership-training" groups. The Catholics who ran these groups became organizers, fund-raisers, and leaders, developing skills they could apply to politics as well as parish life.[25]

At the same time, active parishioners acquired a political education at church. Debating societies and study circles enabled working-class Catholics, many of whom lacked a formal education, to discuss issues such as temperance and socialism and develop their own opinions. The Irish Americans in St. Michael's Catholic Club, formed in 1906, presented papers at weekly meetings and invited a prominent public figure to speak once a month. In 1912, the Holy Name Society of St. Charles in Woonsocket formed a School for Social Studies to sponsor lectures and encourage debate on "social, industrial and economical" issues. Women's clubs engaged with increasingly political themes, shifting the topics of their lecture series from art and history to women's rights and current events in the 1910s and '20s. By 1918, the Union of Catholic Parish Clubs was sponsoring a lecture bureau, essay contests, and two debating leagues for its male members. Some Catholics became accomplished speakers through institutions like these. In 1923, a team of Italian Americans from the Church of the Holy Ghost beat a Boston group in a debate about the League of Nations. The *Visitor* proudly attributed the victory to the popularity of the Holy Ghost Lyceum, whose weekly lecture series "turns out orators and debaters as a Ford factory does Fords."[26]

Belonging to a lay society also was an exercise in self-government. Parish groups regulated themselves by writing constitutions and bylaws. The West

Warwick Catholic Women's Club had to learn Robert's Rules of Order, and the Junior Holy Name Society received instruction in "parliamentary law."[27] Each group had officers who were elected annually or as often as every six months, and some took these elections quite seriously. Men who sought office in the Union of Catholic Parish Clubs in 1917 had to campaign among a membership of four thousand. Lay society elections carried special value for women, barred from voting in lay trustee contests as well as public elections. The Women's Guild at St. Edward's not only chose a slate of general officers but even held elections for its subcommittees.[28] As this example suggests, the benefits of parish organizing were particularly valuable for women, who often lacked other formal means of political expression. Through their parish societies they established contacts, developed leadership skills, and seized opportunities for community service. As we shall see, women such as Isabelle Ahearn O'Neill, the state's first female legislator, used such networks to go even further and build political careers.

Catholic women and men cemented powerful solidarities by participating in parish life. Blessed Virgin sodalities and Holy Name societies, for example, brought together members on a regular basis and created bonds that extended beyond the walls of the church. These societies took communion as a body on designated Sundays and marched through the streets, placing a religious seal on their group identity. There was no more powerful statement of Catholic cohesion than the triennial Holy Name parade, which by the late 1920s attracted more than 35,000 marchers and 100,000 spectators. Links forged at church reinforced those created in the community and, for some parishioners, through the political machine or the union hall. And they functioned as what the *Visitor* called "religion in action," sending outsiders a clear message about Catholic power.[29]

In short, parishes were places where new Americans acquired tools that they could, and did, apply to community activism, workplace protest, and electoral politics. It was no coincidence that prominent unionists and politicians were active in parish life. Aspiring politicians knew they would encounter public dignitaries at church dedications, priests' funerals, and lay society banquets. They also recognized that being an active Catholic sent a positive message about their values, and that a congregation provided a ready-made constituency. Two legendary Irish American politicians—Patrick J. McCarthy and Isabelle Ahearn O'Neill—proved particularly adept at using Catholic networks to build public careers.

P. J. McCarthy was born in County Sligo in 1848. At age two he fled the potato famine with his Gaelic-speaking parents and six older brothers, only to lose both parents to typhus shortly after their arrival in Boston. McCarthy spent his early years shuffling between relatives and orphanages and working as a farm laborer, peddler, foundry worker, printer, carpenter, mason, painter, and brass finisher—while acting in dramatic societies and attending a night school for working boys at Harvard. In 1868, this working-class Renaissance man moved to Providence to seek his fortune.[30] McCarthy, like so many of his compatriots, looked to politics as a means of upward mobility when good private-sector jobs proved elusive. Relatively few of the Irish arrived with industrial skills, but they generally spoke English, were familiar with Anglo-American governing institutions, and had a strong activist tradition as a result of their struggles with the British. When McCarthy found access to electoral politics in Rhode Island difficult because of the special restrictions on immigrant voting, he turned to the Catholic Church as an alternative political space.

Upon moving to Providence, McCarthy joined the Cathedral of Saints Peter and Paul, where he taught Sunday School, sang in the choir, and joined the Christian Doctrine Society. It was there he received his first taste of government, later recalling that "Parliamentary Law governed the proceedings with much exactness." He also joined the Brownson Lyceum, a "literary and debating society composed of Catholics only" and a base of agitation for immigrant voting rights. McCarthy eventually left the cathedral for St. Michael's, where he met Annie McGinney, his future wife, and joined the parish's Catholic Total Abstinence Union (CTAU). McCarthy served on the union's constitution and bylaw committee and traveled around the state to promote temperance. As he later wrote, "The society afforded scope for ambitious young men to study and practice Parliamentary Law. . . . As one of the Board of Directors of the Rhode Island Union, I came prominently before the Catholic people of the State."[31]

Armed with his Catholic contacts and the Harvard law degree he earned in 1876, McCarthy rapidly ascended Rhode Island's political ladder. He served three terms on the city council, followed by two terms in the general assembly, and in 1906 he made history when he was elected Providence's first foreign-born mayor. McCarthy's rise to power reflected his witty oratory and solid reform credentials as well as his masterful use of Catholic resources. As a young man he had developed contacts, learned parliamentary rules, and honed his speaking skills by participating in lay societies. As a rising politician, he had courted coreligionists by speaking to parish groups and joining organizations like the Catholic Club and Holy Name Society. As the *Visitor* later noted, "His strong faith won the admiration of his ecclesiastical superiors as well as the esteem of the Catholic people."[32]

Isabelle Ahearn O'Neill, another political pioneer, used Catholic networks to affirm her respectability and promote her career. O'Neill was born in 1881 to Irish immigrants in Woonsocket, a mill city in northern Rhode Island, the youngest of ten children. After attending the Boston College of Drama and Oratory and Dr. Sargent's School of Physical Education in Cambridge, she returned to Providence in 1900 to teach parochial school and open her own School of Oratory, Drama and Physical Education. Her marriage to John Aloysius O'Neill lasted only three years, but as a strict Catholic she never divorced him. After her separation she returned to the theater, performing in vaudeville and summer stock and acting in locally produced silent films such as "Joe Lincoln's Cape Cod Stories." Her Providence acting venues ranged from Catholic parish halls to the city opera house. In the 1910s she became an active woman suffragist, and once the Nineteenth Amendment was ratified, she threw her talents into campaigning for Democratic candidates.[33]

In 1922, O'Neill made history as the first woman elected to the Rhode Island General Assembly. Her acting career and marital status made her a somewhat risqué choice, but her solid Catholic background and maternalist agenda affirmed her respectability. Her Catholic memberships included the Immaculate Conception choir, St. Michael's Rosary and Altar Society, St. Gabriel's Aid Association, and St. Joseph's Hospital Women's League. Like other female politicians of her day, she built her career on issues such as pensions for widowed mothers, better pay for teachers, and protections for female workers. Not limiting her outreach to her Irish American peers, she courted the state's polyglot electorate by delivering speeches in French and Italian. After eight years in the House of Representatives, she moved on to the state senate and served there as deputy Democratic floor leader, the first woman in the nation to hold this position. Another career highlight came in 1924, when she acted as temporary chair of the Democratic National Convention. Throughout her career, O'Neill was known for her outspoken and principled stands. As one columnist noted, "She has made it a practice to be heard from regularly and at frequent intervals ever since she was 17 years old." Despite her unconventional life, O'Neill's coreligionists seized on her as a model of Catholic womanhood, often inviting her to speak to parish groups on such topics as "Women in Politics."[34]

Religion in Action

Individuals like O'Neill and McCarthy were unusual in the level of prominence they achieved, but many of their coreligionists drew on the skills and solidarities formed at church to become active at the grassroots level. Parish societies were ready-made units that could take on neighborhood problems

CATHOLICISM AND WORKING-CLASS ACTIVISM IN PROVIDENCE · 61

or engage with city politics; by the turn of the twentieth century, Catholics—with the blessing of their priests and bishops—deliberately were using the parish as a bridge between private devotion and public activism. The 1905 state census revealed that almost 52 percent of Providence residents (and just under 51 percent of all Rhode Islanders) were Catholic. Confident in their new status as the majority, they unleashed a movement to secure a proportionate share of political power. As the *Visitor* (the official mouthpiece of the diocese) complained, "We have never received at the hands of the State that consideration which is due to the great number of Catholics. . . . There are many things still due to us from the state and these we should insist upon getting." The *Visitor* was right. Catholics were the majority, but they still lacked protections at the workplace, full access to the vote, and social acceptance in the community.[35]

Led by the Irish and endorsed by the Church hierarchy, lay societies responded by launching a Catholic rights movement. The Knights of Columbus formed a committee to defend Catholics' "right to consideration and justice," and Holy Name Society president James Cahill urged coreligionists to focus on the "promotion and defense of Catholic interests." Before long, lay societies were acting as informal lobbies and conducting voter-registration drives on issues that concerned parishioners as workers, immigrants, and Catholics. Their efforts reflected a concurrent movement by the new American Federation of Catholic Societies (AFCS) to promote the interests of the Church and its members nationwide.[36]

It was a major grievance that many Providence parishioners could not participate in city elections because of the municipal property rule. For decades Catholic editors and politicians had protested this law on both secular and religious grounds. The vote was, in the *Visitor*'s words, not only a "sacred right" but also a "very important test of citizenship."[37] The city's Democrats, socialists, and unionists also were campaigning against the property rule, but the *Visitor*'s distinctive contribution was to bring God into the debate. Its editors argued the property rule was not only undemocratic but also unchristian in that it discriminated against Catholics and prevented them from executing their "sacred duty" to cast ballots. This duty took on new urgency as the AFCS urged Catholics nationwide to use their votes to defend the Church.[38]

The plight of industrial workers was another relevant issue for a Church whose congregants were largely blue collar, and the *Visitor* waged a vigorous campaign for workers' rights. "To defraud laborers of their wages is one of 'the four sins crying to heaven for vengeance,'" the newspaper warned in

1902. Instead, the *Visitor* urged, employers should apply Christian principles to the industrial world by granting workers higher wages, shorter hours, and a voice in management. During economic downturns, the state should step in by providing public-works jobs and social insurance.[39]

The *Visitor's* blue-collar boosterism resulted from fears that disgruntled workers would turn to socialism, from recognition that well-paid workers were more likely to promote Catholic values by forming large families, and from a commitment to human rights and social justice. These priorities reflected local concerns and churchwide directives, the latter articulated in Pope Leo XIII's *Rerum Novarum* (1891) and Pius XI's *Quadragesimo Anno* (1931). These encyclicals spelled out the Church's position on economic justice by condemning socialism and communism on one hand and unbridled capitalism on the other. Inspired by the encyclicals and the growth of the labor movement, and competing with a "trade-union gospel" articulated by socially conscious Protestant ministers in cities like Philadelphia, the American Catholic Church embraced workplace reform and adopted a friendlier attitude toward mainstream unions. Thus it was consistent with national and international Catholic policy for the *Visitor* to argue for higher wages and shorter hours, workers' compensation, and curbs on monopoly—and to do so with the moral authority religion provided.[40]

Like its counterparts in the AFCS and other dioceses, the Providence hierarchy discouraged socialism while promoting "responsible" labor organization. Many local clerics preferred a corporatist approach to labor relations, in which employers and workers recognized their mutual interests and worked out disputes through arbitration, yet they were tireless defenders of the "God-given" right to organize and supported walkouts they considered justified. Throughout this period, the newspaper underscored its support for workers by reporting on union news and carrying the union label. This strategy clearly convinced some unionists the Church was an ally. In 1924, for example, the Woonsocket Central Labor Union asked Bishop William Hickey to persuade local employers to stop favoring nonunion workers. Such connections were evident in less formal ways as well. In 1910, marchers in the Providence Labor Day parade doffed their hats as they passed St. Mary's.[41]

Given the Church's friendly stance, and the overwhelmingly Irish American composition of the labor movement, it was not surprising that many prominent unionists were active Catholics. No doubt some felt they could bolster their reputations (and those of their unions) by being seen at church or in Catholic societies. At a time when many Americans perceived labor activists as dangerous radicals and Irish Americans as drunken rowdies, membership in a group like the CTAU testified to an organizer's sobriety and civic-mindedness. One such man was Patrick Henry Quinn, who started his career in the finishing room at Clyde Print Works and served as district master workman for the state Knights of Labor. He went on to become a lawyer and "man of public importance," chairing the state Democratic Party and running unsuccessfully for governor in 1914. It is likely that his solid record of Catholic service, which included the presidencies of the Rhode Island CTAU and Catholic Club, legitimated his labor activism and fostered his political career.[42] Other unionists such as Lawrence Grace—teamster, state AFL leader, Sacred Heart parishioner, and member of the Holy Name Society and the antisocialist Militia of Christ—agreed the Church was a vehicle for working-class interests. In a 1912 speech to the School for Social Studies at St. Charles, Grace declared all successful labor legislation would "owe its success as much to the prayers as to the activities of men who remain devoted sons of Mother Church."[43]

In addition to benefiting from Catholic networks, Providence labor activists drew on religious rhetoric in their crusades for economic justice. Religion traditionally has been a "weapon of the weak," a shared language and source of moral authority for people without access to formal means of power. Providence workers wielded this weapon with finesse. In 1908, union leaders issued a "Ten Commandments for Labor" that included the rule: "Thou shalt not labor more than eight hours for one day's work, nor on the Sabbath nor on any of the holy days." The following year, the socialist *Labor Advocate* published its own "Ten Commandments," among them the admonition: "Thou shalt consider the Golden Rule superior to the rule of gold."[44] In its Progressive Era campaign for higher wages and shorter hours, the city's *Union Worker Magazine* spoke of "the right of the individual not only to exist, but to live by his toil, the sacredness of the capital which the Creator has granted to mankind." Statements like this combined time-honored Judeo-Christian principles with a new rhetoric of industrial citizenship.[45]

By the 1930s, efforts to marshal religious resources in service of a working-class agenda had paid off. Voters repealed the municipal property restriction in 1928, and in 1935 a new era dawned in which Democrats and their union allies controlled state government and legislated on behalf of the working class. These victories reflected broader developments both local and national, but the ability of laypeople to mobilize for change through their parishes had played an important role. To be sure, there were serious limits to working-class immigrants becoming political through a Catholic Church that was hierarchical and often inconsistent. Women in particular received mixed signals. They were encouraged to be activists but also to observe traditional gender roles, to promote some laws that could improve their lives (mothers' pensions and protective labor laws) but to oppose others (legalized birth control and the Equal Rights Amendment). The Church was progressive on economic matters such as higher wages and social insurance, but within limits. Priests promoted mainstream unions and moderate labor laws that would humanize capitalism, but they railed against left-wing unions and parties whose agendas were more transformative. Yet many Catholics recognized that parishes offered resources radical movements could not in a winner-take-all electoral system biased against third parties, and they chose what they considered to be the best available option. Moreover, some drew on the skills and networks formed at church to become political in ways of which their spiritual and secular leaders thoroughly disapproved. As the following example demonstrates, the results could be explosive.

Trouble at Holy Ghost

On a warm Sunday in July 1920, Providence police officers received an unexpected summons to the Church of the Holy Ghost on Federal Hill. Some one hundred Italian women were trying to forcibly remove a priest from the church, and it took a posse of armed officers to stop them. According to an account in the local newspaper *Il Corriere del Rhode Island,* "The people absolutely want to remove Father Belliotti, and they are intent on doing so at whatever cost and by whatever means."[46] The reporter was right. Over the next months the police regularly were called in to keep the peace as parishioners assembled for demonstrations aimed at ousting Rev. Domenico Belliotti and the Scalabrini Fathers who ran the parish.[47] At an August assembly, *Il Corriere* reported, the appearance of one priest "unloosed such an uproar of screams and protests that it had the actual character of a riot." "No more Scalabrini!" the parishioners screamed. "Either you get out or we will drive you out with force!" When Bishop Harkins removed Belliotti, only to replace him with another Scalabrini priest, some parishioners concluded force was the only solution. On the morning of Sunday, November 7, police officers arrested seven parishioners who had interrupted a service by shouting for the priest's removal and demanding the keys to the church.[48]

This dramatic series of events was the culmination of a fifteen-year battle between the Scalabrini Fathers, a northern Italian order, and the southern Italian laypeople of Holy Ghost. For some time, members of the largely working-class parish had been complaining the priests were materialistic snobs rather than humble servants of God. "No one would think that they are Priests," the church's Holy Name Society grumbled. "Their demeanor, their clothes . . . their well-combed and perfumed hair, their manner of living . . . the levity with which they speak of their ministry . . . everything in them gives unmistakable signs that their faith is lukewarm, if not entirely gone." Particularly galling was Belliotti's habit of wintering in Florida to improve his health, leaving his assistants to tend to the flock in cold, gray Providence.[49]

Worse still, parishioners charged, the Scalabrini were dismissive of Italian patron saints and their feast days. In July 1906, one year after he assumed leadership of the congregation, Belliotti had raised the parish's collective dander by tangling with the Madonna of Mount Carmel festival, one of the most popular celebrations on the community's religious calendar. On this day, Italian Americans would parade through the streets, stop at church for Mass, then continue their procession. Demonstrations like these, which historian Robert Orsi calls "religion in the streets," claimed neighborhood space as sacred space and asserted lay control over expressions of faith.[50]

On the appointed day in 1906, celebrants arrived at Holy Ghost one hour late to find the priest annoyed and their reserved seats filled. As they told the story in a heated petition to Harkins, "The reverend father . . . became irritated and cursed Her name and also the day that he donned the priestly garments. . . . He replied . . . that we did not control him and that if we said another word, he would not let us enter the church and that furthermore he saw no difference between the Blessed Virgin and St. Rocco or any other saint." Such words were deeply offensive to a people for whom patron-saint worship was central to religious practice and ethnic identity. The 1906 affair was one in a series of conflicts that rocked Holy Ghost and the city's other national parishes during the first decades of the twentieth century.[51]

These long-simmering tensions exploded in the summer of 1920. The departure of Father Vincenzo Vicari, a popular assistant priest not affiliated with the Scalabrini, unleashed another flood of impassioned letters and petitions to the bishop and even the Vatican. Holy Name president Daniele Ionata (an Italian-born weaver) and his fellow members demanded the return of Vicari, whom they credited with "rescuing from this religious sloth thousands of Italians" through his inspiring sermons and his sympathy for the poor. Belliotti, by contrast, conducted himself "as the manager of a business establishment instead of a pastor," charged a letter signed by five parish women. "He is never willing to raise his hand or do anything whatsoever unless he is compensated." Moreover, the women complained, the priest claimed "that there is no one above him in this diocese and he can do whatever he pleases without being accountable to anyone."[52]

The controversy posed a major problem for the spiritual lives of Holy Ghost Catholics and the institutional health of the diocese. Parishioners pled with the bishop to help them at what they termed a "terrible moment." "We have been minimized, insulted, beaten, arrested, denounced to the civil authority as a flock of primitives and criminals," charged a petition bearing 626 names. "And after so much, after such a disgrace to our name, to our dignity . . . we are . . . to be compelled to return to our executioners." This seemed intolerable, and many worshippers threatened to leave the parish if Vicari did not return. "The church will close with no one attending any-more," one Catholic warned the bishop. "God is present at other churches, and also at home," noted Errico Bellifante, a laborer and active parishioner. Bellifante's statement sent diocesan officials a message that was disturbing on two counts. Disgruntled Italians might flock to the Protestant missions that peppered their neighborhood, but they were just as likely to practice their faith in a "domus"-centered religion that recognized homes as valid sites of worship.[53]

Given the size of the movement, both threats were cause for concern. Even though community spokesmen dismissed the uprising as the work of a discontented fringe, at least eighteen hundred individuals and eighteen church societies had signed petitions demanding the Scalabrini's ouster and Vicari's return. A movement of this magnitude threatened the viability of Rhode Island's flagship Italian parish. Bishop Hickey, who had assumed lead-ership of the diocese only recently, did not wish to sacrifice the advances his predecessors had made among the Italians. He refused to bring back Vicari, whom some suspected of fomenting the uprising, but he finally found an acceptable leader who restored peace to the turbulent parish. He also created a new Federal Hill church, devoted to the same Madonna of Mount Carmel whose feast day had touched off the trouble fifteen years earlier.[54]

To understand the rebellion at Holy Ghost, one must begin with the rebels. A statistical sample (using census records, city directories, and tax lists to find ninety-six, or 15 percent, of the people who signed the longest surviving peti-tion) reveals a great deal about the protesters and their motives.[55] The petition-ers were a relatively stable group in that the majority were married, more than one-third owned homes or small businesses, and the average age was thirty-nine. This was not a group of young, rootless transients, yet it was a distinctly working-class community. Of those people whose occupations could be found, almost half were common laborers and most others held jobs best described

as blue collar. Given the working-class character of the rebellion, it is not surprising that economic issues played a role. When the parishioners complained
about the priests' expensive habits and winters in Florida, they expressed class
tensions that divided the congregation and the larger community.

This also was an uprising of new Americans. Of those petitioners whose
birth and citizenship could be determined, sixty were Italian immigrants and
the other two were the children of immigrants. Even though the foreign-born
had been in the country an average of seventeen years, only one-third had
become citizens. It was only natural, then, that disagreements over assimilation and ethnicity informed the affair. The conflict between the Scalabrini
and the congregation reflected regional tensions that typically divided older
immigrants from northern Italy and newer arrivals from the south (although
Belliotti himself was Sicilian). The dispute over the Madonna of Mount Carmel festival, which had ignited the troubles in 1906, was quite typical of
conflicts that arose when priests discouraged an Old World, popular religion in favor of an Americanized or institutional form of worship. Conflicts
like this pitted recent arrivals against community leaders as well as priests.
Speaking for their middle-class readers, *L'Eco del Rhode Island* denounced
the uprising as "unwisely indecent and ludicrous" and *Il Corriere* feared it
would "dishonor us in the eyes of the Americans."[56] Whereas civic leaders
associated Americanism with orderly behavior and upward mobility, the
protesters may have felt they were acting in distinctly American ways by
rebelling against injustice.

Gender too played an important role in the uprising, and here a disclaimer
about the sample is in order. The women and men collected petitions separately and the women amassed almost twice as many signatures; yet the
petition that survives in full is the men's. Moreover, even though 14 percent
of the names on the full petition appear to be female, the sample is skewed
toward men because they are easier to find in public records. As a result, only
nine of the ninety-six petitioners discussed here are women, but this should
not obscure the central role they played as demonstrators, petitioners, and
letter writers. The rebellion provided a rare opportunity to voice frustrations
with an institution where they formed the bulk of the faithful but worshiped
under the direction of male clerics, as well as to protest discrimination in the
larger community. Yet this was by no means a single-sex rebellion. In fact,
the passionate involvement of parish men challenges the assumption that
Italian religiosity was primarily a female affair.

Finally, this was an uprising by people who lacked other institutionalized means of self-assertion. Only ten petitioners in the sample had jobs

that were likely to be unionized. At least thirty-nine were aliens and thus nonvoters, and that does not include the thirty-six whose citizenship could not be determined. Even if all had been citizens, only thirty-seven (just over one-third of the sample) owned enough property to vote in city elections. In short, many people in this community lacked access to recognized political vehicles such as the union and the ballot. They turned instead to the Church to express resentments over gender inequities, economic oppression, and mounting pressure to assimilate during the First World War. At the start of the war, thousands of Italian Americans had taken to the streets of Federal Hill for two weeks of rioting; the trigger had been the rising price of pasta, but the underlying cause had been long-simmering grievances over economic and social discrimination in the new country. Six years after the Macaroni Riots, community resentments had turned inward and exploded within the Church.[57]

The uprising at Holy Ghost reveals a great deal about class, religion, and politics in the first decades of the twentieth century. First, it testifies to the importance of the Church in ethnic, working-class neighborhoods. Even as the controversy revealed deep fissures within the congregation, it sent the message that religion mattered. Second, the conflict testifies to the complex ways in which churches served as political organizing sites. As we have seen, by the early twentieth century, Catholics were using their parishes as spaces in between the pew and the polls or the picket line—tapping into the resources religion provided to raise external challenges to employers and elected officials. Yet as the conflict at Holy Ghost demonstrates, parishes also served as stages on which internal tensions played out. Episodes like this send an important message to historians seeking a more nuanced understanding of the relationships between religion and protest in working-class communities. The Catholic Church was indeed a hierarchical institution where priests and bishops wielded significant power; and in Providence the hierarchy heartily approved of laypeople's using parish resources to lobby for better working conditions and electoral access. Yet clerics could not always control how parishioners would direct the skills and convictions acquired at church. The uprising at Holy Ghost was an unsanctioned social movement created by working people who had learned to be leaders by serving in the church's Holy Name Society, to be organizers by raising funds to build the parish hall, and to have confidence in their opinions by joining the parish's popular debating club. Like other forms of parish-based activism, it was an inclusive social movement that enabled women as well as men, immigrants as well as natives, and aliens as well as citizens to be public actors. And it was a vehicle that mobilized people who lacked other institutions through which to advance their interests. Dramas like this played out in parishes across America during the industrial age. Historians should take more notice.

Notes

1. This essay is adapted from Evelyn Savidge Sterne, *Ballots and Bibles: Ethnic Politics and the Catholic Church in Providence* (Ithaca, NY: Cornell University Press, 2004), with the permission of Cornell University Press.

2. Marvin E. Gettleman, *The Dorr Rebellion: A Study in American Radicalism, 1833–1849* (New York: Random House, 1973), 101–2; and Patrick T. Conley, *Democracy in Decline: Rhode Island's Constitutional Development, 1776–1841* (Providence: Rhode Island Historical Society, 1977), 328–29.

3. Conley, *Democracy in Decline,* 315, 328.

4. Ibid., 48, 274; Chilton Williamson, *American Suffrage: From Property to Democracy, 1760–1860* (Princeton, NJ: Princeton University Press, 1960), 243–45; and William G. McLoughlin, *Rhode Island: A History* (New York: W. W. Norton, 1986), 128.

5. Alexander Keyssar, *The Right to Vote: The Contested History of Democracy in the United States* (New York: Basic Books, 2000), 45; and Superintendent of the Census, *Report upon the Census of Rhode Island, 1865* (Providence, RI: Providence Press, 1867), lv.

6. Ray Allen Billington, *The Protestant Crusade 1800–1860: A Study of the Origins of American Nativism* (New York: Rinehart, 1938), 132; Gettleman, *Dorr Rebellion,* 8–9, 45; and Francis W. Goddard, *The Political and Miscellaneous Writings of William G. Goddard* (Providence, RI: Sidney S. Rider and Brother, 1870), 58–59, 68, 89–90, 151.

7. "Native American Citizens! Read and Take Warning!" (1842), Broadside File, Rhode Island Historical Society, Providence, RI (hereafter cited as RIHS).

8. *Proposed Constitution of the State of Rhode Island and Providence Plantations* (Providence, RI: Knowles and Vose, 1842).

9. For a fuller discussion of the Bourn Amendment, and the politics behind its repeal, see Sterne, *Ballots and Bibles,* 60–70.

10. General Assembly, *Acts and Resolves of the General Assembly of the State of Rhode Island and Providence Plantations* (Providence, RI: E. L. Freeman, 1887), 296; *Providence Journal Almanac, 1889* (Providence, RI: Providence Journal, 1889), 33; and Chilton Williamson, "Rhode Island Suffrage since the Dorr War," *New England Quarterly* 28 (1955): 43. The long-term impact of the municipal property requirement was calculated by the author based on a forty-year analysis of voting statistics in the annual *Providence Journal Almanac.*

11. Keyssar, *Right to Vote,* 120–23, 133.

12. Bureau of Industrial Statistics, *Census of the Foreign-Born Population of Rhode Island. Bulletin 1. Part 1 of the Annual Report for 1907* (Providence, RI: E. L. Freeman, 1907), 1081; Bureau of Industrial Statistics, *Church Statistics and Religious Preference.*

Bulletin 2. Part 1 of the Annual Report for 1907 (Providence, RI: E. L. Freeman, 1907), 274; and John S. Gilkeson Jr., *Middle-Class Providence, 1820–1940* (Princeton, NJ: Princeton University Press, 1986), 7.

13. Robert A. Orsi, *The Madonna of 115th Street: Faith and Community in Italian Harlem, 1880–1950* (New Haven, CT: Yale University Press, 1985), xv.

14. Teresa Anne Murphy, *Ten Hours' Labor: Religion, Reform and Gender in Early New England* (Ithaca, NY: Cornell University Press, 1992); Jama Lazerow, *Religion and the Working Class in Antebellum America* (Washington, DC: Smithsonian Institution Press, 1995); William R. Sutton, *Journeymen for Jesus: Evangelical Artisans Confront Capitalism in Jacksonian Baltimore* (University Park: Pennsylvania State University Press, 1998); and Mark S. Schantz, *Piety in Providence: Class Dimensions of Religious Experience in Antebellum Rhode Island* (Ithaca, NY: Cornell University Press, 2000).

15. Gary Gerstle, *Working-Class Americanism: The Politics of Labor in a Textile City, 1914–1960* (New York: Cambridge University Press, 1989); Ken Fones-Wolf, *Trade Union Gospel: Christianity and Labor in Industrial Philadelphia, 1865–1915* (Philadelphia: Temple University Press, 1989); Jon Gjerde, *The Minds of the West: Ethnocultural Evolution in the Rural Middle West, 1830–1917* (Chapel Hill: University of North Carolina Press, 1999); John T. McGreevy, *Parish Boundaries: The Catholic Encounter with Race in the Twentieth-Century Urban North* (Chicago: University of Chicago Press, 1996); Mel Piehl, *Breaking Bread: The Catholic Worker and the Origin of Catholic Radicalism in America* (Philadelphia: Temple University Press, 1982); David M. Emmons, *The Butte Irish: Class and Ethnicity in an American Mining Town, 1875–1925* (Urbana: University of Illinois Press, 1989); and Mary Lethert Wingerd, *Claiming the City: Politics, Faith, and the Power of Place in St. Paul* (Ithaca, NY: Cornell University Press, 2001). See also William Issel, *Church and State in the City: Catholics and Politics in Twentieth-Century San Francisco* (Philadelphia: Temple University Press, 2012), for a discussion of how alliances between labor activists and the Catholic Church influenced policy and public debate in San Francisco.

16. Richard J. Callahan Jr., *Work and Faith in the Kentucky Coal Fields: Subject to Dust* (Bloomington: Indiana University Press, 2009); Matthew Pehl, "'Apostles of Fascism,' 'Communist Clergy,' and the UAW: Political Ideology and Working-Class Religion in Detroit, 1919–1945," *Journal of American History* 99, no. 2 (September 2012): 440–65; and Jarod Roll, *The Spirit of Rebellion: Labor and Religion in the New Cotton South* (Urbana: University of Illinois Press, 2010).

17. *Le Jean-Baptiste*, 23 January 1903; Richard A. Walsh, *The Centennial History of Saint Edward Church, Providence, Rhode Island, 1874–1974* (n.p., n.d.), 54; *50th Anniversary, 1907–1957. Golden Jubilee. St. Bartholomew's Parish. Providence, Rhode Island* (n.p., n.d.); *Providence Visitor*, 22 May 1935; and John F. Sullivan and Vincenzo F. Kienberger, *Storia della Parrocchia di S. Anna, Providence, R.I. In Occasione del Giubileo d'Argente Sacerdotale del Parroco, 1900–1925* (n.p., n.d.), 18.

18. Sullivan and Kienberger, *Storia della Parrocchia di S. Anna*, 18; "Report of St. Ann's Day Nursery and Industrial School, 1918," St. Ann's Papers, Providence Catholic

Diocesan Archives, Providence, RI (hereafter PCDA); Robert W. Hayman, *Catholicism in Rhode Island and the Diocese of Providence, 1886–1921* (Providence, RI: Diocese of Providence, 1995), 507–8; and John H. McKenna, *The Centenary Story of Old St. Mary's, Pawtucket, R.I., 1829–1929* (Providence, RI: Providence Visitor Press, 1929), 46.

19. McKenna, *Centenary Story of Old St. Mary's*, 45–46; and Stephen Almagno, *The Days of Our Years: Saint Bartholomew's Parish, Providence, Rhode Island, 1907–1969* (n.p., n.d.), 21.

20. Walsh, *Centennial History of Saint Edward Church*, 134–49.

21. *Providence Journal*, 30 October 1910.

22. Paula Kane, *Separatism and Subculture: Boston Catholicism, 1900–1920* (Chapel Hill: University of North Carolina Press, 1994), 112.

23. Leslie Woodcock Tentler, "Present at the Creation: Working-Class Catholics in the United States," in *American Exceptionalism? US Working-Class Formation in an International Context,* ed. Rick Halpern and Jonathan Morris (New York: St. Martin's Press, 1997), 138.

24. Lay control over church governance had declined nationwide by the turn of the twentieth century, and papal encyclicals issued between 1878 and 1901 directed the church hierarchy to exert more control over lay activities. Yet in reality, the extent to which clerics supervised lay affairs varied greatly depending on the personality of the bishop and priest. Bishop Matthew Harkins, who led the Diocese of Providence from 1886 to 1921, allowed his lay societies a considerable degree of autonomy. See Sterne, *Ballots and Bibles*, 123–24.

25. Walsh, *Centennial History of Saint Edward Church*, 53; and John P. McGuire, *History of Holy Trinity Parish. Central Falls, Rhode Island* (privately printed, 1939), 36–40.

26. Hayman, *Catholicism in Rhode Island*, 609–10, 703; *Woonsocket Evening Call*, 4 November 1912; and *Visitor*, 14 June, 27 September 1918, 11 May 1923.

27. *Constitution and By-Laws of the Catholic Women's Club of West Warwick* (n.p., n.d.), 8, West Warwick Catholic Women's Club Papers, PCDA; and Michael L. Coffey to Hickey, 19 September 1930, Holy Name Society Papers, PCDA.

28. Walsh, *Centennial History of Saint Edward Church*, 49–50; *Visitor*, 19 October, 16 November 1917; and Jay P. Dolan, *The Immigrant Church: New York's Irish and German Catholics, 1815–1865* (Notre Dame, IN: University of Notre Dame Press, 1975), 233.

29. *Visitor*, 6 October 1922, 28 September 1928.

30. Mary Josephine Bannon, ed., *Autobiographic Memoirs of Hon. Patrick J. McCarthy* (Providence, RI: Providence Visitor Press, 1927), 1–2, 5–6, 9–16, 28–32, 278–80, 286.

31. Ibid., 32–33, 35, 193, 280; and *Providence Journal*, 14 December 1888.

32. Bannon, *Memoirs of Hon. Patrick J. McCarthy*, 43–45, 279–81, 286–87.

33. Emily Stier Adler and J. Stanley Lemons, "The Independent Woman: Rhode Island's First Woman Legislator," *Rhode Island History* 49, no. 1 (February 1991):

3–6; Mary Carey McAvoy, "Isabelle Ahearn O'Neill: Little Rhody's Lone Theodora," *Woman's Voice* 26 (March 1931): 12, 31; Katherine Gregg, "Isabelle Ahearn O'Neill: A Starring Role at the State House," in *Women in Rhode Island History* (Providence, RI: Providence Journal, 1994), 16; and "Autobiography" and "Scrapbook, 1897–1918," Isabelle Ahearn O'Neill Papers, RIHS.

34. McAvoy, "Isabelle Ahearn O'Neill: Little Rhody's," 12, 31; Gregg, "Isabelle Ahearn O'Neill: A Starring Role," 16; "Autobiography" and "Scrapbook, 1897–1918"; and *Visitor*, 9 March 1923.

35. Bureau of Industrial Statistics, *Church Statistics*, 274; and *Visitor*, 15 September 1906, 27 April 1907.

36. *Visitor*, 13 May 1910, 23 September 1910. For more on the AFCS and similar efforts in other cities, see Sterne, *Ballots and Bibles*, 141–44.

37. *Visitor*, 13 October 1916, 29 October 1926.

38. Ibid., 8 December 1922, 3 April 1924.

39. Ibid., 21 June 1902, 17 December 1904.

40. Charles R. Morris, *American Catholic: The Saints and Sinners Who Built America's Most Powerful Church* (New York: Random House, Vintage Books, 1997), 150–51; Fones-Wolf, *Trade Union Gospel*; and Dolan, *Immigrant Church*, 329–40, 342–43.

41. Eugene Benoit and Charles A. Winsor to William Hickey, Woonsocket, 2 October 1924, Woonsocket Central Labor Union Papers, PCDA; and *Visitor*, 9 September 1910.

42. Thomas Williams Bicknell, *The History of the State of Rhode Island and Providence Plantations* (New York: American Historical Society, 1920), 4:36; *Providence Journal*, 29 January, 19 February 1894; Evelyn Sterne, "All Americans: The Politics of Citizenship in Providence, 1840–1940" (PhD diss., Duke University, 1999), 90–91; and Scott Molloy, *Trolley Wars: Streetcar Workers on the Line* (Washington, DC: Smithsonian Institution Press, 1996), 167.

43. Scott Molloy, "No Philanthropy at the Point of Production: A Knight of St. Gregory against the Knights of Labor in the New England Rubber Industry, 1885," *Labor History* 45 (2003): 4; *Providence Journal*, 29 October 1937; Piehl, *Breaking Bread*, 36; Hayman, *Catholicism in Rhode Island*, 703; and *Woonsocket Call*, 16 November 1912.

44. James Scott, *Weapons of the Weak: Everyday Forms of Peasant Resistance* (New Haven, CT: Yale University Press, 1985); *Union Worker Magazine*, June 1908, 6; and *Labor Advocate*, 15 January 1913.

45. *Union Worker Magazine*, March 1913, 10.

46. *Il Corriere del Rhode Island*, 17 July 1920 (trans. Robert W. Hayman).

47. The Scalabrini Fathers were known more formally as the Missionaries of St. Charles Borromeo, an order that Bishop Scalabrini of Piacenza in northern Italy formed in 1887 to train priests for missionary work among expatriates. His particular goal was to resolve the church-state conflicts that resulted from Italian unification by working with Italians abroad in cooperation with the foreign ministry. This required

priests to promote a nationalism that may not have resonated with parishioners who clung to regional loyalties. Peter D'Agostino, "Clerical 'Birds of Passage' in the Italian Emigrant Church," paper delivered at the Organization of American Historians Conference, Indianapolis, IN, 4 April 1998, 10, 15, 20; and Hayman, *Catholicism in Rhode Island*, 174–76.

48. *Il Corriere del Rhode Island*, 17 July 1920, 14 August 1920 (trans. Robert W. Hayman); Hayman, *Catholicism in Rhode Island*, 211; and *Providence Journal*, 14 October 1920, 8 November 1920.

49. Holy Name Society of Holy Ghost to Donato Sbarretti, Providence, 19 September 1921 (trans. Robert W. Hayman), Holy Ghost Papers, PCDA; and Hayman, *Catholicism in Rhode Island*, 210.

50. Orsi, *Madonna of 115th Street*, xiii.

51. *The Parish of the Holy Ghost. Providence, Rhode Island, 1889–1989. 100th Anniversary* (Tappen, NY: Custombook, 1989), 19; Hayman, *Catholicism in Rhode Island*, 210; and Societa di Mutuo Soccorso Maria S.S. Del Carmine to Matthew Harkins, Providence, 23 September 1906, Holy Ghost Papers.

52. Hayman, *Catholicism in Rhode Island*, 190; Holy Name Society to Sbarretti, and Irene De Battista et al. to William Hickey, Providence, c. June 1920, Holy Ghost Papers.

53. Errico Bellifante to William Hickey, Providence, 18 June 1920, Holy Ghost Parishioners to William Hickey, Providence, 14 January 1921, and R.S. to William Hickey, Providence, 12 July 1920 (trans. Robert W. Hayman), Holy Ghost Papers; and *Il Corriere del Rhode Island*, 14 August 1920 (trans. Robert W. Hayman). For a discussion of the religious implications of the Italian American home, or "domus," see Orsi, *Madonna of 115th Street*, ch. 4.

54. John Zuccarelli, "The Priest the Immigrants Did Not Want," *Rhode Island Echo*, 2 February 1978; Holy Ghost Parishioners to Hickey, Antonio Ciaveglio to William Hickey, Providence, 2 August 1920, Holy Ghost Papers; and Hayman, *Catholicism in Rhode Island*, 211, 213.

55. The sample is taken from the longest surviving petition, bearing 626 names and submitted by Italian-born jeweler Mauro Corona. Mauro M. Corona et al. to William Hickey, Providence, 17 January 1921, Holy Ghost Papers.

56. *L'Eco del Rhode Island*, 18 November 1920 (trans. Robert W. Hayman); and *Il Corriere del Rhode Island*, 17 July 1920 (trans. Robert W. Hayman).

57. For more on the Macaroni Riots, see Sterne, *Ballots and Bibles*, 105–7; Joseph W. Sullivan, *Marxists, Militants and Macaroni: The I.W.W. in Providence's Little Italy* (Kingston, RI: Rhode Island Labor History Society, 2000); and Russell J. DeSimone, "Providence's 'Macaroni Riots' of 1914," *Italian Americana* 32, no. 2 (Summer 2014): 133–45.

3

Faith Powers and Gambling Spirits in Late Gilded Age Metal Mining

JAROD ROLL

Charles Fox Parham, a central figure in the development of Pentecostalism, was neither the first nor the last person to find fortune in the metal mining boomtown of Galena, Kansas. Although blessed with momentary notoriety in 1901 after his students at Topeka's Bethel Bible College received the divine gift of unknown tongues, Parham had settled into a modest and mildly disappointing career as an itinerant evangelist preaching about the healing power of the Holy Spirit. In August 1903 he met Mary Arthur, a woman with chronic eye and digestive problems, at a mineral spring in western Missouri known for its therapeutic qualities. Arthur's apparently miraculous recovery after praying with Parham so astounded friends and relatives that her husband, E. L. Arthur, a leading merchant of mining equipment in Galena, invited the preacher to their home. In the Arthurs' "large and commodious" Victorian parlor, Parham held a series of services in October that proved popular among the town's middle-class Methodists. To provide more space when the gatherings became too large for the house, the Arthurs erected a tent in their yard. There, at the corner of Fourth and Galena Streets, Parham's ministry changed in ways that neither he nor his middle-class followers had expected. Reporting in January 1904 on the "three months of religious fervor" that followed, a local newspaper doubted "whether in recent years anything has occurred that has awakened the interest, excited the comment or mystified the people of this region as have the religious meetings held by Dr. C. F. Parham, familiarly termed 'the Divine Healer.'" The paper claimed that Parham healed "over a thousand people and converted more than eight hundred" after he opened his services on the Arthurs' lawn, where "soon the streets in that vicinity were crowded nightly with people who were anxious to see and hear the wonderful man who was healing the 'halt, the maimed and the blind' without money and without price."[1] Parham had never before preached to so many people so eager to see and even believe in miracles.

The Arthurs' two-story home occupied a large corner lot a few blocks from Galena's teeming business district. It was a new neighborhood that had been built up with money earned from the local mining boom of the 1880s and 1890s. The Arthurs, who owned a profitable hardware business, built their home around the turn of the century. From their west-facing front parlor, they gazed upon a neighborhood of respectable middle-class families who lived in large homes much like theirs. Looking east or north from their back porch, however, the Arthurs faced an entirely different scene. Their backyard abutted Galena's largest, most lucrative field of zinc and lead mines, a roaring and rumbling industrial riot where hundreds of miners risked life and limb to dig wealth from hard rock. These miners and their families made up the majority of those who joined the fervor of Parham's healing tent. Yet none of them expected the revival to lead to any significant new religious movement or church. Rather, they took Parham's claims of miracles and spirit power in the context of their ordinary lives, which revolved—in one way or another—around the zinc and lead mines that loomed on the edge of town.

Primitive and chaotic, the Galena mines lay in the Joplin district, a hundred-mile swath of ore deposits that cut across the borders of Kansas, Missouri, and Indian Territory. With more than six hundred mines, the district led the nation in zinc production and ranked third in lead, both essential base metals in high demand during the rapid industrial expansion of the Gilded Age. Unlike in other mining districts where large corporations exercised monopolistic control over highly capitalized operations, however, the companies that worked the Joplin district's shallow but unpredictable metal fields were small, owner-operated outfits. Most of the successful mines began as rudimentary prospecting shafts dug by poor but ambitious men who relied on their own muscle power and an appetite for speculative risk in the pursuit of wealth. Although the majority of district miners worked for wages in 1903, they did so in the hopes of saving enough capital to invest in their own chances as prospectors. It was dangerous work, both physically and financially; many men succeeded, but many more failed or died trying. For some, success itself proved fatal. Miners who exploited discoveries in the area's silicate rock formations worked in air laden with silica dust, which caused deadly lung damage, particularly silicosis. Despite these odds, the district's miners labored with faith in the district's promise as a "poor man's camp," where, with hard work, a willingness to take risks, and some good fortune, the "poor man of today may be her rich man of tomorrow."[2]

The willing crowds of mining families that gathered in the streets around the Arthur home transformed Parham's small prayer sessions into something new: a mass, public healing revival that changed the course of Pentecostalism. Parham soon moved the service into Galena's 2,000-seat Grand Leader Building. For weeks, a local newspaper testified, he preached two times daily to "crowded houses" where "cures that are looked upon almost in the light of miracles have been performed." While some worshippers spoke in tongues, most sought miraculous healing. The revival soon spread from Galena throughout the other mining camps of the Joplin district, where working-class families responded to the promise of divine blessing as eagerly as their peers in Galena. Parham and his new followers founded a church, the Apostolic Faith Mission, and together took the message into Texas, where, in Houston in 1905, they met William Seymour, an African American holiness preacher who would take Parham's teaching to Los Angeles and, in early 1906, lead the revival on Azusa Street that made Pentecostalism into a movement that would become of international significance.[3] That history would not have happened the same way, if at all, without the people on the streets of Galena and the other camps of the Joplin district, whose enthusiastic participation and creative belief turned Parham's rather ordinary middle-class faith-healing ministry into a religious force that spoke to the spiritual and physical needs of ambitious workers who ran big risks at the end of the Gilded Age.[4]

Told one way, from Parham's perspective, the story of the Galena revival marks a noteworthy but relatively minor moment in the rapid rise of American Pentecostalism. Most scholars of the movement mention it, if only briefly, as a scene in the course of Parham's career between the events of his Topeka ministry and his meeting with Seymour in Houston. With a lens focused on Parham, these accounts give minimal attention to the people of Galena and its environs. When historians have explained Parham's sudden and unprecedented popularity in Galena, they follow the more general historiographical framework, laid out in the introduction to this volume, often used to explain similar instances of fervent faith among working people in modern America: their credulity for the supernatural was born of economic deprivation and social dislocation. According to Robert Mapes Anderson, the people of Galena hungered for old-time Protestant revival because their mining town had become utterly profane and sinful. James R. Goff, Parham's biographer, explained that the people of Galena were weary of the economic fluctuations and social disruption caused by the mining industry and thus "ready to believe."[5] These tellings, in short, explain the revival as the spiritual escape of working-class Americans from the pressure and pain of living at the rough edge of industrial capitalism.

Told another way, from the perspective of the working-class families who so readily listened to Parham, the story of the Galena revival reveals a much longer pattern of creative faith among the mining communities of the "poor man's camp," whose inhabitants sought miracles in their dangerous effort to wrest individual wealth from the ground. It is a story of working-class belief, not as a cognitive process of assent to theological propositions or the embodiment of received rituals of lived religion, but as the dynamic, active orientation of human consciousness and culture through expectant material practice. Understood this way, acts of belief are at once sacred and secular, metaphysical and somatic, cultural and economic.[6] The people on the streets of Galena were not *ready* to believe, they *already* believed, not in the novel theology of divine healing and spirit power that Parham preached, of course, and in many cases not in any theology or religion whatsoever. Rather, they believed in the possibility of miraculous transformations of personal fortune that their experience of late nineteenth-century capitalism offered. Their belief world—protean, eclectic, and dynamic—encompassed a broad field of vernacular epistemology assembled while seeking individual aggrandizement amid hard rock. Joplin miners dealt in luck and chance and courted the regular working of all kinds of supernatural powers in their lives, most crucially in the speculative labors that at once promised to make poor men rich but also threatened complete ruin, financial and physical.[7] They redirected Parham's career by grasping onto certain parts of his theology, particularly his message that believers could bring the forces of heaven to bear on the material world to effect miraculous change, most especially on and in their own bodies. Parham's promises of spirit power and tangible miracles fit squarely within the occult alchemy of working-class prosperity at the heart of the "poor man's camp" faith.

This essay contends, in short, that the story of the Galena revival is about the power of working-class enchantment with the magic of capitalism at the end of the Gilded Age. As such, it suggests an important field of analysis for historians of working-class religion, particularly during the rapid and tumultuous period of economic change between 1865 and 1915. While one scholarly tradition portrays mass faith in this era as compensation for material hardship, another, newer tradition emphasizes how religious belief provided many workers a potent means of resistance against capitalism.[8] The Galena revival points to a third alternative, located in the broad space between the pew and the picket line: of working-class religious innovation as an empowering expression of some poor people's belief in the chance-world of capitalism.

Beginning in the 1850s, the zinc and lead fields of the Joplin district, scattered along the geological line where the Missouri Ozarks flatten onto the prairies of present-day Kansas and Oklahoma, provided a rare opportunity for miners with little capital to acquire and develop their own mining interests. Highly capitalized, mechanized mining companies, like those that took control of western precious metal mining, saw little incentive in developing the district's fragmented, shallow bodies of base metal ore, which held much less value per volume relative to gold and silver. Instead, very small companies of a few working miners, in most cases owner-operator partnerships with low capital costs and flexible operations, leased mineral rights on plots of land, anywhere from two hundred square feet to five acres, where they prospected for ore for a period of five to ten years. Terms were fair. Miners retained their leases so long as they worked the ground earnestly and consistently. They paid royalties to the landowner on any ore mined from the leasehold, ranging from 5 to 20 percent of market value, depending on the ground's expected productivity. The opportunity attracted several thousand miners between 1850 and 1890, mostly native-born white men from older lead-mining districts in eastern Missouri, Illinois, and Wisconsin. In 1902 the census counted more than three hundred separate companies in the district, most of which worked only one mine each; together they sold more than $8 million worth of ore. "One of the most striking features is the large number of individual owners who have a mine," a 1916 report declared. Such success was becoming harder to achieve at the time, although even then, over fifty years after the district opened, there was "still a chance for the individual to rise, in the time-honored fashion, by a combination of luck and hard work." "All of the capital that was required" to own a mine in the Joplin district, a local historian wrote in 1912, "was a pick, a shovel and two willing hands."[9] One could control access to these material requirements, but as for luck, one could only hope, or perhaps pray.

Although the majority of prospectors never became mine owners, the possibility of doing so at a time of profound industrial change nationwide fired powerful hopes in poor men with either mining experience or some familiarity with the industry. Examples of successful operators, like Galena's Charles Frye, stood as obvious evidence of what was possible. With his own funds, Frye discovered and exploited a run of lead that sold for more than $40,000 in the early 1890s.[10] But there was more to believing than simply seeing. Tales of sudden wealth, passed by word of mouth and printed in local newspapers, filled men's imaginations with a canon of rags-to-riches stories that emphasized physical effort, chance taking, and good fortune. "The successful few are heard of not once, but time and time again," the Missouri state mine inspector reported in 1889. "The story of how one man digging a well for water in his backyard found, instead of water, a vein of ore from which he took out $100,000, is told around almost a hundred thousand times," the staid inspector lamented, with equal parts dismay and exaggeration. In 1899 a mining newspaper told the story of John Newlin, who, on his way from Iowa to Arkansas to buy a farm, "listened to the wonderful stories of how poor men had become millionaires in the" Joplin district. "He was enchanted" and decided "to try his luck in the mines." Newlin bought a pick and shovel, secured a lease, and "struck ore near the surface." Now, the report concluded, he "counts his money by the thousands." The inspector disdained the "gambling spirit" that such stories encouraged. Yet, an abiding faith in the chances of striking pay dirt overshadowed any doubts that more sober outside commentators might introduce. After all, a Joplin newspaper reminded readers in 1907, "It requires just one 'last shot'" at prospecting "to change a man of meager means into a man of a million."[11]

The speculative, risk-taking miners' culture made district camps into dynamic, supercharged communities. Like other mining camps, Galena experienced dramatic growth, from 3,500 inhabitants in 1890 to over 12,000 in 1900, and featured rude enterprises common to most boomtowns, from saloons to gambling houses to brothels. Fights were common, murders not infrequent. "Saturday night in Galena is a carnival of money spending," one report noted around 1900, because that was when companies and prospectors sold the week's ore, and men who worked for wages got paid. An 1899 report reckoned that "more money is paid out every Saturday night in Galena than in any other town its size in the world." In one week at the height of the market, three thousand miners received over $40,000 on a single Saturday. The raucous celebrations that followed would last until local church bells began ringing the following morning. Such outcomes laid fresh evidence of the promise of the "poor man's camp" tradition on a weekly basis. Mining results dominated life in the camps of the Joplin district; the chances of hitting pay dirt dominated the minds of miners. "Everyone in the district is concerned with the mines," an 1897 prospectus noted. "Those who have nothing, hope to get rich; while the rich expect to become richer."[12]

This aggressive entrepreneurial culture informed a politics of opportunistic individualism among local miners. They were notoriously opposed to labor unions. Although some miners set up assemblies of the Knights of Labor in the early 1880s, these groups were small, with a few dozen members and seemingly out of line with the more general political culture of the Knights, which upheld an ethic of sobriety, manly restraint, and respectability. The Webb City assembly, for example, sold stock in a speculative prospecting venture. Although billed as a cooperative effort, the wealth-seeking drive that inspired the scheme fit poorly with the dominant ethos of the Knights. In an attempt to entice Terence V. Powderly himself to invest, one miner revealed an expectation not commonly heard in a labor organization: "A man may be poor here one day & rich the next," he confided. By the late 1880s, all but one of the assemblies had disbanded, mainly because they refused to support the organization's strikes. Unlike other miners who embraced unions in this period, these men saw their future as owner operators, not wage-working cogs.[13] The Western Federation of Miners (WFM), which represented the nation's metal miners after its formation in 1893, made no headway in the district, despite serious organizing efforts from 1899 onward. The WFM considered the organization of the district a priority because Joplin miners became notorious as strikebreakers throughout the western metal camps beginning with the strike in Leadville, Colorado, in 1896.

Joplin miners read the labor shortages caused by WFM strikes as risky but lucrative opportunities to earn high wages. "It is the money I'm after," miner Scott McCollum explained when asked why he went to Leadville. Many, like Albert Torr, who worked as a strikebreaker in northern Idaho in 1899, used their earnings to invest in prospecting stakes in Joplin.[14] By 1903, when Parham arrived in Galena, the miners of the Joplin district were highly sought after by western metal companies looking for workers to defy the WFM. Labor agents from Colorado, Arizona, Nevada, and California recruited in the district that autumn, offering potential strikebreakers daily wages that ranged from $2.50 to $4.50 per day. Hundreds accepted, despite modest WFM organizing gains in the summer of 1903, when organizers set up five new locals around Joplin. By the time the WFM organizer returned in early 1904, however, none of the locals survived. Former members declared "that they could get along without organization."[15] The miners of the Joplin district were not tricked or coerced into their antipathy toward unions. Rather, their antiunionism was the result of their faith in the promise of the poor man's camp. As a private detective explained to Colorado mine owners in 1896, "The miners in this country do not believe in Unionism (Labor Unions)." What they believed in was the lure of individual reward.[16]

The quest for pay dirt demanded that miners gamble with their own bodies. As in other districts, miners in the Joplin district suffered frequent injuries and sometimes death while at work, whether from cave-ins, rock falls, or accidents with tools or equipment. Respiratory illness, however, posed the most treacherous threat to their health. In the late 1890s, prospectors discovered an area where mineral deposits ran in thin seams through very hard silicate rock, a zone known locally as the sheet ground. Miners made money in the sheet ground, but only after using more intensive extraction methods, like dynamite blasting. Dynamite loosened mineral but also created thick clouds of silica dust in the mine. Whether miners owned these claims or worked there for wages, they inhaled vast amounts of silica that shredded deep lung tissue, which caused silicosis and complicated forms of tuberculosis. Once a miner contracted silicosis, he could expect to live ten years, maybe less. A 1915 study found that over 60 percent of all miners in the district had either silicosis or tuberculosis or both.[17] Although the direct cause of silicosis was poorly understood until that study, everyone knew that mining was extremely dangerous, often deadly. None knew this better than miners themselves and their families, but the chance to wrest life-changing rewards from hard rock led thousands headlong into those dangers anyway.

This culture of male risk taking relied on the work of women to provide stability and security. Many miners were married. Because mining companies in the district were too small to provide company stores, women not only directed domestic economies but also raised animals and planted gardens for food. Some women also ran boardinghouses as a way to earn money. Others provided for children when husbands and fathers died in mine accidents, which happened often, or had been incapacitated by injury or disease. More commonly, women struggled with difficult living conditions as men regularly invested any cash in mining ventures. In 1889, the state mine inspector met a miner who lived with his wife and one-year-old daughter in a rented house with "a very poverty-stricken appearance, no carpet on any of the floors, poorly furnished and lacking in cleanliness." The man was working a leasehold with three partners from which he had earned ninety dollars in 1888. Rather than improve the living conditions of his family, the miner invested the surplus back into the mine. "The trouble is," the inspector concluded, "the savings which could certainly buy a comfortable home are dumped into holes in the ground, which possibly may result in gains of thousands, but which probably and generally result in the loss of all." While some women, like the wife of John Newlin mentioned previously, tried to stop their husbands from making these gambles, others embraced the culture of risk and reward. "Everybody that come here then had to work hard but they didn't complain none," a miner's wife in what would become Ottawa County, Oklahoma, explained. "Watchin' new mills go up an' the new mines go down wuz as excitin' as watchin' kids grow an' everything wuz like that—growin' over night."[18] Women's efforts to build long-term security amid reckless presentism helped generate belief in mining miracles, although from the very different perspective of those most likely to bear the costs of the "poor man's camp."

Local churches reflected this tension in the district's mining culture. No one denomination predominated in the district's fragmented religious terrain, which was overwhelmingly Protestant. Galena's Christians divided more or less equally between four denominations: Northern Baptist, Disciples of Christ, Presbyterian USA, and Methodist Episcopal, the largest church in town. Assorted "other Protestant" groups were also present. Joplin's 30,000 residents, meanwhile, could choose from a dizzying kaleidoscope of religious groups: Seventh-Day Adventist, Baptist (Northern, Southern, and Free), Christian Scientist, Congregationalist, Disciples of Christ (the city's largest denomination), the Church of Latter-Day Saints, Lutheran, Methodist (Northern, Southern and Free), Presbyterian (USA and Cumberland), Episcopalian, Spiritualist, Roman Catholic, and the Salvation Army. As we have seen, many miners followed other pursuits on Sunday mornings. Men in Joplin were 25 percent less likely to belong to a church in 1906 than their male counterparts nationally. Women made up the majority of those in the pews.[19] Yet many of these denominations, particularly the Methodists, represented significant wealth and occupied ornate church buildings—"monster stone edifices," according to one laudatory report. Their wealth and opulence depended entirely on proceeds from the local mining economy; Saturday, in other words, funded Sunday. "With money earned by underground toil the hard-working miners have here and there aided in the erection of ministerial palaces," a news report boasted, "to be heralded throughout the country as the centers of a devout devotion." But devotion to what? Rather than challenge the gambling spirits of local miners, churches encouraged the entrepreneurial ethos of the poor man's camp. According to this survey of Joplin's religious life, "Men worth hundreds of thousands are every Sunday seen to grasp the calloused hand of a mine-laborer and say, 'God bless you, my brother.'"[20]

Some miners sought out non-Christian spiritual powers in their search for economic fortune. Successful prospector and mine owner C. R. O. Baker claimed that his "belief and faith" in Spiritualism "led to his princely discovery" in the ground. Baker, "well known in the Joplin mining district," explained that he received "assurance from some source which he is unable to explain to the ordinary laymen that he was near the great riches." He eagerly offered to introduce other miners to "the great powers which guide him."

Meanwhile, "hundreds" of miners regularly consulted Professor Babboo, "the great palmist," who predicted the location, extent, and direction of ore deposits by reading the palms of prospectors and mine operators, "rich and poor alike."[21] From the largest mainstream denominations to the most marginal sites of faith, miners in the Joplin district, both the already successful and the aspirant, frequently called on the spirit world to aid their effort to make themselves rich.

The power of this enchantment with economic speculation shaped religious reform groups as well as mainstream churches. As the camps of the district developed into towns, a thriving middle class of merchants and professionals prospered alongside the mining industry. Although their livelihoods depended on the risky enthusiasm of local miners, many desired to live in communities that reflected the era's model of social respectability: sober, pious, physically and emotionally restrained men and women who performed traditional separate-spheres gender roles. The Methodists who gathered in the Arthur home to hear Parham in late 1903 felt this unease. They sought moral revitalization through the holiness movement, a three-decades-old radical reform effort within Methodism. Holiness adherents challenged the perceived worldliness of the church, exemplified in Joplin by the "monster stone edifices," and called instead for empowering individual believers in their fight against evil. According to historian Grant Wacker, their teachings sought "to eradicate 'inbred sin' and thereby to break the stranglehold of selfish desires." The emphasis on the purification of true believers opened many worshippers to "the theology and practice of divine healing for the body." This more radical phase of the holiness movement, where Parham's career took root, was particularly appealing to middle-class women such as Mary Arthur who struggled to uphold Victorian social codes in communities dominated by vulgar and dangerous pursuits of wealth.[22]

With Arthur's support, Parham's Galena revival began as a therapeutic alternative for wealthy but unhappy Christian women, but unwittingly reinforced the connections between economic prosperity and metaphysical good fortune. "The high social standing and excellent reputation of Mrs. Arthur has done much in bringing Parham before the public in a favorable light," a local newspaper reported. Among those to attend the first meetings at the Arthur home was the wife of Charles Frye, "one of the best known mine operators." "Mrs. Frye had been a constant sufferer for years but states that she is now in excellent health through the prayers of Mr. Parham and his band." But Parham's well-to-do Galena supporters were not content to purify their own lives. They insisted on amplifying Parham's ministry. The

Arthurs and Fryes led the push within the Galena Chamber of Commerce to rent the Grand Leader Building for his use. They also likely gave him direct financial support. By lending their money and influence, these holiness families made clear their hope that Parham's revival would lead to a new moral awakening.[23]

Public support from leading citizens, particularly mine operators like Frye, whose ascent from prospector to owner epitomized what was possible for local miners, signaled an association between the events at Parham's healing services and economic success in the poor man's camp that working-class people readily accepted. "The list of those who have been benefitted" by Parham's "faith powers," the report continued, "have done much to cause the public to regard the man with an almost superstitious awe."[24] Parham's own well-tailored suits and refined diction reinforced that association. His services thus fit snugly within a local tradition of appealing to miraculous forces for personal empowerment and prosperity. For example, the newspaper issue that described Parham's "three months of religious fervor" also featured an adjacent article, "Spirit Messages," about recent spiritualist meetings in Joplin; both stories ran on the front page. The latter article quoted a recent message from a spirit called Van Dee, "a monk who lived hundreds of years ago," who explained that "if you can get the natural mind in full accord with the soul force within you then there is no limit to your power."[25] People outside of middle-class parlors rarely had access to this kind of intentional spiritual power, however. That changed, along with Parham's popularity, when the evangelist moved his service onto the Arthurs' yard, where all could hear his message and participate, even the miners who daily walked past the Arthur home to seek their fortune in the mine that rumbled while he preached.

Howard Goss was one of the miners drawn to Parham's promise of divine empowerment. Goss had moved to Galena in 1898 when his father sold the family farm in the Missouri Ozarks to invest in a mining venture, which soon failed. "All our savings disappeared," Goss recalled. At the age of fifteen, he went to work in the mines, probably as a shoveler, the most common underground occupation in the district for young men. Companies paid shovelers to load newly blasted ore from the mine floor into large cans to be hoisted to the surface. Because the district's fragmented ore bodies offered no long-term reliability, companies paid shovelers by a contract piece rate per can to encourage speed. Rates varied according to the price of ore; shovelers received between four and eight cents per can, which each held between 1,000 and 1,250 pounds of ore. In 1915, a Bureau of Mines official figured that Joplin shovelers moved an average of 44,000 pounds of ore a day, which would have earned between $1.56 and $3.12, depending on the rate. In 1912, shovelers earned an average of $2.90 a day. Some shovelers loaded one hundred cans a day—100,000 pounds or more—for which they could earn as much as eight dollars. They took pride in their earning power and the masculine physical prowess required to achieve it. According to observers, "The young and vigorous men prefer to shovel, as it pays best."[26] Shovelers performed hard, dangerous work but, if they had enough physical and mental power, could earn good money, possibly for investing in their own speculative venture one day.

Able to marshal both his body and mind, Goss excelled at underground work. "Physically, I was a natural athlete . . . alert and strong," he later recalled. Mining demanded more than muscle, however. Goss developed a heightened sense of awareness in the mine workscape, a vexed space where all workers ran enormous risks. "I soon became used to the 'voices' of the mines—the rumblings of the earth," Goss said, "and got to understand their portent." The mines of the Joplin district could feed a man's ambitions or destroy him, often literally. One day, "just after the powder men had set off a blast," he recalled, "a great pile of falling stone partly buried me," cutting his head and knocking him unconscious. Goss got lucky; rock falls killed dozens of miners each year. He went back to work, but soon faced death again when the cage lowering him and a coworker into the mine suddenly plummeted 125 feet to the bottom of the shaft, where a pool of water cushioned their impact. The balance of risk that Joplin miners ran, between the pursuit of money and the material perils it required, forced many to think hard about the whims of fortune. "While I was falling," Goss explained, "I saw all of my sins depicted before me on the wall of that shaft." Although he did not then believe in God, Goss sensed powerful spirits at work in the ground. As he recovered, shaken by this brush with his own mortality, Goss learned of Parham's revival, where people he knew claimed to have "experienced God's healing for various of their diseases." Intrigued, Goss went to see for himself. "After attending the services," he explained, "it soon became evidence to me that some superhuman power was at work there." Goss wanted that power to work through and for him.[27]

Parham's message about the miraculous physical gifts of the Holy Spirit reached a hungry audience among miners who pushed their bodies to the brink in order to make money. Parham evoked the ready accessibility of Christ's full gospel, "attended with signs, wonders, mighty deeds, divers miracles and the gifts of the Holy ghost," for those who believed. These were not symbolic gifts, he emphasized, but tangible, physical displays of God's power that worked on and through the bodies of ordinary people. All that was required was faith. "The healing of the sick is as much part of the gospel as telling" of heaven, Parham preached. Far more than speaking in tongues, the physical manifestations of Holy Spirit baptism held the imaginations of miners like Goss who prized bodily strength and "mighty deeds" as the poor miner's route to riches. "During the altar service one night I watched an old Indian chief receive the Baptism of the Holy Spirit," Goss recalled. The elderly man "stood tilted rigidly backwards," yet remained perfectly balanced and unmoving, while he praised God for more than an hour. "Unusually strong as I was," Goss explained, "I knew that it was beyond ordinary human power to perform this feat, or many of the other things which I saw take place before my eyes," including the healing of injury and illness. "I soon became fully convinced that there was a Supreme Being, and that His power was at work in our town" and that the "power to heal was . . . through His power, as the Son of God from Heaven." He converted to what Parham then called the Apostolic Faith and received Holy Spirit baptism. Shortly after accepting Parham's version of Christianity, Goss was promoted to manage a mine, a dramatic economic advancement he linked to his conversion.[28]

As Goss understood it, physical restoration was only one aspect of a more bountiful physical existence that God intended for believers to enjoy. This interpretation fit a growing pattern in Parham's ministry to expand from the healing of illness and injury to a more positive message about enjoying God's abundance. "'Whatsoever things ye desire when ye pray,'" Parham preached the following summer, quoting the Gospel of Mark, "'believe that ye have them and ye shall have them.'" It is impossible from the available sources to know whether Parham's encounter with the miners in Galena influenced this theological move, but his message was not so far from what the spirit Van Dee had said in Joplin. In the poor man's camp, a miner's main asset, his greatest source of capital, was his body. Miners found in Parham's services a means to both repair and enhance their physical abilities, and thus breathe new life into their quest for individual gain. By January 1904, Parham was leading meetings in "almost a dozen of the different mining camps of this district, all of which are attracting large crowds."[29] What began in a nerve-racked middle-class parlor had become, through acts of working-class belief in the "poor man's camp," a wide-open revival that offered miners the potential of spiritual empowerment in their very physical efforts to achieve economic prosperity.

Although Parham left for Texas in early 1905, the revival he started in Galena continued and gradually coalesced in more formal church groups, which dealt closely with the perils and promise of mining. Parham returned in late 1905 and early 1906 to lead reunion revivals, but middle-class women and working-class men dominated the new groups. Mary Arthur and Howard Goss became leaders in the Galena church, known as the Apostolic Faith Mission. Opal Stauffer, who had accompanied Parham to Houston where she prayed with William Seymour, returned to lead the Christ Church Association, as the Joplin church was called. In 1906, Stauffer married Efton Wiley, a local miner and church member. Although Wiley became pastor of the church in 1909, he "continued to mine." So did his brother, Everett Wiley, an evangelist who preached throughout district mining camps. Their ministry grappled directly with the tensions of underground work. In 1907, Russell Casey, "a well known miner," which meant he was probably an owner operator, and an adherent to the Apostolic Faith, got trapped in his Joplin mine when the roof collapsed. "We knew by many sudden deaths what such accidents meant," Mary Arthur explained, "and no one expected to see him alive again." While a group of miners worked to reach him, a small group of Pentecostals prayed "for a brother in Christ . . . until deliverance came, and he was brought out alive." Casey's ribs were crushed, but "God had saved him and he was still alive . . . giving God glory for his deliverance."[30]

Middle-class support for Parham soon faded in the Joplin district, however. He suffered from the sensational, negative coverage of Seymour's Azusa Street revival, even though Parham publicly denounced what he considered the fanaticism of his former student's ministry. As Pentecostalism emerged as distinct from the holiness movement, imaginations conjured a variety of claims about the apparently unrestrained group. In September 1907, five of Parham's followers were arrested for murder in Zion City, Illinois, the community founded by the late healer Alexander Dowie. They were accused of preventing a seriously ill woman from seeking medical attention and instead forcing her to pray for relief from her affliction, from which she later died. A Joplin reporter asked Parham, who was holding revivals in Galena and Joplin at the time, whether the case was a direct result of his teachings. The "founder of peculiar religion," as the subsequent article called him, denied any responsibility. But the case clearly damaged his reputation. "His meetings in Galena and neighboring cities attracted thousands who attended nightly," the paper reminded readers, and noted with newfound embarrassment how "a surprisingly large number of his listeners became believers in the faith."[31] Many of those believers now turned on Parham. A week later, the same Joplin newspaper led its Sunday morning edition with a front-page story about the pitiable plight of R. R. Preston, a Galena merchant, who declared, "Parham has wrecked my home." The Prestons had become followers of Parham in late 1903. But since then, Preston told the paper, his wife, Dora Preston, had become "so terribly influenced with the teachings of Parham that she was neglecting her home and duties to be near the man." He planned to divorce her, but blamed Parham "for my ruination financially, besides the sorrow and disgrace he has wrought upon myself and family." If middle-class families looked to the Apostolic Faith for spiritual restoration, this was surely not it. Preston's admission, the report noted ominously, was only "the latest version of the many charges which are being brought to the attention of the public in regard to the workings of Charles F. Parham."[32] Although he continued to live in nearby Baxter Springs, Kansas, until his death in 1930, Parham's personal influence in the Joplin district was finished.

Yet faith in the power of God to overcome material limitations not only endured in the Joplin district but flourished as the area became an important hub in early Pentecostalism. In the autumn of 1910, D. C. O. Opperman, E. N. Bell, and Goss directed a two-month Bible school in Joplin intended to train Pentecostal evangelists. This group of activists, including Efton Wiley and Opal Wiley, then spearheaded a series of meetings throughout the Ozarks that led to revivals in Springfield and, in 1911, in Yellville, Arkansas, a zinc-mining boomtown not unlike Galena. Goss, the Wileys, and other evangelists from the Joplin district attended the formation of the Assemblies of God in Hot Springs, Arkansas, in 1914, which incorporated the Apostolic Faith Mission and the Christ Church Association. Goss quit mining to join the executive board of the Assemblies of God alongside Bell, who became the first chairman of the denomination. Efton Wiley continued to mine for zinc and lead in Joplin as well as preach to an Assembly made up of mining families.[33]

Even so, the poor man's camp faith in the miracle of working-class prosperity had transformed Parham's preaching more than Parham's preaching had transformed the culture of the poor man's camp. Most of the miners in the district, and even most of the miners who experienced Parham's revival, did not become Pentecostals. The 1926 census of religious bodies counted only sixty-eight members of the Assembly of God in Joplin.[34]

Although changes to the local mining industry altered the terms of risk and reward, miners continued to embrace the work with the same individualistic enthusiasm that they once invested in prospecting. After 1910, mining companies replaced the old system of prospector leases with a regime of wage labor that revolved around piece-rate shoveling. Poor miners could no longer hope to invest in their own mine, but instead locked their focus on the high wages that shovelers could earn. Neither the WFM, nor any other miners' union, made any serious progress organizing the district despite repeated efforts. The discovery of the richest zinc field yet in Ottawa County, Oklahoma, in 1915, when wartime demand pushed metal prices and miners' wages to record highs, made the lure of working-class prosperity as attractive as ever. Shoveling provided a means for individual miners to pursue big pay but took a terrible toll on their bodies. While battered bones and torn tissue diminished many, shovelers were especially vulnerable to silicosis. The harder a shoveler worked, the more he earned, but the harder he worked, the faster and deeper he needed to breathe, which increased the amount of silica dust he inhaled. Just as the gambling spirit propelled miners in the Joplin district, silicosis haunted them, whether they worked as owner operators, prospectors, wage hands, or shovelers. Both Everett Wiley and Efton Wiley died of tuberculosis, probably the result of silicosis; Everett died in 1912, Efton in 1916.[35] Despite this knowledge and new, increasingly strenuous efforts by local elites to restrain worker behavior, miners continued to seek high wages no matter the health risk, to themselves or the public.

In 1920, Charles Morris Mills, a social worker for the Interchurch World Movement, conducted a three-month investigation of social conditions in Picher, Oklahoma, the district's newest boomtown. He was trying to understand why Picher had the highest mortality rates from tuberculosis in the nation. Mills found 12,000 miners gripped by an "individualistic spirit" that encouraged rampant "economic opportunism," especially in pursuit of the "economic prize of the shoveler's wages." To his disappointment, Mills concluded that local churches did nothing to counteract such destructive, high-risk, hypermasculine behavior. Rather, he noted, "the church has confined itself to a narrow, emotional type of old-fashioned theology instead of living and serving as the social, recreational and inspirational center." Unless religious leaders pushed back against the selfish, short-term mindset of the miners, he warned, "a feverish unsteadiness will continue to warp the social instincts and ideals of men."[36] He misunderstood the relationship between working-class aspiration and the nature of religious power in the district. Most miners seem to have not wanted a church at all, let alone one that would pacify them. Rather, they sought spiritual powers with worldly purchase. They got what they wanted from the "emotional" worship that Mills derided: a faith that promised physical miracles for lives strained in pursuit of economic ambition. "Every minister of the city is a red-blooded he-man," a Picher community appraisal stated in 1927, "chaps who have worked for their living in the past, and many of them continue to do as now, although they preach on Sunday."[37] In the 1920s as in Parham's day, the miners of the Joplin district interpreted the efficacy of religion through a lens shaped by their working-class faith in the prosperity that capitalism made possible. That lens gave material form to supernatural workings, nowhere so needed as in the mines, where poor men pursued the chance of individual wealth amid the most pressing physical limitations, of the earth and of their own bodies. That history of working-class belief remained powerful in the "poor man's camp" even during the hard times of the Great Depression. Following the passage of the National Industrial Recovery Act in 1933, the International Union of Mine, Mill and Smelter Workers (as the WFM renamed itself in 1916) organized several locals in the district that together went on strike in the summer of 1935. Within a week, hundreds of union and nonunion miners organized a back-to-work movement that broke the strike. The back-to-work miners held their first meetings in Cardin, Oklahoma, in the Pentecostal church.[38]

To conclude, this volume represents a new wave of scholarship on working-class religion in modern American history. Beginning with Ken Fones-Wolf's *Trade Union Gospel*, that growing body of work, conceived in the bottom-up style of the new labor history, has shown how a diverse range of American workers—white and African American, rural and urban, northern and southern—interpreted evangelical Christianity in creative and independent ways to meet their social, cultural, and often political needs. One of the most important findings in this field is that often workers' interpretations of religion emerged from, and further encouraged, resistance to capitalism. This essay shows how working-class interpretations of Christianity could also emerge from laborers' faith in the promise of capitalism. To limit the implications of the new history of working-class religion to the labor movement or radical politics is to blunt its greatest point, that American workers mobilized spiritual faith for their own ends in an innovative process of believing that was the product of both intellectual work and physical practice. That some workers looked for miraculous help in their struggle to gain individual prosperity, as shown here, only makes the new emphasis on their spiritual creativity more compelling, particularly in view of the role of religion in the later relationship between American workers and the new conservatism.

The story of Parham's Galena revival is at heart a story about the power of working-class belief as a creative act that mediated the tension between ideas and things, the religious and the profane, and the supernatural realm and the material world in an economic context that promised individual transformation. Miners in the Joplin district created and acted within a belief world born of rampant ambition and strict physical limitations. It was a distinctly working-class world where poor men sought economic transubstantiation through a combination of risk taking, stubborn determination, and brutally hard work. Their aim—turning poverty into wealth—was both easy to imagine and so difficult to achieve. Their efforts required immense labor power and good fortune. For the latter, these miners regularly courted supernatural forces. Parham's ministry offered one potential source that miners adapted to meet their needs. Then they kept digging and kept shoveling in search of hard-rock metal. They were not alone among American workers in drawing on the spirit world in the face of industrial capitalism. The rigors, challenges, and aspirations that working people experienced within that system both encouraged and demanded claims on the miraculous: to transcend material inadequacy, to alter profound imbalances of earthly power, and to transform one's life in an enchanted world of astounding wealth and immense hardship.

If the belief world of Joplin miners did not foment resistance, neither did it encourage acquiescence to poverty. Many historians have been quick to read Pentecostalism and other ecstatic forms of Christianity as pie-in-the-sky escapism and otherworldly compensation for earthly deprivation. Some Pentecostal denominations certainly encouraged that view at times. Others, by contrast, have preached a prosperity gospel that lent divine power to the worldly quest for material wealth. Charles Parham's quite accidental and unexpected success in the Joplin district suggests that the salience of this view had much less to do with the work of theologians and evangelists than it did a much more popular faith in the possibility of miraculously transforming one's worldly circumstances. Galena miners already believed in the power of capitalism to make poor men rich before Parham arrived in town. Their faith in individual economic miracles played a crucial role in the creation of Pentecostalism, not the other way around.

Notes

1. James R. Goff, *Fields White unto Harvest: Charles F. Parham and the Missionary Origins of Pentecostalism* (Fayetteville: University of Arkansas Press, 1988), 69–93; Mary A. Arthur, "Beginning History of Galena Church," n.d., 1–5, item 10228208, Flower Pentecostal Heritage Center, Springfield, MO; Sarah E. Parham, *The Life of Charles F. Parham, Founder of the Apostolic Faith Movement* (Joplin, MO: Tri-State, 1930), 87–91 (first quote on 91); "Three Months of Religious Fervor," *Daily News Herald* (Joplin, MO), 24 January 1904 (remaining quotes).

2. Ethel E. Goss, *The Winds of God: The Story of the Early Pentecostal Days (1901–1914) in the Life of Howard A. Goss* (New York: Comet Press, 1958), 6–8; Arrell M.

Gibson, *Wilderness Bonanza: The Tri-State District of Missouri, Kansas, and Oklahoma* (Norman: University of Oklahoma Press, 1972), 3–50, 68 (first quote); "Opportunities for Poor Men," *Joplin Daily Globe*, 24 February 1907 (second quote).

3. "Blindness and Cancer Cured by Religion," *St. Louis Globe-Democrat*, 1 January 1904; Parham, *Life of Charles F. Parham*, 95–127; Goff, *Fields White unto Harvest*, 90–104; Stanley Wayne, "Early Revivals," in *Perpetuating Pentecost: A Look at the Formation and Development of the Southern Missouri District Council of the Assemblies of God* (Springfield: Southern Missouri District Council of the Assemblies of God, 1989), 6–8.

4. Grant Wacker and Jonathan R. Baer have both shown how early Pentecostals focused much more on healing and the body than on speaking in tongues. See Wacker, *Heaven Below: Early Pentecostals and American Culture* (Cambridge, MA: Harvard University Press, 2001), 3; and Baer, "Perfectly Empowered Bodies: Divine Healing in Modernizing America" (PhD diss., Yale University, 2002), 1–9.

5. Robert Mapes Anderson, *Visions of the Disinherited: The Making of American Pentecostalism* (New York: Oxford University Press, 1979), 58–59; Goff, *Fields White unto Harvest*, 90–93 (quote on 92); Wacker, *Heaven Below*, 4–5, 214; Vinson Synan, *The Holiness-Pentecostal Tradition: Charismatic Movements in the Twentieth Century* (1971; Grand Rapids, MI: William B. Eerdmans, 1997), 89–92; Randall Stephens, *The Fire Spreads: Holiness and Pentecostalism in the American South* (Cambridge, MA: Harvard University Press, 2008), 189–91; Harvey Cox, *Fire from Heaven: The Rise of Pentecostal Spirituality and the Reshaping of Religion in the Twenty-First Century* (Reading, MA: Addison-Wesley, 1995), 49.

6. My use of *belief* here draws on efforts by theologians, historians, and anthropologists to build an understanding of human agencies of faith that incorporates the dynamic relationship between both intellectual and material religious culture while scanning aspects of the human experience not usually considered relevant to more limited concepts of "religion." See David Morgan, "Materiality, Social Analysis, and the Study of Religions," in *Religion and Material Culture: The Matter of Belief*, ed. David Morgan (London: Routledge, 2005), 73; Kevin Lewis O'Neill, "Pastor Harold Caballeros Believes in Demons: Belief and Believing in the Study of Religion," *History of Religions* 51 (May 2012): 299–316; Richard J. Callahan Jr., *Work and Faith in the Kentucky Coal Fields: Subject to Dust* (Bloomington: Indiana University Press, 2009), 8–10, 129–51; Danilyn Rutherford, "The Enchantments of Secular Belief," paper presented to the Martin Marty Seminar for the Advanced Study of Religion, University of Chicago Divinity School, October 2008, http://divinity.uchicago.edu/religion-and-culture-web-forum-archive-20092008; and James Carse, *The Religious Case against Belief* (New York: Penguin, 2008), 2–108.

7. Working from limited secondary sources, Grant Wacker alluded to a possible connection between the risk-taking attitude of miners in the Joplin district and the popularity of Pentecostal revivals there but curiously overlooked the central role of the Galena revival in Parham's career and the vital work of converts from Galena and

Joplin in the revivals leading up to Azusa and later in the founding of the Assemblies of God. See Wacker, *Heaven Below*, 214. Similarly, Richard Callahan has shown how Kentucky coal miners produced powerful religious meaning that melded natural and supernatural forces through their very physical experience of industrial capitalism during the same period. The creative religious interpretations of those miners also contributed to the development of Holiness and Pentecostal belief, although with less emphasis on miraculous prosperity than among their counterparts in Kansas and Missouri. See Callahan, *Work and Faith in the Kentucky Coal Fields*, 129–57.

8. For an extensive overview of this literature, see the introduction to this volume.

9. John R. Holibaugh, *The Lead and Zinc Mining Industry of Southwest Missouri and Southeast Kansas* (New York: Scientific, 1895), 5–7; Gibson, *Wilderness Bonanza*, 68–78; *Sixteenth Annual Report of the State Lead and Zinc Mine Inspector of the State of Missouri* (Jefferson City, MO: Tribune, 1903), 295; U.S. Bureau of the Census, *Special Reports: Mines and Quarries, 1902* (Washington, D.C.: Government Printing Office, 1905), 217–19, 244–47; "Zinc Boom Builds Cities Over Night," *Cleveland Plain Dealer*, 31 October 1916 (first two quotes); John T. Livingston, *A History of Jasper County Missouri and Its People*, vol. 1 (Chicago: Lewis, 1912), 150 (last quote).

10. Holibaugh, *Lead and Zinc Mining Industry*, 16.

11. *Eleventh Annual Report of the Bureau of Labor Statistics of the State of Missouri* (Jefferson City, MO: Tribune, 1889), 336–37 (inspector quotes); "Rich in Zinc and Lead," *Butte Weekly Miner*, 8 June 1899 (Newlin quotes); "Opportunities for Poor Men," *Joplin Daily Globe*, 24 February 1907 (last quote).

12. U.S. Bureau of the Census, *Twelfth Census of the United States: Population: Part I* (Washington, DC: Government Printing Office, 1901), 163; "A Kansas Mining Town," n.d. [1899] (first two quotes), Kansas Mining Town Collection, Library Archives, Missouri Southern State University, Joplin; William R. Draper and Mabel Draper, *Old Grubstake Days in Joplin: The Story of the Pioneers Who Discovered the Largest and Richest Lead and Zinc Mining Field in the World* (Girard, KS: Haldeman-Julius, 1946), 18 (third quote).

13. John F. Loftus, Joplin, to Terence V. Powderly (quote), 24 December 1879, Reel 2, *Terence Vincent Powderly Papers, 1864–1937* (Glen Rock, NJ: Microfilming Corporation of America, 1975); Jonathan Garlock, *Guide to the Local Assemblies of the Knights of Labor* (Westport, CT: Greenwood Press, 1982), 86–87, 132–33, 246–47; *Proceedings of the General Assembly of the Knights of Labor* (Philadelphia: General Assembly, 1887), 1353.

14. "Why They Went," *Joplin Daily Globe*, 6 November 1896 (quote); "Albert Torr," *Joplin City Directory*, 1907, www.ancestry.com.

15. "Wanted," *Joplin Daily Globe*, 13 September 1903 and 22 September 1903; D. C. Copley, "Official Proceedings of the Thirteenth Annual Convention, Western Federation of Miners, Salt Lake City, 1905," 258–59 (final quote), Bound Volume 166, Records of the Western Federation of Miners/International Union of Mine, Mill and Smelter Workers, Archives, University of Colorado at Boulder Libraries.

16. "Operative T. Z. P. reports from Joplin, Mo.," 9 September 1896 (first quote), file folder 47, box 2, MSS 334, Leadville Strike Reports, History Colorado, Denver. For a full treatment of strikebreaking miners from the Joplin district, see Jarod Roll, "Sympathy for the Devil: The Notorious Career of Missouri's Strikebreaking Metal Miners, 1896–1910," *LABOR: Studies in Working-Class History of the Americas* 11, no. 4 (Winter 2014): 11–37.

17. A. J. Lanza and Edwin Higgins, *Pulmonary Disease among Miners in the Joplin District: A Preliminary Report*, Bureau of Mines Technical Paper 105 (Washington, DC: Government Printing Office, 1915), 38–39 (quotes); Edwin Higgins, A. J. Lanza, F. B. Laney, and George S. Rice, *Siliceous Dust in Relation to Pulmonary Disease among Miners in the Joplin District, Missouri*, Bureau of Mines, Bulletin 132 (Washington, DC: Government Printing Office, 1917), 65–68.

18. *Eleventh Annual Report of the Bureau of Labor Statistics of the State of Missouri*, 336–38 (first two quotes); Velma Nieberding, *History of Ottawa County* (Miami, OK: Walsworth, 1983), 74–92; "Of Work (Mrs. B)," Appendix B: The Tri-State People Speak, 15 (final quote), in Tri-State Survey Committee, "A Preliminary Report on Living, Working and Health Conditions in the Tri-State Mining Area (Missouri, Oklahoma, and Kansas), 1939, Countway Library of Medicine, Harvard University.

19. U.S. Bureau of the Census, *Special Reports: Religious Bodies, 1906, Part 1: Summary and General Tables* (Washington, DC: Government Printing Office, 1910), 314–17, 376–77, 381–407.

20. "Joplin a City of Churches," *Joplin Daily Globe*, 24 February 1907.

21. "Guided by Spirits He Locates Lead Bonanza," *Joplin News Herald*, 16 March 1910; "The Great Palmist," *Joplin Daily Globe*, 13 June 1899.

22. Grant Wacker, "The Holy Spirit and the Spirit of the Age in American Protestantism, 1880–1910," *Journal of American History* 72 (June 1985): 48 (quotes). See also Jackson Lears, *No Place of Grace: Antimodernism and the Transformation of American Culture, 1880–1920* (1981; Chicago: University of Chicago Press, 1994), xvi, 16.

23. "Three Months of Religious Fervor," *Joplin Daily News Herald*, 24 January 1904 (quotes). On the popularity of healing among women, see Heather D. Curtis, *Faith in the Great Physician: Suffering and Divine Healing in American Culture, 1860–1900* (Baltimore: Johns Hopkins University Press, 2007), 85–91, 122–41.

24. "Three Months of Religious Fervor," *Joplin Daily News Herald*, 24 January 1904.

25. "Spirit Messages," *Joplin Daily News Herald*, 24 January 1904.

26. Goss, *Winds of God*, 7–8 (first quote on 7); Clarence A. Wright, *Mining and Treatment of Lead and Zinc Ores in the Joplin District, Missouri: A Preliminary Report*, Technical Paper 41, Bureau of the Mines (Washington, D.C.: Government Printing Office, 1913), 17, 36–38; A. J. Lanza, "Silicosis and Pulmonary Tuberculosis: Some Observations Based on Recent Investigation of Metal Mines in Southwest Missouri" (second quote), report enclosed in A. J. Lanza to Rupert Blue, Surgeon General, January 8, 1915, folder 5153 (Jan.-Apr. 1915), box 558, and A. J. Lanza, "Pulmonary Disease among Miners in the Joplin District, Missouri, and Its Relation to Siliceous Dust in the Mines, Final Report," folder 5153 (1922–1923), box 561, both in File 5153,

Central File, 1897–1923, RG 90, Records of the U.S. Public Health Service, National Archives, College Park, MD.

27. Goss, *Winds of God*, 7–11. For an excellent evocation of the spiritual and physical world of mining, see Callahan, *Work and Faith in the Kentucky Coalfields*, 8–10, 102–12, 120–28.

28. Charles Parham, "Healing," *Apostolic Faith*, August 1905 (first two quotes); Goss, *Winds of God*, 7–8, 14–17, 28 (remaining quotes).

29. Parham, "Healing," *Apostolic Faith*, August 1905 (first quote); "Three Months of Religious Fervor," *Joplin Daily News Herald*, 24 January 1904 (last quote); Parham, *Life of Charles F. Parham*, 93–102.

30. Glenn Gohr, "The Wiley Family and the Beginnings of Pentecost in Southwest Missouri and Northwest Arkansas," *Assemblies of God Heritage* (Spring 1999): 28–32; Arthur, "Beginning History of Galena Church," n.d., p. 5 (quotes two through four), item 10228208, and Wayne, "Early Revivals," in *Perpetuating Pentecost*, 7–9 (first quote on 8), item 100116441, both in Flower Pentecostal Heritage Center.

31. "Followers of Charles Parham, of Apostolic Faith Fame, Arrested," *Joplin Daily Globe*, 21 September 1907.

32. "'Parham Has Wrecked My Home,' Says R. R. Preston, Galena Merchant," *Joplin Daily Globe*, 29 September 1907.

33. Daniel C. O. Opperman, "Diary," item 10223077, Flower Pentecostal Heritage Center; Gohr, "Wiley Family," 28–32; Glenn Gohr, "D. C. O. Opperman and Early Ministerial Training: Short-Term Bible Schools," *Assemblies of God Heritage* (Winter 1990–91): 8–10; U.S. Bureau of the Census, *Special Reports: Religious Bodies, 1906*, 279.

34. U.S. Bureau of the Census, *Religious Bodies: 1926, Volume 1: Summary and Detailed Tables* (Washington, D.C.: Government Printing Office, 1930), 442–43.

35. Lanza and Higgins, *Pulmonary Disease among Miners in the Joplin District*, 38–39; Higgins, Lanza, Laney, and Rice, *Siliceous Dust in Relation to Pulmonary Disease among Miners in the Joplin District, Missouri*, 65–68; Gohr, "Wiley Family," 28, 31.

36. Charles Morris Mills, "Joplin Zinc: Industrial Conditions in the World's Greatest Zinc Center," *Survey* 45 (1921): 658 (first two and fourth quotes), 661 (third quote), 663 (fifth quote).

37. Frank D. Hills, "The Picher of Tomorrow," in "Program, Twelfth Birthday Anniversary, City of Picher, May 6, 1927" (1927; repr. 1975), Folder 1 "Historical pamphlets, ca. 1975–1976," R754 Picher (Okla.) Collection, ca. 1975–1995, State Historical Society of Missouri Research Center, Rolla.

38. George G. Suggs Jr., *Union Busting in the Tri-State: The Oklahoma, Kansas, and Missouri Metal Workers' Strike of 1935* (Norman: University of Oklahoma Press, 1986), 33–55.

4

Discovering Working-Class Religion
in a 1950s Auto Plant

MATTHEW PEHL

In 1961, the Detroit Industrial Mission (DIM) published a provocative essay titled "Work: Curse or Joy?" For the previous four years, the Protestant ministers associated with DIM had labored on assembly lines at Detroit-area auto plants, assessing and analyzing the impact of industrialization on faith and life. They had reached an unsettling conclusion: "In general," DIM asserted, "[workers] hate their jobs" and find work "a distasteful necessity." Managers seemed oblivious or defensive, insisting that their workers were happy; or, if they were unhappy, they could find another job. Unions, meanwhile, appeared to have adopted the philosophy that "work in most of modern industry is Hell . . . [and] this essential hellishness cannot be changed." Work, according to union leaders, might be made bearable, but could not be made enjoyable or fulfilling. Indeed, throughout the 1950s, a series of studies revealed that, underneath the collective-bargaining triumphs of the United Automobile Workers (UAW) and the rising financial security of autoworkers, alienation and even a sense of dehumanization were pervasive. "There is nothing more discouraging than having a barrel beside you with 10,000 bolts and using them all up," one worker told two sociologists. "Then you get another barrel with another 10,000," and the Sisyphean task begins anew. According to DIM, the entire dilemma stood opposed to the "Biblical tradition," which viewed work as "a source of joy" and made people into richer, deeper, fuller human beings. Was not something wrong with the very soul of modern labor, DIM asked, if so many people were dehumanized by their work?[1]

For DIM, the human experiences of industrial work were best interpreted through the lens of contemporary Christianity. Alienation, DIM ministers believed, had come to define the daily sinews of modern existence, but this condition was, at its root, largely symbolic of the disconnection between humans and God. Therefore, DIM argued, the alienation workers felt toward their jobs could best be healed by bridging the alienation between God and humanity. This conviction inspired DIM ministers to themselves labor on assembly lines, where they hoped to model their faith in action and to nurture a stronger link between what they perceived to be the very estranged realms of "the church" and "the world." For the historian, DIM's "experiment" (as it was called) is significant for two reasons. First, it provides a telling example of the impact of liberal theology on both the attitudes and practices of Christian ministry in the mid-twentieth century. Second, and more important, DIM ministers, as sojourners on the shop floors of America's preeminent industrial metropolis, provide a rare, detailed, and nearly anthropological portrait of working-class religion as it was felt and lived.[2]

DIM's records and publications are, thus, invaluable sources in the cultural history of religion, but they are not without the normal limitations of bias and belief. For if religion provided DIM's lens on labor, class subjectivities ground the glass and fitted the frame. DIM began its ministry with a belief in the universality and classlessness of Christianity, but in fact, its articulation of religion was decidedly middle class. DIM evolved out of spiritual "retreat centers" in rural Michigan and seminary classrooms in Princeton, not the organic experience of industrial work in blue-collar communities. To their credit, DIM's ministers grew evermore self-critical of their own limited perspectives after extended exposure to life in the plants. Still, DIM's class-bound framework shaped its understanding of working-class religion in critical ways. Primed to promote a religion marinated in modernism and enveloped in existentialism, DIM bristled at the supposedly narrow, fatalistic, or fundamentalist "sects" that many workers seemed to prefer. Gendering both Christianity and labor as masculine, it offered no insight into the religious lives of working-class women, either in the plants or in the churches. Assuming that the "classless," white, Protestant churches of Cold War America were synonymous with "authentic" Christianity, DIM failed to appreciate the diversity and complexity of the Catholic, African American, and Southern-born white evangelical workers it encountered.

Like DIM, these workers also viewed labor through a religious lens. But the differences of inflection and interpretation are highly revealing of distinctly class-based cosmologies. In 1957, when Ford worker Pat Hamilton was asked to reflect on the intersection between his life as an industrial worker and his faith as a Catholic, he began by acknowledging the frank reality of his day-to-day existence. "Life in a factory," Hamilton admitted, "despite all the modernization, can be very depressing." But Hamilton's understanding of this dilemma differed significantly from DIM. Postwar Catholicism, with its emphasis on self-discipline and self-denial, and its glorification of sacrifice, suffering, and duty, certainly created stern demands on Hamilton's behavior (he avoided "shop talk" and "lewd stories"), but it also inspired his spirit. Without faith, Hamilton implied, people could bear the drudgery of auto work only by chiseling extra time out of a lunch break, slowing the pace of production, or lashing out in acts of petty theft and sabotage. The insight is telling. DIM's ministers wanted to reinvent the experience of industrial work, to prophetically critique the whole system as unethical and dehumanizing. Hamilton entertained no such illusions. Rather, he recommended receiving the sacraments often and praying daily. Religion was meaningful to Hamilton because it allowed him to endure ongoing struggles with dignity and purpose. It promised comfort and continuity, not a new and challenging paradigm. Whereas DIM viewed religion as a transformative tool of spiritual reinvention and social renewal, working-class believers like Hamilton experienced religion as solace and inspiration in the hard struggle to make meaning out of the realities of laboring lives.[3]

DIM's frustration with, and misunderstanding of, workers' cosmologies suggests the vital role that religion played in making and shaping social class in mid-twentieth-century America. While some aspects of class analysis are purely material (income, education, housing options, job opportunities, and so on), DIM's experience reminds us that class is also a subjective, historical identity created over time and expressed in culture. And, for both DIM's ministers and the workers they observed, religion was one of the central cultural idioms in defining, articulating, and performing social class. Placed side by side in the factories of America's preeminent mid-century industrial center, DIM ministers and Detroit autoworkers inhabited the same space. But their conflicting religious interpretations of this space—and the work performed in it—illustrates that they did not inhabit the same world.[4]

DIM was established in 1956 by the Reverend Hugh White, an Episcopal priest at St. Martin's parish in Detroit. White, a student of English industrial missions and the "worker priests" of France, was intrigued by trends in European theology (especially the burgeoning ideas of "Christian existentialism") and their application to the more immediate worldly problems confronting postwar Detroit.[5] White recruited Scott Paradise, who had worked with the Sheffield Industrial Mission in England, to bring his experience to the Motor City. Initially, Paradise found that DIM's approach was "distinctly Episcopalian"; however, the program rapidly became ecumenical, and the character of the ministry shifted as it absorbed and incorporated similar "industrial" missionary efforts by other mainline Protestant bodies. Of these, the most important would prove to be the Presbyterian Industrial Project (PIP). PIP originated among idealistic and energetic students at Princeton Theological Seminary in 1954. These students—George Coleman, David Lowry, and Orrie Hopper—decided to form a "triple pastorate" in Ecorse, a declining, blue-collar suburb southwest of Detroit; they began work at Ecorse Presbyterian Church in the fall of 1956. While Colman, Lowry, and Hopper worked out of the church, two other Princeton Seminary graduates—Jesse Christman and Jim Campbell—took jobs on an assembly line at the nearby Cadillac plant. They also maintained contact with the Methodist Phil Doster, who took a plant job at McLouth Steel in 1957 and was later formally adopted by DIM. These "working," or plant-based ministers, were looking to unite the theological innovations of the church with the "real" world of the laity by sharing the experience of auto work. In the process, they hoped to gently engage workers and their managers in thoughtful conversations about industrial ethics, the spiritual promises of creative work, and the meaning of life.[6]

Upon entering the auto plant, DIM's ministers recognized—apparently to their surprise—that religion was ubiquitous. "Preachers in factories are not unique phenomena," they correctly noted. Indeed, DIM's idea of bringing the ministry onto the shop floor was nearly as old as the American industrial system itself. As early as the 1830s, some ministers were holding prayer meetings in industrial workplaces, and the impulse to shape religious messages into worker-specific (even class-conscious) contexts gained considerable momentum throughout the Progressive Era.[7] In Detroit, a number of activists for the budding UAW—including Lloyd Jones, a onetime "Ford preacher" from Kentucky, and William Bowman, one of the UAW's first African American organizers—were either active or former ministers. Claude Williams, the Detroit Presbytery's "minster to labor" during World War II, formed numerous "shop tabernacles" in the city's burgeoning war plants to preach a potent blend of Bible-centered political radicalism. And, in direct anticipation of DIM, the Methodist Rev. Owen Geer of Dearborn created the Detroit Religion and Labor Seminar (DRLS) in 1946. By 1947, DRLS was educating over twenty middle-class seminarians in issues of labor unionism and working-class life, including the requirement that seminarians labor at industrial jobs in area factories.[8]

DIM, however, appeared fairly oblivious to this history. Instead, DIM ministers were struck not by their continuity with the past, but by the strangeness of contemporary worker religion and their own estrangement from it.

According to DIM, the many "sect-group pastors" who earned their keep as autoworkers dominated religion in the factory. Evangelical, fundamentalist, and Pentecostal pastors had indeed been a part of the cultural ecosystem of the auto plant since at least the Southern "great migration" surrounding World War II; during the war, some observers counted upward of three thousand evangelical "shop-floor preachers" working at war plants. DIM ministers clearly and emphatically distanced themselves from the robust emotionalism and biblical literalism of what they dismissively referred to as "the sects." By contrast, DIM viewed its own religion as a mature and thoughtful expression of "the church." DIM ministers saw themselves as very different from their blue-collar fellow pastors: "We didn't preach," they note, "or carry Bibles."[9]

Hyperconscious of their differences from the workers they aspired to inspire, DIM ministers quickly came to feel that their association with churches produced anxiety, uneasiness, and even a measure of hostility among some workers. Scott Paradise, for instance, sensed an "intense discomfort" in his visits to the shop floor. He theorized that the rawness of union politics and the bruising nature of work caused some workers to view him as a "judge," which produced in these workers an "underlying sense of guilt." On the other hand, Paradise also realized he was often used as a pawn in a game, in which some workers hoped to playfully embarrass more "sinful" coworkers by exposing their high jinks before a symbol of respectability and morality. Workers' views of "preachers," Christman reported, focused on moralistic behavior and social utilitarianism: they "don't go in bars, and . . . don't swear. [H]e's a leader, and sets an example to others." As outliers of shop-floor morality, DIM concluded, preachers were common enough, but remained essentially "outside" working-class culture.

These observations may have been rooted in more complex, class-based cultural power struggles than the DIM ministers fully realized. While mid-century auto factories were often described as zones of a secularized "rough culture," religion nevertheless remained a vital component in the lives of large swaths of the working class. Workers did not resent religion itself, then; they resented being preached at, especially by well-meaning outsiders. As Princeton-educated theologians, DIM minsters would naturally arouse the suspicions of workers who might jealously guard the boundaries of cultural autonomy. This insight explains why, when a worker revealed Campbell's and Christman's ministerial background, the social dynamic immediately shifted:

> Phil and I were discussing Bible reading, someone else having brought it up. [Another worker] made several extremely crude remarks about this practice

and also about those who engage in it. I asked him why he felt this way and pushed him a little about why he should be so hostile to the idea that some might find Bible reading helpful. Before I knew it he was accusing me of trying to get him to go to Church and telling others, "HEY, HE'S TRYING TO GET ME TO GO TO CHURCH." It was almost as if he were saying "now, I've finally found him out."

Perhaps this particular worker genuinely disliked religion and held no personal faith. But his broader message to other workers was clear: "Middle-class outsiders are (once again) trying to change and/or police our culture." Class and the power structure it represented, not religion, was the real point of contention.[10]

As DIM's ministers were realizing, workers ultimately held an entirely different conception of religion itself. To DIM, "religion" was an unfolding intellectual process of searching, questioning, and exploring, not a finished end. But workers' "religion," as DIM read it, was a closed system: rigid, literalistic, and moralistic. After inquiring among unskilled and semiskilled workers about their perceptions of the afterlife, one DIM minister wrote that workers never gave the issue consideration, "unless these thoughts are the naively accepted doctrines of some religious sect or group." Contemporary ministers who shared similar theological and class backgrounds echoed DIM's conclusion. Cleo Boyd, a mainline pastor with a declining church in inner-city Detroit, set out to explore the flourishing "storefront" tabernacles of Appalachian migrants in 1958. The theology of working-class evangelicals, according to Boyd, was "one of old time fundamentalism with a literalistic interpretation of the Bible. These beliefs permeate the society. . . . Their concept of God is that of a stern, punishing God, Who, for all His severity, holds forth the bright promise of life hereafter to the well-behaved poor." Hundreds of these storefronts were known to exist throughout Detroit in the late 1950s and early 1960s. In a single neighborhood on Detroit's lower-east side, forty-two of the fifty-five churches were in storefronts. DIM ministers worked on assembly lines next to some of these Southern-born migrants, but their conceptions of religion, so deeply rooted in class experiences, were worlds apart.[11]

The conservatism of working-class religion, as DIM saw it, mirrored many workers' social and political attitudes. Scott Paradise noted that workers were much more likely to idolize the wealthy and disparage government spending than union leaders. Asking one group of workers about integration, Paradise noted that all "bragged" about their willingness to work with African

Americans, but none wanted blacks living in their neighborhoods. DIM was tapping into an important and troubling aspect of mid-century working-class culture. Other studies from the time confirmed the weak links many workers had to the liberal ideological precepts of both the UAW and the Democratic Party. Despite the vigorous efforts of union leaders to encourage greater politicization, researchers into UAW political attitudes found most union members "continue to be indifferent, uninvolved, lacking enthusiasm and conviction."[12]

Meanwhile, the daily reality of factory work steadily wore away at workers' sense of purpose, vitality, and humanity. Scott Paradise felt workers were "profoundly ambivalent" about life in the plant, taking pride in their job but despising the labor itself. One man even told him, "I die every morning when I come through those gates." Campbell and Christman also reported a conversation with one coworker who claimed he hated the plant. "I never tell anyone I work at Cadillac," this worker admitted. "I don't guess there are more than four members of my family that know I work in the factory. I even have two sets of wallets and key-cases." In DIM's eyes, the combination of a rigidly moralistic and "otherworldly" religion combined with deadening labor to retard and cripple the spirit of most workers. In 1960, DIM articulated this connection in frank and startling terms: "THE MORALIST GOD AND THE FACTORY SYSTEM," DIM declared, were "ONE AND THE SAME":

> The religious background of most of the men around us is that of the southern sect groups. A few have behind them old world Catholicism. Most are estranged in one way or another from this background. . . . They have good reason for leaving it. . . . The religion with which [many workers] are deeply imbued and from which they have fled but not escaped is the religion of merit, of holiness in moralistic terms, of earned righteousness, of do's and don'ts, mostly the latter. . . . The workingman faces the same thing in the work and the religion available to him. God and the factory are one and the same. The man is dominated by them and coerced by them, but he hates them both, because they have refused him his manhood.

By the fall of 1960, DIM's ministers had come to despair over the possibility of spiritually "elevating" the experience of factory work. "And yet," they argued hopefully, "we believe that the Christian faith can be relevant to the millions of skilled and unskilled workers in America."[13]

In fact, faith *did* remain relevant to many workers—but in fashions that DIM could not or would not acknowledge. Across town at the Dodge Main Body Shop, at the same time that DIM was bemoaning the inadequacy of working-class evangelicalism, workers boasted of "being the only automobile manufacturing plant in the world, where Bible classes are held at noon daily." Frank Favor, a Dodge welder, had launched the program, and had brought a minister into the plant to provide "some spirited and instructive advice, pertaining to ways and means, of efficiently serving 'The Good Lord,' here in this vale of tears, so that we may be happy with Him in the next." From DIM's point of view, the Dodge workers' close attention to Bible study and their "otherworldly" focus on the afterlife would have been proof of the debilitating literalism and moralism that crippled the working-class soul. But the workers themselves clearly felt differently. As Favor pointed out, workers who heard the shop preacher "came away with a spiritual uplift, that mere words fail to properly describe."[14] Like the Catholic Ford worker Pat Hamilton, these Dodge workers saw religion as a source of inspiration, uplift, and meaning. That DIM's interpretation differed so strongly suggests that the full complexities of working-class religious culture remained hidden from its view.

DIM's ministers were unusually bright, perceptive, and sensitive observers of working-class religious culture. They sympathized deeply with workers and generally approached the task of working-class ministry with refreshing humility. Nevertheless, their basic analysis of working-class religiosity suffered from the restrictions of their own racial, religious, gender, and class assumptions.

First and foremost, "working-class religion" was far more pluralistic and diverse than DIM acknowledged. DIM went looking for fellow white Protestants, but in the process missed the most significant segments of Detroit's workers. Catholics, especially, were far more numerous than Protestants, were extremely disciplined in religious practice, and were much more likely to hold blue-collar jobs than mainline white Protestants. Nearly two-thirds of Detroiters were Catholic during the 1950s, and, of this number, roughly 60 percent were skilled or semiskilled workers. Even middle-class Catholics seemed to demonstrate what one landmark study from the early 1960s called "an affinity for working-class values": prizing collectivism and security, for instance, over individualism and entrepreneurial risk taking. Catholics, in other words, were critical to shaping working-class religious culture in cities like Detroit.[15]

Ordinary working-class Catholics *lived* religion in a way that merged their spiritual and laboring identities. In 1950, the *Michigan Catholic* told the story of one notable working-class prayer group composed of men and women who "toil in office, shop and factory in Detroit's Boulevard district." Every

Wednesday, several dozen of these workers attended Our Lady of the Rosary church to say prayers, "[t]ired and hungry though they may be." By the mid-point of the decade, Ford workers had organized ten different weekly rosary groups (totaling several hundred participants), which met during the lunch hour, on the workers' time. Likewise, Most Holy Trinity parish witnessed a remarkable demonstration of working-class piety in March 1954. Holy Trinity's pastor, Clement Kern, responded to requests of downtown newspaper truck drivers for a more convenient service by establishing a 2:30 A.M. mass. Incredibly, 250 workers attended this middle-of-the-night service, enjoying Fr. Raymond Clancy's inaugural sermon on St. Joseph, "Patron of the Working Man." By the end of the month, Kern added an extra program of 2:15 A.M. confessions every Monday. It is worth reiterating that these religious programs were begun *at the request* of working-class laypeople themselves. These voluntary, self-directed groups indicate the value and satisfaction that Catholics derived from their religious practice.[16]

Moreover, Detroit's Catholics—both clergy and laity—had long been at the vanguard of "social Catholicism" and labor reform. During the 1930s, more than 2,500 lay Catholics joined the Association of Catholic Trade Unionists (ACTU) to promote both unionism and Christianity, while the archdiocese founded nearly forty parish-based "labor schools" to advance Catholic social theory and train workers in the business of running a union local. By 1946, the ACTU had consolidated what labor historian Philip Foner called an "informal alliance" with Walter Reuther, and served a key role in helping Reuther win the presidency of the UAW that year. Interestingly, in the summer of 1956, at nearly the same moment that Hugh White was organizing the Detroit Industrial Mission, the Detroit ACTU disaffiliated from the national body and reorganized as the Detroit Catholic Labor Conference (DCLC). William Ryan, the ACTU president who presided over this transformation, offered revealing reasons for the change. Ryan noted that, although other ACTU chapters took "specific legislative, political and economic positions by a majority vote of their membership," the Detroit group consistently argued that individual members alone should decide how to use what they learned from the ACTU. Explaining the break in Detroit's ACTU newspaper, *Wage Earner*, Ryan averred that *individuals* should speak and persuade, not organizations. "If a 'Catholic mind' is to be developed," Ryan wrote, it would be done by "convincing enough Catholics that a thing is right."[17]

Given the DCLC's promotion of industrial justice, individual conscience, and ethical persuasion, one might assume that it would be a natural partner for DIM. By the late 1960s, DIM would indeed collaborate with a Catholic priest, but in the 1950s, such cooperation was not even imagined, revealing that DIM ministers instead viewed Catholicism with vague derision, as evidence for their overall thesis that workers' religion was moralistic, hidebound, and suffocating. Scott Paradise complained that "overchurched Catholics" eagerly reported all the kindnesses they extended to nuns—as if such deeds somehow "bought" them a moral advantage—while lapsed Catholics avoided him doggedly. Paradise also discovered that one of the few subjects that easily got working men talking about God was overpopulation and birth control; to his bewilderment, Catholic workers passionately argued that artificial birth control perverted God's plan. To Paradise, the takeaway was simply that working-class Catholicism was a deterrent to "deeper" religiosity, rather than constituting a valid religiosity in itself.[18]

African Americans, likewise, were largely ignored or minimized in DIM's analysis of working-class religion, despite the profound importance of African Americans to the economic, social, and religious transformations that confronted Detroit at mid-century. During the 1950s, as white residents flooded out of the city, African Americans continued moving in: by 1960, 45 percent of all Detroiters were black, an overwhelming working-class population. Moreover, African Americans were, characteristically, deeply religious. Local African American journalist Ulysses Boykins, for one, observed that religion "played a far greater part in the community, civic, business and social life than any other social factor" in black Detroit; he counted nearly two hundred black churches in 1948, although this number seemed to mushroom in the subsequent decades.[19]

During the 1940s, a number of these churches had emerged as centers of political and working-class activism. Charles Hill, pastor of Hartford Avenue Baptist Church, happily observed that "the colored clergy tell their flocks to obey the Lord and obey the CIO." The NAACP's Gloster Current agreed with Hill, observing that "[m]any colored deacons who were previously anti-CIO have now swung around and are all out for the CIO." Like their Catholic counterparts, a number of these churches ritually combined religious and class identities. As early as 1943, several Detroit churches were hosting an "FEPC Sunday" to demonstrate support for fair employment laws. Annual membership drives for the NAACP were routinely kicked off on Sunday mornings. In 1952, UAW Ford Local 600—one of the largest and most progressive union locals in the country, with strong representation from African American Ford workers—sponsored the NAACP membership drive launched at Detroit's influential Bethel AME church, a program that offered especially sharp evidence of the blurring between racial, religious, and class identities in black churches. Yet, as with Catholics, DIM never seemed to ally or communicate with either black churches or black workers.[20]

While DIM was supportive of racial equality as a basic principle, its ministers may not have even recognized working-class African American religion as "religion." Like the white "sects" and "old world" Catholicism, African American religion emphasized emotional experiences, a direct connection with a personal god, and inspiration to endure the struggles of a fallen world. Detroit's African American religion journalist, Isaac Jones, spoke for most church people when he defended the importance of emphatic preaching: "Sermons heard from pulpits," he asserted, "have a great effect on one's heart and soul." Sermons by leading black preachers were characteristically described in the *Michigan Chronicle*'s "Church Pages," as "uplifting," "stirring," or "dynamic." In other words, they gave working-class congregations a strong connection to beauty, joy, community, and transcendence.[21]

Church music, too, was a source of emotional power. Frances Carter, an organist at Detroit's John Wesley AMEZ Church, noted that the "old hymns of zion and folksongs" transformed the service: "[T]hey produce such a release of emotions . . . that it looks as if some people have lost their minds. This emotion, however, is contagious. It seems as if the building itself has come alive. People laugh through their tears, walk the aisles, fling their bodies around and just generally shout!" Tellingly, Carter observed that, throughout the 1950s, her church—a more middle-class congregation with pretentions to respectability—viewed folk hymns as "the lowest form of church music." Yet, the power and joy of these working-class songs could not be denied. As Joseph Washington stated in his study of African American religiosity, the "combination of suffering and music" bound black churches together.[22]

Working-class African American religion also maintained strong ties to rural folk culture, which DIM would probably have dismissed as "premodern" or "superstitious." When Richard Dorson visited African American communities throughout Michigan in the 1950s, tales of traditional conjuring—or "hoodoo"—remained vibrant. One of Dorson's informants, a woman named Lulu Powell, claimed she "never believed in this hoodooism business," but after becoming sick with cramps and heavy sweating, her husband called in a hoodoo doctor named Young. After communicating with a spirit named "Dr. McCoy," Young told Powell she had been poisoned at a church fish fry by another woman jealous for her husband's affections. "[S]he cured me," Powell claimed. The *Michigan Chronicle* featured advertisements for these urbanized "hoodoo doctors" throughout the 1940s and 1950s. "If you need help," the Rev. Mme. Parker advised, "see the woman of God who knows that prayer is the key TO SUCCESS!" "Bishop" A. Ewell, DD, implored, "COME AND SEE A WOMAN THAT GOD HAS SPOKEN TO," and promised solicitors "Blessed Articles direct from Jerusalem." Particularly popular in the 1940s was a medium named Prince Herman, who claimed that "so-called sickness, lack of money, strained conditions, jealousy, infatuations, crosses, home conditions, bad luck, etc. are all overcome by the application of the mysterious element or principle that overcomes all obstacles." Prince Herman even broadcast nightly, half-hour nostrums through a local radio channel.[23]

African American workers were hardly alone in seeking personal connections, pragmatic results, and miraculous revelations as a basic component of religiosity. Belief in the "miraculous"—the direct intervention of God to address personal problems—saturated working-class religion more generally. Three-fourths of the Southern whites interviewed for one study believed in faith healing. According to Jessie Blankenship, a native West Virginian whose husband worked in a Detroit steel plant, her father was healed of a terrible illness after her mother wrote to a radio preacher and "laid hands" on her father while the preacher preached. Although she had not personally been to a faith healer, she "would go to one" if she was sick. Likewise, Laverne Highsby worked in a Tennessee shirt factory and a tool company in Indiana before finally settling in Detroit. She too "definitely believes in [faith healers]." One of her relatives prayed to Billy Graham on the radio after doctors gave up on him, and prayer saved a leg and hip; the doctors declared "it was a miracle."[24]

Miracle stories similarly abounded in Catholic culture. In fact, clergy and members of the church hierarchy insisted upon their authority to judge the veracity of miracles with a defensiveness that hints at the variety and autonomy of miraculous belief among the laity. In 1954, the *Michigan Catholic* cautioned, "There are many self made faith healers," especially Protestant healers, that bore a superficial resemblance to traditional Catholic beliefs about the nature of miracles. "Of course," the newspaper continued dismissively, "such pretensions are false." In 1957, the newspaper again pointed out that the Catholic Church maintained an exacting standard in ascertaining miracles, and that few Protestant healings "would stand the searching test that the Catholic Church applies" to miraculous claims. Almost as an afterthought, the 1954 article reminded Catholics that they "may never attend non-sectarian or non-religious healing services." But the very existence of these instructions in the diocesan newspaper implies that lay Catholics' understanding of miracles resembled the beliefs of white and black Protestant workers.[25]

If DIM ministers ignored or minimized the diversity of working-class religion, they expressed open anxiety regarding working-class gender identities. Cold War culture in general roiled with a deep anxiety over the swift demographic and economic changes unleashed by World War II. On the eve of American entry into the war, 202,960 Detroit-area women worked for wages; by 1955, that number had leaped to 383,900. While the majority of women in the mid-1950s worked retail jobs, 15 percent of Detroit's manufacturing workforce was female. Catholic workers at the Dodge Main plant in Hamtramck were certainly aware of women's presence on the shop floor; nearly eight hundred women assembled electrical systems in Dodge Main's wire room. More, there is scattered evidence that some of these female Dodge workers explicitly brought their Catholicism into the workplace. In January 1954, wire-room worker Helene Barwick took a break from her work to listen to Bishop Fulton Sheen's radio program. "Good as usual," she noted in the Dodge Main newspaper. "Next week his talk is to be about 'Workers.' Musn't miss this broadcast."[26]

Nevertheless, DIM's shop-floor ministers apparently could not even imagine women as "workers." Instead, in 1960, they concluded emphatically that the "GREATEST PROBLEM IN THE LIFE OF THE ASSEMBLY LINE WORKER IS TO BE A MAN." Working-class religion, in DIM's reading, had become intertwined with a broader crisis in working-class masculinity:

> Neither the elements of [the assembler's] job nor his relationships therein afford him much opportunity to be a man whom others respect and who respects and esteems himself. And so he attempts to prove his manhood by other means; by drinking the other fellow under the table, by philandering, by success in petty arguments, by violence, by cleverness in gambling. He pathetically tries to prove it by building up his chest and arm muscles, and then by wearing tight T-shirts. . . . When he returns home his wife is reading romance stories concerning actors or statesmen or business and professional men, or watching TV on which a factory worker never appears as hero and rarely as an extra. . . . He is nothing—He is not even a man. . . . At the plant basically he is a statistic, at home a shadowy figure in the chair watching TV with his beer bottle beside him. . . . But Father and Man he is not.

For DIM, the social and cultural forces that eroded masculinity were linked to the moralism they so disliked in working-class religion. In breaking free from the shackles of an outworn fundamentalism and embracing the "new theology," DIM implied, working-class men could reclaim both pride in their work and authority in their homes.[27]

Interestingly, DIM's anxiety over masculinity and its muteness on issues of relevance to working-class women is contrasted by one of the most notorious preachers in mid-century Detroit, "Prophet" James Jones. Born in a Birmingham slum, Jones arrived in Detroit in 1938 and founded the Church of Universal Triumph, the Dominion of God. By the mid-1950s, Jones commanded fifty thousand followers. Converting an abandoned movie theater into his temple, Jones staged nightly, televised services that could stretch well past midnight. He boasted an elaborate, extravagantly expensive wardrobe, offered faith healing and prophecy, and lived in a regal chateau among Detroit's African American elite.[28] From DIM's perspective, Jones would have appeared a flimflam artist; yet he was communicating important, affirming messages that the black working class needed to hear. An observer at one of Jones's services in 1961 highlighted the prophet's special connection with African American women. In his sermon, Jones preached that man must labor because of sin. However, he quickly shifted his focus directly to the women in attendance. "Now you and I know that man doesn't labor," Jones clarified; "It's women who labor. . . . But when the great day comes, we will be freed from the bondage of the flesh and won't need to work any more." Jones offered no political solution to the predicament of working-class women. But he recognized a spiritual and psychological reality that escaped DIM's ministers. For even as working-class women entered the workplace, they also often retained primary responsibility for child rearing, homemaking, and religious instruction. These demanding circumstances obviously affected women workers' quality of life. In a survey of UAW members in the late 1950s, very few women described themselves as "highly satisfied" with their lives; more typical were responses showing 62 percent of women (versus 26 percent of men) claiming that they worried "a lot." Asked about their chances "to enjoy life," women dissented twice as often as men. Working-class women, especially, needed the feelings of acknowledgment, sympathy, and uplift offered by Jones. No analysis of working-class religiosity could be complete without taking these spiritual needs into account.[29]

By 1960, after four years in the plants, Jesse Christman, Jim Campbell, and Phil Doster had undergone their own type of conversion experience: all had become thoroughly convinced that "a distinct working class" existed, as did a "distinct cleavage between the world of the assembler and the world of those economically, vocationally, educationally, and socially above him." Such sentiments, they well knew, were "rather frowned upon in our country, so convinced are we in our idealization of our society that ours is truly a classless society." But the ministers' experiences of industrial work had dramatically changed their understanding of the relationship between religion and social class. No longer did they envision Christianity as a universal truth that transcended social divisions and cultural norms. Instead, they stepped away from their sojourn on the shop floors of Detroit with a jarring sense of the stark particularities, and the troubling divide, between middle-class and working-class religions.[30]

The evolution in the thinking of DIM's ministers from optimism to confusion to frustration can be observed in some detail. During the first months of their employment, Doster, Campbell, and Christman agreed that work was ennobling, and remained hopeful about the chances for building fellowship and community. "Somehow," they wrote, "as one walks out of the factory after his shift along with the other workers, there is a deep sense of participation. Perhaps," they added soberly, "this is a romantic reaction soon lost to the man whose stay in the factory lengthens." Indeed, as the ministers experienced the cyclical and unstable nature of auto work, and as they learned more about the work itself, these sentiments faded considerably. All three men suffered periodic yet unpredictable bouts of unemployment. Some of what these men experienced was the result of bad timing: 1957 and 1958 were recession years that hit the auto industry especially hard, and automation was further reducing job rolls. On the other hand, autoworkers commonly faced employment insecurity. In December 1957, Doster claimed that he was adjusting better to the work, but he worried that the "pious members of the working force do not control the environment," and observed that "positive comments" were "hard to deliver while working." A couple of weeks later, he "found himself unable to speak to the religious questions, statements, and comments brought by the other men."[31]

Christman, likewise, struggled with himself over his hostile and critical responses to a slower-moving coworker. After a few weeks, he was sharing beers with coworkers after the Friday shift. Campbell's reaction was even more extreme. He became obsessed with a workplace dispute, though he openly expressed "guilt and resentment on this." Campbell also described "how easily the spirit of revenge grows in himself, with regard to other workers. Felt that his emotions were much closer to the surface." Slowly, these mainliners were beginning to understand for themselves some of the social, psychological, and cultural dynamics that characterized working-class life. The ability of working experiences to shape ideas and behaviors "are not idle observations about others," they insisted. "We have felt them ourselves—increasing pettiness, souring of personality, deadening of creativity, fading self-esteem, heightened tension and temper." They expressed amazement that so many men endured the experience intact. "God is at work," they thought. "But not through religion."[32]

Of course, what they meant is: not through *their* religion. Not through religion they way they had always defined it. After three years of experience, DIM concluded that plant ministers and church ministers were "living in two distinct worlds, worlds which did not seem to intersect in a significant fashion and worlds which we seemed unable to bring together in meaningful dialogue with the project." The "experiment" had reached a breaking point. Plant-based ministers like Campbell, Christman, and Doster accused their fellow mainline Protestants of conflating Christianity as a religion with the American middle class as a culture. Indeed, they took this charge much further. If the paternalistic foreman and moralistic preacher were two sides of the same coin, then so, too, was the well-heeled corporate executive just another version of a well-fed bishop. The established mainline church, "in which congregations like subsidiary plants, feed statistics and money into the mass corporate institution, reflects more inhumanity than humanity, more anonymity than community, more mechanization than militant conviction about life and its meaning." Protestant churches were filled with men in gray-flannel suits. Little wonder that workers viewed this religion as an alien, even menacing, cultural force.[33]

DIM was ultimately unable to claw through its own dense web of middle-class values to truly share the religious world of the working class. But, in making the effort, its ministers left a vital record of workers' cosmologies in the mid-twentieth century. More important, DIM's experience reminds historians of the power and importance of class as a historical construct. Too often, historians of religion have been eager to minimize—even ignore—class in favor of other sociohistorical identities like race, ethnicity, or denomination. DIM illustrates the dangers of this tendency. Indeed, if anything, DIM's ordeal suggests that class is perhaps even more central to shaping religious experience than these other social markers. Historians should pay heed, and bring the tools of class analysis more fully into religious studies.

Notes

1. "Work: Curse or Joy?," *Life and Work*, September 1961, copy in Parishfield Records, 1948–71 (hereafter PR), box 2, folder "Detroit Industrial Mission, 1958–1967," Bentley Historical Library (hereafter BHL), Ann Arbor, MI; Charles R. Walker and Robert H. Guest, *The Man on the Assembly Line* (Cambridge, MA: Harvard University Press, 1952), 54, 70, 76–77. See also Ely Chinoy, *Automobile Workers and the American Dream*, 2nd ed. (Urbana: University of Illinois Press, 1992).

2. The papers of the Detroit Industrial Mission are archived at the Walter P. Reuther Library of Labor and Urban Affairs, Wayne State University, Detroit, MI (hereafter LLUA). The Parishfield Records, BHL, also contain significant material on DIM.

3. *Michigan Catholic*, April 4, 1957.

4. My understanding of class is indebted to E. P. Thompson, *The Making of the English Working Class* (New York: Vintage Books, 1966), 9–10. For examples of recent publications on the subject of religion and class, see Evelyn Savidge Sterne, "Bringing Religion into Working-Class History: Parish, Public, and Politics in Providence, 1890–1930," *Social Science History* 24 (Spring 2000): 149–82; Laurie Maffly-Kipp, David G. Hackett, R. Laurence Moore, and Leslie Woodcock Tentler, "Forum: American Religion and Class," *Religion and American Culture* 15 (Winter 2005): 2–30; Sean McCloud, *Divine Hierarchies: Class in American Religion and Religious Studies* (Chapel Hill: University of North Carolina Press, 2007); Robert Bruno, *Justified by Work: Identity and the Meaning of Faith in Chicago's Working-Class Churches* (Columbus: Ohio State University Press, 2008); Richard J. Callahan Jr., *Work and Faith in the Kentucky Coal Fields: Subject to Dust* (Bloomington: Indiana University Press, 2008); and the special issue *Labor: Studies in Working-Class History of the Americas* 6 (Spring 2009).

5. For the theological and cultural context, see David A. Hollinger, *After Cloven Tongues of Fire: Protestant Liberalism in Modern American History* (Princeton, NJ: Princeton University Press, 2013). DIM was associated with, and in some ways emerged from, the Parishfield religious retreat, in Michigan; most issues of Parishfield's newsletter, *The Sword and the Shield*, discuss the impact of this "new theology."

6. "PLANT PHASE REPORT OF: The Ecorse Project," TS, April 1958, and "PIP-D Report to Presbytery," TS, Fall 1960, both in Detroit Industrial Mission Records (hereafter DIM), LLUA, box 3, folder PIP-D. See also *Life and Work* (Summer 1965) for background on Doster.

7. For background, see Teresa Anne Murphy, *Ten Hours' Labor: Religion, Reform, and Gender in Early New England* (Ithaca, NY: Cornell University Press, 1992); Jama Lazerow, *Religion and the Working Class in Antebellum America* (Washington, DC: Smithsonian Institution Press, 1995); William R. Sutton, *Journeymen for Jesus: Evangelical Artisans Confront Capitalism in Jacksonian Baltimore* (University Park: Pennsylvania State University Press, 1998); Ken Fones-Wolf, *Trade Union Gospel: Christianity and Labor in Industrial Philadelphia, 1865–1915* (Philadelphia: Temple University Press, 1989); Kathryn J. Oberdeck, *The Evangelist and the Impresario: Religion, Entertainment, and Cultural Politics in America, 1884–1914* (Baltimore: Johns Hopkins University Press, 1999); and David Burns, *The Life and Death of the Historical Radical Jesus* (New York: Oxford University Press, 2013).

8. "I Was a Ford Preacher," *United Automobile Worker,* November 15, 1940; on Bowman, see August Meier and Elliott Rudwick, *Black Detroit and the Rise of the UAW* (New York: Oxford University Press, 1979), 43; on Williams, see Erik S. Gellman and Jarod Roll, *The Gospel of the Working Class: Labor's Southern Prophets in New Deal America* (Urbana: University of Illinois Press, 2011); on Geer, see "Summer Seminar in Industrial Church Work," TS, in Liston Pope Social Ethics Collection, Archives and Manuscripts, RG 73, box 97, folder 3, Yale Divinity Library, New Haven, CT.

9. "Notes on the Industrial Contacts of the Ecorse Church Group, April 1958," in DIM, box 3, folder "Ecorse Project Reports."

10. Scott Paradise, *Detroit Industrial Mission: A Personal Narrative* (New York: Harper and Row, 1968), 12–13; "Christman-Plant Phase Report 1–10–59" and "Comments of men at Cadillac relative to class structure . . .," DIM, box 3, folder "Ecorse-study papers."

11. "Life, Death and Destiny in the Minds of Workers," TS (n.d.), DIM, box 3, folder PIP-D, phase reports; Cleo Boyd, "Detroit's Southern Whites and the Store-Front Church," in Metropolitan Detroit Council of Churches, Records, 1920–1971, box 12, folder "Detroit's Southern Whites . . .," LLUA; see also Mayor's Commission for Community Action, Working Papers, "Religion and the Store Front Church" (September 1963); "Franklin Settlement Progress Report," TS, December 1965, in National Federation of Settlements and Neighborhood Centers, Records (hereafter NFSNC), Social Welfare History Archive, University of Minnesota, (hereafter SWHA), box 73, folder 20.

12. Paradise, *Detroit Industrial Mission* 9, 36–37; Arthur Kornhauser, Harold L. Sheppard, and Albert J. Mayer, *When Labor Votes: A Study of Auto Workers* (New York: University Books, 1956), 298.

13. James Campbell, "Digest of 'Are Workers Middle Class?,'" (May 1959), DIM, box 3, folder "Ecorse-study papers"; phase reports, "Report to Presbytery," Fall 1960, and "The Gulf between Church and World," both in DIM, box 3, folder PIP-D, phase reports; Paradise, *Detroit Industrial Mission*, 32.

14. *Dodge Main News*, January 28, 1956.

15. J. David Greenstone, "A Report on the Politics of Detroit" (Cambridge, MA: Joint Center for Urban Studies of the Massachusetts Institute of Technology and Harvard University, 1961), 1–5; Gerhard Lenski, *The Religious Factor: A Sociological Study of Religion's Impact on Politics, Economics, and Family Life* (Garden City, NY: Doubleday, 1961), 34–44; and Albert J. Mayer and Harry Sharp, "Religious Preference and Worldly Success," *American Sociological Review* 27 (April 1962): 227.

16. *Michigan Catholic*, 3 August 1950, 18 and 25 March 1954; Genevieve M. Casey, *Father Clem Kern, Conscience of Detroit* (Detroit: Marygrove College, 1989).

17. See Matthew Pehl, "The Remaking of the Catholic Working Class: Detroit, 1919–1941," *Religion and American Culture* 19 (Winter 2009): 37–67; "NCWC News Service" (1956); George Higgins to Bill Ryan, 5 July 1956; *Wage Earner*, August 1956, and *Work,* August 1956, all in George Gilmary Higgins Papers, 1932–2002, subject files: ACTU, 1949–1968, American Catholic Research Center, Catholic University of America, Washington, DC.

18. Paradise, *Detroit Industrial Mission* 9, 36–37.

19. Detroit Urban League, "A Profile of the Detroit Negro, 1959–1967"; Ulysses Boykins, "Handbook of the Detroit Negro" (Detroit: Minority Studies Associates, 1948), microfilm edition, 37–38.

20. "Conversation with Charles A. Hill," and "Conversation with Gloster Current," both in "Survey of Racial and Religious Conflict Forces in Detroit," TS, September 1943, in Civil Rights Congress of Michigan, box 71, folder "Survey," LLUA; *Michigan Chronicle*, 25 September 1942, 15 May 1943, 8 February 1947, 15 February 1947, 3 May 1952.

21. Isaac Jones, "Sermons I Shall Remember," *Michigan Chronicle*, 19 January 1952; see also "Church Pages," *Michigan Chronicle*, 15 February 1947 and 4 January 1947.

22. Bruno Nettl, "Preliminary Remarks on Urban Folk Music in Detroit," *Western Folklore* 16 (January 1957): 38–39; Frances E. Carter, "The Function of Folk-Songs in the A.M.E. Zion Church Service," 1967 (111), 6, folklore archive, LLUA; Joseph Washington, *Black Cults and Sects* (Garden City, NY: Doubleday, 1972), 77.

23. Richard M. Dorson, *Negro Folktales in Michigan* (Cambridge, MA: Harvard University Press, 1956), 114; *Michigan Chronicle*, 25 September 1943, 5 January 1952; these ads were common. On the transformation of black folk religion in the urban North, see Yvonne P. Chireau, *Black Magic: Religion and the African American Conjuring Tradition* (Berkeley: University of California Press, 2003).

24. Ellen J. Stekert, "Southern Mountain Medical Beliefs" 1969 (154), TS, folklore archive, LLUA.

25. *Michigan Catholic*, 18 March 1954 and 11 July 1957. On Catholic beliefs in healing, see Robert A. Orsi, *Thank You, St. Jude: Women's Devotion to the Patron Saint of Hopeless Causes* (New Haven, CT: Yale University Press, 1996).

26. Detroit Metropolitan Area Regional Planning Commission, "Employment of Women in the Detroit Region" (Detroit, 1959), 15–20; *Dodge Main News*, 16 January 1954. For context on women workers at the Dodge plant, see Kevin Boyle, "The Kiss: Racial and Gender Conflict in a 1950s Automobile Factory," *Journal of American History* 84 (September 1997): 496–523.

27. "Report to Presbytery, Fall 1960" and "Life, Death and Destiny in the Minds of Workers," TS, (n.d.), both in DIM, box 3, folder PIP-D, phase reports; Paradise, *Detroit Industrial Mission*, 46.

28. Washington, *Black Sects and Cults*, 116–17; John Kobler, "Prophet Jones: Messiah in Mink," *Saturday Evening Post*, 5 March 1955, 72–78.

29. Neal Brian Westveer, "An Evening with the Prophet Jones," TS, 1961 (17), folklore archive, LLUA; Arthur William Kornhauser, *Detroit as the People See It: A Survey of Attitudes in an Industrial City* (Detroit: Wayne University Press, 1952), 91. Kornhauser, *When Labor Votes*, 176–82.

30. "Christman-Plant Phase Report 1-10-59" and "Comments of men at Cadillac relative to class structure . . .," DIM, box 3, folder "Ecorse-study papers."

31. "Plant Phase Report of: The Ecorse Project," TS, April 1958, in DIM, box 3, folder "Ecorse Project Reports."

32. "Ecorse Project Group, 12-9-57," TS, in DIM, box 3, folder "Ecorse Project Reports"; "Report to Presbytery, Fall 1960," DIM, LLUA, box 3, folder PIP-D.

33. "Report to Presbytery, Fall 1960," DIM, LLUA, box 3, folder PIP-D.

5

Black Power and Black Theology in Cairo, Illinois

KERRY L. PIMBLOTT

On March 14, 1970, hundreds of people from across Cairo, Illinois, converged on St. Columba's Catholic Church where the United Front, an ecumenical citywide Black Power coalition, held its weekly "spiritual rallies." Teenagers arrived on bikes, deacons greeted visitors at the door, and community elders took their seats in the pews. Once the crowd had settled, the United Front choir led those present in a rousing rendition of a well-known spiritual. As they reached a crescendo, the organization's charismatic leader, the Reverend Charles Koen, ascended the stage and turned his King James Bible to the book of Nehemiah. The passage from which Koen derived his sermon chronicled the return of Nehemiah, a Jewish official in the court of the fifth-century BCE Persian ruler Artaxerxes, to Jerusalem after the fall of the Babylonian Empire. Nehemiah arrived to find his homeland in disarray, the landscape and people indelibly marked by the scars of conquest and colonialism. Jerusalem's inhabitants appeared distraught, impoverished, and defenseless. The city's walls were broken down and its gates burned with fire. Koen encouraged his listeners to observe the parallels between present-day Cairo and Jerusalem in the wake of captivity. Both, he explained, were "fallen" cities whose ungodly rulers had succumbed to corruption and greed, bringing down judgments in the form of economic decay, crumbling infrastructure, and grinding poverty. Further, in both communities an oppressed people had worked in unison to rebuild, setting the city back on a godly foundation. Black Cairoites, Koen argued, would not integrate into an unjust order nor would they wait for colonial rulers to rebuild their city for them. Like the Israelites, they would work

independently to resurrect Cairo, building their own cooperative parallel institutions through which jobs could be created, profits redistributed,
and a new set of human relations forged. In this manner, Koen argued, a
new and righteous society was being birthed out of the ashes of the old.[1]

Koen's sermon captures an important and largely overlooked strain of Black
Power politics. Fusing left nationalism with grassroots religious revivalism,
the exhortations of this small-town working-class radical rub uneasily against
interpretations of Black Power as having abandoned the spiritual moorings of
earlier civil rights campaigns. Scholars in the field of Black Freedom Studies
generally agree that churches served as key staging grounds for Civil Rights
protest and important repositories of an oppositional ideology and culture
that sustained participants.[2] In contrast, the rise of Black Power is often cast
as a moment of disjuncture in which a new generation of activists increasingly questioned the relevance of the black church, embracing the Nation of
Islam and secular humanist traditions.[3] Although scholars occasionally note
the participation of clergy and congregations in local struggles, the growing
subfield of Black Power studies remains in need of substantive analyses of the
extent and significance of this involvement as well as the broader influence
that theological considerations may have had on the movement's ideology
and tactics.[4]

Using Cairo, Illinois, as a case study, this chapter contends that the thesis
of Black Power's de-Christianization must be tested on the ground, with
scholars paying attention to local struggles as they evolved over time, and
in response to changing social and economic conditions. Thus, I trace the
religious contours of Cairo's black freedom struggle from the 1950s to the
1970s to illustrate that while Black Power's reliance upon the black church
was consistent with earlier campaigns, the United Front's theology nevertheless reflected a significant departure from the established Civil Rights credo.
Whereas civil rights leaders expressed a firm belief in the redemptive power
of Christian nonviolence and moral suasion to topple the *walls* of segregation that served to divide communities and bar African Americans from full
participation, Cairo's Black Power advocates were less optimistic. Instead,
they looked to Nehemiah's account of a formerly captive people rebuilding
a *wall* of self-preservation and security as a metaphor for their own black
nationalist politics of self-determination, armed self-defense, and community
control.

Not all local movements centered on the black church during the Black
Power era, though Cairo was far from unique. As the following section dis-
cusses, the religious tenor of protest traditions in Cairo was not inevitable,

but rather the result of the ingenuity of grassroots organizers forced to navigate the peculiar challenges of movement building in a declining river city. Foremost among those challenges was the Depression-era collapse of Cairo's black civil society, spurred by the premature onset of capital flight, deindustrialization, and population decline. In a pattern that subsequently came to haunt larger Rust Belt metropolises, the instability of black working-class employment contributed to the out-migration of Cairo's small black middle class as well as a significant erosion of the black public sphere that had sustained earlier forms of political activity. As freedom struggles gained steam after WWII, black Cairoites necessarily looked to their churches—among the few remaining black-owned institutions—to fill the void in political leadership and resources left in the wake of the urban crisis. In this manner, the United Front's mobilization of black churches as well as the Nehemiah story's call to "build the wall" also serves as an important bellwether, prefiguring the more recent upsurge in African American faith-based economic development initiatives aimed at reconstructing postindustrial cities.

When Cities Fall

Located at the confluence of the Ohio and Mississippi Rivers, Cairo's decaying facades and stately mansions are the legacy of a prosperous and bygone era in which the city served as a vital hub for transcontinental trade. Cairo's foundation and rise during the mid-nineteenth century paralleled the development of a national market, exploiting the North-South trade in agricultural staples and manufactured commodities as well as emergent markets to the west. The two rivers that intersected in Cairo—the Mississippi and Ohio—were integral to this period of economic expansion, functioning as the nation's first interstates for the transportation of goods both domestically and internationally. Town boosters expected Cairo to become a thriving metropolis and in 1852 these hopes were bolstered when the city was selected as the southern terminal for the Illinois Central Railroad. By 1900, Cairo boasted seven railroads and its place as an important transfer point for packet lines heading south. With such fortuitous geographic location and excellent transportation links, Cairo became southern Illinois's largest city and an important transshipment hub for the storage and processing of cotton, lumber, and flour as well as the manufacture of finished products.[5]

    Black migration and community building in Cairo coincided with the city's commercial height in the late nineteenth century. The first significant wave of migrants arrived during and immediately following the Civil War as Union forces established a military base and "contraband camp" in the city. Enslaved men and women fled across the two rivers, swelling Cairo's black population from just 47 in 1860 to 1,849 in 1870. These trends continued in the closing decades of the nineteenth century as the black community ballooned to 5,000 by 1900—a robust 40 percent of Cairo's population. Black migrants from the agrarian South underwent the process of proletarianization, joining white wage laborers in small manufactures and nonindustrial commercial enterprises tied to the city's river and rail networks. Still others entered low-paid personal service and domestic labor, including the majority of black women who worked in white households as laundresses, cooks, and servants. While discriminatory employment practices limited the range of opportunities open to African American workers, unskilled positions abounded, allowing for the development of a relatively stable black working class and a new black middle class that catered to a predominantly black clientele. In turn, these transformations provided the foundation for a wave of community building propelled by rigid practices of racial exclusion and segregation in public accommodations. By the turn of the twentieth century, black entrepreneurs owned and operated their own grocery stores, barbershops, funeral parlors, laundries, dance halls, saloons, restaurants, hotels, and an opera house. In turn, black Cairoites of all social classes engaged in institution building, forming their own churches, schools, sports teams, mutual-aid societies, fraternal orders, newspapers, political clubs, labor unions, and a local branch of the National Association for the Advancement of Colored People (NAACP).[6]

Collectively, these community-building initiatives gave rise to an autonomous black public sphere or, more precisely, a black counterpublic through which black Cairoites were able to preserve a sense of community and culture, share grievances, and launch political movements.[7] The foundation of Cairo's black counterpublic was its churches, which like other Ohio River Valley communities were principally affiliated with the historically African American Methodist and Baptist denominations. By the turn of the twentieth century, Cairo's three largest African American congregations were Ward Chapel AME Church, First Missionary Baptist Church, and Mt. Moriah Missionary Baptist Church. Established in 1863, Ward Chapel was the city's oldest black congregation and by the early twentieth century its imposing edifice on Seventeenth Street claimed over four hundred parishioners. The Methodists' commitment to an educated ministry, restrained worship, and a theology that promoted the virtues of temperance, frugality, and industry as keys to racial advancement appealed to members of the city's emergent professional and business class who were often migrants from other urban communities in the Midwest and Upper South. In contrast, Baptist congregations tended to attract rural migrants from the Deep South and reflected their preference for charismatic leadership and ecstatic forms of religious expression.[8] Such churches functioned as springboards for the formation of a wider black counterpublic that, by the early twentieth century, included a broad array of both religious and secular institutions. Church members were leaders in the formation of the first free schools that accepted black students as well as fraternal orders and mutual-aid programs. The latter were often initiated by churchwomen who were leading members of denominational mission boards and women's auxiliaries as well as secular organizations affiliated with the Cairo City Federation of Colored Women's Clubs. Clergy and lay leaders also took the lead in forming black Republican clubs and later the NAACP, holding mass meetings in their churches and involving their congregants in discussions of electoral politics and civil rights. However, during the early twentieth century, these important advancements were eroded as Cairo entered a period of prolonged economic decline foreshadowing events that would take place subsequently in Rust Belt metropolises.[9]

Cairo's transformation from bustling river city to impoverished backwater was a gradual process set in motion by broader changes within the national economy. The first signs of the coming crisis occurred in the transshipment industry, which was demoralized by a steady decline in river traffic during the late nineteenth century. Consequently, black workers who had relied on river and rail employment began to witness stagnating incomes and dwindling job opportunities, challenges that were further compounded during periods of financial crisis and environmental catastrophe. These conditions discouraged the development of large-scale industry in Cairo and catalyzed a spate of plant closures during the 1920s, which resulted in the loss of more than one thousand wage-earning positions and an almost 40 percent cut in the county's total manufacturing base. The Great Depression proved the final blow to Cairo's disintegrating economic base. With more than half of the town's workers on relief rolls in 1934, Cairo survived solely on direct federal intervention in the form of New Deal programs. Black workers, already struggling under the effects of job discrimination as well as extensive layoffs in the river, rail, and manufacturing sectors, bore the brunt of the fiscal crisis. As late as 1940, temporary public-works projects offered the only relief from real black unemployment rates that hovered dangerously close to 40 percent. Escalating joblessness fostered out-migration and discouraged new waves of migrants from settling in the city. At a moment when wartime investment and migration contributed to a demographic explosion in the metropolises of the Upper Midwest, Cairo witnessed its population decline from 14,407 in 1940, to 12,123 in 1950, and then to 9,348 in 1960. A 1948 study by the

Illinois Interracial Commission found that black workers who remained in Cairo and were able to secure employment found themselves consigned to "unskilled and service jobs with low wage scales" where the avenues for career advancement were "blocked pretty effectively by the discriminatory practices" of employers. The report failed to underscore the equally important role of Cairo's trade unions, which almost universally excluded black workers from membership. Conditions were arguably worse in the public sector where African Americans were customarily barred from most municipal and federal positions. While some of these discriminatory practices could be traced back to the late nineteenth century, others—like the shift to hiring exclusively white mail carriers—were implemented in immediate response to the collapse of the city's commercial and manufacturing base. Accordingly, black workers faced hardening job discrimination on top of declining job prospects, forcing the majority into day labor, seasonal work, or unemployment.[10]

The transformation of Cairo's black workers into an expendable and permanently surplus labor force also contributed to a decline in the fortunes of the city's small black middle class and the erosion of the black public sphere. Dependent almost exclusively on African American consumer spending, black entrepreneurs felt the effects of declining household incomes. After the Great Depression, businesses that offered anything but the most basic and essential services were forced to close their doors. As a result, a large segment of the black middle class left the city, resulting in the collapse of many of the social and political institutions they had helped sponsor, including clubwomen's associations, newspapers, mutual-aid societies, and the local branch of the NAACP. Traditional black working-class institutions also struggled to survive. Labor unions were devastated by the effects of plant closures, depriving workers of a vital tool in the battle for racial and economic justice. In the broader context of shrinking municipal budgets and widespread practices of racial segregation and exclusion, the decline of these vital institutions spelled disaster for black civil society and the vibrant counterpublic it had sustained, leaving many local residents without access to a political voice, adequate health care, housing, food, educational resources, and employment.[11]

Black Churches Face the Urban Crisis

As black civil society collapsed under the weight of discrimination and economic upheaval, the impossible task of meeting the immense needs of a distressed urban community fell back on one of the few remaining autonomous institutions: its churches. The performance of these extensive and varied responsibilities by Cairo's black churches hinged on their ability to work collaboratively, an undertaking that was aided by the comparatively homogeneous quality of African American religious traditions in the city. In contrast to many larger Upper Midwest metropolises, Cairo did not experience the rapid process of religious diversification associated with the influx of rural African American migration during the interwar years.[12] Here, there were no Holiness, Spiritual, Islamic, or Judaic sects, although a small number of black Cairoites did join Pentecostal and Catholic congregations. Rather, Cairo maintained its strong orientation toward the historically African American Methodist and Baptist denominations. A 1957 study of religious traditions in the city illustrated the extent of this uniformity with more than three-quarters of black respondents indicating that they were members of a local church: 70.4 percent were Baptist and 13.5 percent Methodist.[13] This cohesive religious culture provided a vital resource for local activists, serving as the foundation of a much narrower but significant black counterpublic in the postindustrial city.

While black freedom fighters in more cosmopolitan Upper Midwest communities necessarily deployed secular political discourses designed to bridge a plurality of religious constituencies, their counterparts in Cairo did just the opposite, turning to that "old-time religion" to express their grievances and mobilize local residents.[14] When investigators from the Works Progress Administration (WPA) visited the city in 1941, they observed that even the smallest congregations maintained a plethora of clubs and societies. Facing their own financial challenges due to diminished tithes and offerings, Cairo's black congregations adopted a collaborative and ecumenical approach to providing mutual aid and pastoral care.[15] Beginning at the height of the Great Depression, black clergy established an Interdenominational Ministers' Alliance and fostered a "city wide union spirit" encouraging church committees to better coordinate the social and spiritual ministries of their congregations. From this new set of institutional arrangements, black church leaders were elevated to a position of civic leadership and charged with championing the needs of the entire community.[16]

This expansion in the black church's role and authority was also important because of the increased marginalization of black Cairoites from formal avenues of political power. During the late nineteenth century, African Americans had exerted considerable influence on local politics through black Republican clubs and ward-based organizing, resulting in a number of key electoral victories and patronage appointments. However, as economic opportunities constricted, the tactical alliance between black and white Republicans fractured, leading to the passage of a series of punitive Progressive Era electoral reforms that undercut the ward-based power of black voters and prevented the election of a single African American candidate to municipal and county office for almost seventy years. Accordingly, Cairo's black churches were also expected to fill an immense political vacuum by providing charismatic leadership, articulating grievances to civic elites, and functioning as staging grounds for mass protest.[17]

Civil Rights and the Making of a Black Christian Radical

When local black freedom struggles began to gain steam in the post-WWII era, they necessarily reflected the aspirations of Cairo's black working class and relied upon the invaluable resources of local churches. Ministers and lay leaders reinvigorated the local branch of the NAACP in 1941, recruiting a mass membership and leading the first major campaigns for the equalization of teacher's salaries and the desegregation of public schools in 1943 and 1952, respectively. Under the presidency of Rev. Arthur Jelks, itinerant pastor of Ward Chapel AME, the NAACP moved its base of operations into local congregations where information could be safely transmitted and community members mobilized for mass direct action. An Alabama native, Jelks began his ministry as a child evangelist serving rural sharecropping and tenant farming communities. His political awakening occurred at fourteen years of age when a white plantation owner, angered by a hailstorm that threatened to destroy the cotton crop, forced all of his tenants out into the fields. When a young pregnant woman with whom Jelks was boarding refused, the plantation owner violently struck her, causing the premature delivery of the child. "It was probably then," Jelks declared, "that I decided to fight for racial justice." For the remainder of his life, Jelks would fuse his ministerial responsibilities with an unwavering commitment to protest.[18] A majority of the NAACP's other branch officers were also recruited from the ranks of the ministerial alliance, church missionary societies, women's auxiliaries, and steward and trustee boards. Among them was the Reverend J. I. Cobb of the Cairo COGIC congregation, Ward Chapel trustees Dr. W. A. Fingal and Dr. James Carroll Wallace Jr., and respected churchwoman and schoolteacher Hattie Kendrick.[19] Although the salary-equalization suit better reflected the goals of the NAACP's Legal Department in Washington, the organization's shift toward a more direct assault on Jim Crow education during the early 1950s galvanized the black working class. Many African American parents viewed school desegregation as a tool to improve educational opportunities for their children and provide a pathway to social mobility. Appealing to state laws banning segregation, black Cairoites filed over eighty transfer requests with local school authorities, staged mass demonstrations, and marched on all-white schools.[20]

These early postwar campaigns resulted in some limited victories, including equal pay for black teachers and the token integration of the city's schools, but they also provoked widespread opposition among prosegregationist whites, igniting a campaign of terror that forced the nascent movement underground. Foreshadowing the "massive resistance" of white Southerners that would follow the *Brown* decision, vigilantes burned crosses in the streets, firebombed the homes of prominent civil rights leaders, and subjected working-class parents to acts of economic and legal harassment. While many attributed the violence to a lower-class and criminal minority, newspaper accounts indicate that some of Cairo's most prominent business owners, trade-union leaders, and ministers were among the nearly twenty men arrested in relation to the cross burnings and bombings. After an all-white grand jury controversially failed to indict any of the men in the summer of 1952, several of the accused joined other civic leaders in forming the Cairo Citizens Association, a forerunner to the White Citizen's Councils that would soon spring up across the South.[21]

As fear of reprisals intensified, the NAACP's membership plummeted and mass direct-action strategies were jettisoned in favor of behind-the-scenes legal gradualism. This shift in strategy was also necessitated by the intensification of disagreements within black congregations over the appropriate use of church resources and ministerial authority, prompting the resignation of Rev. Jelks from his pastorate at Ward Chapel in 1953 and a broader retraction of church support for civil rights activities in the city. As Kendrick, a prominent member of Ward Chapel, recalled, "A part of the church congregation was proud of the firm stand which was being made in civil rights, the other part seemed humiliated."[22] Kendrick attributed the split to intraracial class and political divisions within Ward Chapel in which the majority of the so-called upper tens opposed political engagement because they believed it drew unwanted and dangerous attention and aligned the congregation with the interests of the black working class. "[N]o self respecting member of [the] black bourgeoisie would done belong to that mess," Kendrick declared.[23] As white vigilantes escalated their campaign of terror, even those ministers and congregants that had supported the NAACP began to backpedal, fearing that it was simply "too dangerous." In a letter to Thurgood Marshall in September 1953, W. A. Fingal—Jelks's successor as branch president—bemoaned that "eighty percent of the Negroes dare not attend an NAACP meeting" and were being "taught through the pulpits . . . that this is just stirring up something." According to Fingal, only two of Cairo's nearly twenty black churches were now available for civil rights activities. Without access to the church's meeting space, social networks, and leadership, civil rights activists in Cairo struggled to move beyond episodic campaigns toward a concerted mass movement to improve the quality of life of the city's black and poor residents.[24]

In this context, the ascendance of a nationally televised, pietistic southern campaign for civil rights during the late 1950s and early 1960s helped legitimate the political engagement of black churches and resurrect the stillborn struggle. At the behest of the bishop of the Illinois A.M.E. Conference, Ward Chapel received the youthful and progressive Reverend Blaine Ramsey Jr. in 1959. Ramsey joined Kendrick and other well-established lay leaders in reorienting the congregation and local ecumenical bodies toward civil rights activities. Inspired by the wave of student-led sit-ins that swept the country the following year, Ramsey and Kendrick reached out to local schoolchildren, including sixteen-year-old Charles Koen, in the hope that they might serve as the vanguard of a citywide campaign to upend Jim Crow. Ramsey took Koen, an impoverished youth from Cairo's segregated Pyramid Court public-housing project, under his wing, functioning as a spiritual father and initiating the young leader into the networks and culture of church-based activism.[25] In the summer of 1962, Ramsey invited activists from the Student Nonviolent Coordinating Committee (SNCC) to come to Cairo and launch "Operation Open City," the organization's first northern campaign. When SNCC fieldworkers John Lewis, Mary McCollum, James Peake, and Joy Reagon arrived from Nashville in June, they learned that Koen had organized more than seventy-five local schoolchildren between the ages of twelve and eighteen and formed the Cairo Nonviolent Freedom Committee (CNVFC), modeled after SNCC's philosophy of racial reconciliation and Gandhian nonviolence. Over the coming months, Koen led local schoolchildren in a series of successful sit-ins against discriminatory proprietors culminating in the toppling of Jim Crow segregation in public accommodations. As in earlier postwar struggles, Cairo's black churches functioned as ground zero for mass mobilization, not only providing important organizational resources, but also reinforcing the movement's guiding philosophy through fiery sermonizing, testimonies, hymns, and spirituals.[26]

Operation Open City marked Koen's entrée into the black freedom struggle, and though his politics would alter dramatically over the coming years, he never lost his belief in the salience of religious institutions and discourses to mass mobilization. During the campaign to integrate public accommodations, Koen found himself drawn to SNCC's conception of segregation as "an evil system," which needed to be confronted in order for God's vision of a Beloved Community to be achieved.[27] For CNVFC members, the effects of this "moral sickness" were palpable in Cairo, which they described as "dying" as a result of "unemployment, a low standard of living, [and] serious social problems." Koen and his peers attributed these social problems to the fact that "men's hearts are filled with hatred instead of with love."[28] As a result, the students committed themselves to a philosophy of nonviolence aimed at convicting white proprietors of their sinfulness. Upon being assaulted by one white proprietor, Koen surmised, "No matter what they do or say, we will be able to accept it and forgive them for their cruelness. After they treat us cruel for so long, maybe it will get on their conscience and they'll finally realize what they're doing."[29] This articulation of the power of moral suasion and hope of Christian reconciliation inspired Koen's elders and secured intergenerational and cross-class support for the CNVFC's methods. Toppling the "walls of segregation and discrimination" became a collective goal, reflecting deep-seated anxieties regarding the recent collapse of black civil society and virtual exclusion of African Americans from mainstream institutions.[30] However, for black workers to be able to procure these newly integrated services, the obstacles of mass unemployment and widespread job discrimination would have to be addressed. Accordingly, Koen and other CNVFC members viewed the integration of public accommodations as just the first phase of a much broader battle to establish "a truly Christian city."[31]

By the end of the summer, however, the effort to make a strategic transition from the integration of public accommodations to shop floors was stymied by the expiration of Rev. Ramsey's four-year itinerancy at Ward Chapel and Koen's subsequent departure for ministerial training at McKendree College in Lebanon, Illinois. Lacking two of its leading activists, the Cairo movement stalled once more. As Koen explained: "When it came to employment, everything just dropped. It was like the struggle swept in like a cyclone, picked up the door and windows but left the house intact. . . . When it came to finding jobs for blacks, the struggle ended and though we could eat, swim and skate with whites, we didn't enjoy the luxury. With no job, we were back where we started. Poor."[32] When mass protest erupted again in July 1967, it came in the form of a spontaneous urban rebellion led by black working-class youth frustrated with the slow pace of change. The five years following Operation Open City witnessed a deepening of the economic crisis, as unemployment for African American men reached 16.2 percent, compared to 6.5 percent for white men. By the end of the 1960s, almost three-quarters of all African American families lived on a household income of less than $3,000 per annum, making Cairo's black community among the poorest in the nation. Sparked by the suspicious death of nineteen-year-old soldier Robert Hunt Jr. while in police custody, Cairo's uprising gave voice to feelings of hopelessness and alienation rife among black working-class youth. For two long nights in July 1967, the city exploded, as young men from the Pyramid Courts shot out streetlights, smashed windows, and tossed homemade Molotov cocktails into the storefronts of businesses that refused to hire black workers.[33]

In the short term, the rebels' actions produced some tangible gains, including the appointment of a black assistant to the chief of police, the hiring of black police and fire officers, and a limited expansion in local job opportunities. Most notably, two of the city's largest employers—M. Snower and Company and Burkhart Manufacturing Company, both textile factories—hired additional black workers. Elsewhere, however, hiring practices went largely unchanged with the majority of black workers experiencing little improvement in their plight.[34] Moreover, the decision to use arson as a strategy provoked a broad resurgence in organized white supremacist activity led by local business owners that drove a wedge through the black community, alienating long-standing community leaders and disrupting the religious foundations of earlier struggles.[35]

Black Power Confronts the Postindustrial City

Consequently, the challenges facing Cairo's activists in the aftermath of the rebellion were twofold. First, local organizers needed to develop new approaches capable of addressing not only discriminatory labor practices but also the disastrous consequences of corporate disinvestment and structural unemployment. Because of the advanced nature of the urban crisis in Cairo, black workers could not focus their campaigns exclusively on the integration of existing workplaces or the implementation of affirmative-action programs designed to counteract institutional racism in hiring, promotion, and government contracts. No matter how successful, such strategies were unlikely to produce the number of jobs necessary to counteract black unemployment. Nor could black working-class activists capitalize—as their counterparts in larger industrial metropolises might—on a strategically advantageous position at the point of production or in the ranks of organized labor to exert greater control over workplace conditions and plant location. Rather, black workers in Cairo found themselves on the margins of a postindustrial economy in which large numbers of new jobs had to be created as well as existing positions opened up to ensure their survival.[36]

As local activists contemplated the means to address this colossal task, they faced the additional challenge of securing renewed support from the city's black churches. Earlier struggles demonstrated that the support of local congregations was essential to building effective movements, and with heightened external opposition and growing dissonance within their own ranks, Cairo's leading organizers were more determined than ever to marshal the church's resources and unite the black community around a set of shared objectives.

Koen, now an ordained Baptist minister, was particularly well situated to restore the church to its privileged position in local black freedom struggles by bridging the gap between established civil rights leaders and the new generation of militant working-class youth. Since the 1962 desegregation campaigns, Koen had undergone an ideological transformation, abandoning his earlier faith in liberal integrationism in favor of a Black Power politics that emphasized self-determination, economic empowerment, and community control. Koen's evolution was aided by his sustained involvement with SNCC, an organization that epitomized the shifting political sentiments of many African American activists in the mid-1960s. Koen formally joined the organization in 1966 and went on to lead a series of grassroots struggles in cities across southern Illinois and Missouri. The campaigns aimed to improve economic opportunities for black workers, particularly youth, who experienced the worst effects of the urban crisis. Increasingly, Koen championed selective patronage and cooperative economics as solutions to the problems created by long-term capital flight, deindustrialization, and ongoing job discrimination. Rather than procuring goods and services from discriminatory white proprietors, Koen encouraged black workers across southern Illinois to pool their resources for the purpose of establishing cooperative alternatives that would generate employment and redirect profits back into the black community. These endeavors earned Koen the respect of the SNCC leadership and resulted in his election to the position of national deputy chairman in June 1968.[37]

Koen's transition from civil rights liberalism to the "new nationalism" did not lead to a jettisoning of the black church or African American Christianity. Like many other ministers of his generation, Koen worked creatively to reconcile his evolving political ideology with an abiding faith in black Christian institutions and ideas. Koen's seminary years coincided with a tumult in African American religious history, as black clergy, provoked by urban rebellions and the rise of Black Power, struggled to render the church relevant to the rapidly changing conditions of the communities they served. Embracing the spirit of the age, African American clergy established autonomous black church caucuses, task forces, and ecumenical bodies, most notably the National Committee of Black Churchmen (NCBC) in 1966. Through these new bodies, black clergy endeavored to address the urban crisis by influencing church policy and leveraging denominational resources for use by grassroots organizations. Meanwhile, many black clergy and seminarians became interested in the theological implications of Black Power. Their concern prompted the formation of the NCBC's Theological Commission in 1967 and the publication of James Cone's *Black Theology and Black Power* and Albert Cleage's *The Black Messiah* the following year. These early entrées into the development of a systematic black theology were unified by an important critique of the Eurocentrism of established Christian theology and their extension of an alternative paradigm that centered the black experience and emphasized the liberation motifs of scripture. Both Cleage and Cone situated God on the side of the oppressed and black, arguing that contemporary Black Power struggles represented a contemporary manifestation of the divine's liberatory intent breaking into history. Koen immersed himself in these new religious networks, forming close ties with NCBC leaders and infusing his cooperative political agenda with the moral discourses of an emergent black liberation theology.[38]

During the spring of 1969, Koen returned to Cairo to spearhead a renewed campaign aimed at addressing the basic quality-of-life issues facing black Cairoites. In April, leaders representing each of Cairo's remaining civic organizations—from black churches to civil rights organizations and youth groups—joined to form the United Front, a citywide political alliance with Koen at the helm. Shortly after its formation, the United Front launched a boycott of downtown retailers that discriminated against black workers and initiated plans to develop a wide range of cooperative institutions. While African Americans of all social classes joined the United Front, the majority of the organization's membership was drawn from the ranks of Cairo's large black working class and mobilized through the city's black churches.[39] "The church was the control center of the movement in Cairo," explained United Front member Cordell McGoy. "This is where the rallies were held, marches were organized."[40] As in earlier struggles, clergy and laypersons assumed leadership positions and sacred edifices provided space for the United Front's offices and weekly mass meetings. These democratic assemblages, referred to as "spiritual rallies," adopted the ritualistic style of a camp meeting replete with scripture readings, gospel music, call-and-response oratory, and communal prayer. Through their sermons and writings, Koen and other United Front leaders crafted a grassroots Black Power theology that made sense of the plight of Cairo's black working class as well as legitimated a new strategic agenda capable of transforming conditions in the declining river city.[41]

Let Us Arise and Build

At the forefront of the United Front's Black Power theology were postexilic narratives of nation building little referenced in an African American theological tradition that historically centered on biblical accounts of exodus and exile.[42] For black Cairoites, it was Nehemiah's account of the destructive effect of Babylonian conquest on his ancestral homeland, symbolized by Jerusalem's "broken-down" wall and gates "burned with fire," that best evoked their own city's crumbling infrastructure and subjection to a system of internal colonialism (Neh. 1:3). Some drew explicit parallels between Cairo and ancient Babylon itself, a "fallen city" whose decadent and exploitative regime had brought forth divine judgment. Much like earlier civil rights discourses, United Front leaders attributed Cairo's decline to the moral failings of its white civic elite, and chalked the flight of capital out of the city up to divine punishment for avarice and greed. In contrast with more moderate civil rights leaders, who tended to emphasize the redemptive power of nonviolence and moral suasion to achieve integrationist ends, the United Front channeled the spirit of Nehemiah, calling upon black Cairoites to work independently to *rebuild* the fallen city.[43]

Nehemiah's theme of nation building provided scriptural legitimation for a resurgent black nationalist ideology and self-help strategy during this era. Rather than stressing the integration of existing institutions, United Front leaders insisted on the need to build black-owned alternatives capable of providing jobs and equitable services to the city's black working class. These institutions, which would eventually include a day-care center, housing development program, pig farm, taxi service, women's clothing store, grocery, legal defense agency, and medical clinic, were collectively framed in the United Front's rhetoric as a prophetic expression of Nehemiah's mission to rebuild the walls of Jerusalem.[44]

Paralleling the Nehemiah story, United Front leaders cast the rebuilding of Cairo's crumbling infrastructure as the divine calling of an oppressed and chosen people, an exercise in self-determination and collective action. The restoration of Jerusalem, they argued, had been a fundamentally cooperative enterprise in which all members of the oppressed community—young and old, male and female, rich and poor—labored with common cause. Thus, rather than "begging the white folks" for jobs and freedom, as Koen derisively put it, black Cairoites were encouraged to model themselves on the children of Israel, who "assumed the burdens of one another," by joining together to mend the city's walls (Neh. 4:17).[45] Speaking at a rally in September 1970, United Front leader Rev. Blaine Ramsey, now chair of the Illinois Council of Churches Special Task Force Committee, beseeched his audience to be like Nehemiah, "who returned to that rebel, that torn down community, and said, we are on this wall, we are going to do our work, and we can't come down."[46] Importantly, while scriptural accounts of the exodus situated great leaders like Moses as key agents in accomplishing God's redemptive purpose, the Nehemiah story reflected a more radical and democratic vision in which the labor of the masses was integral. As South African theologian J. N. K. Mugambi explains, "The role of Nehemiah is very different from that of Moses. He encourages the people and facilitates their work."[47] In the years following the assassinations of Malcolm X (a.k.a. El-Hajj Malik El-Shabazz) and Dr. Martin Luther King Jr., this emphasis on collective effort as opposed to heroic leadership was particularly important to activists seeking to sustain the movement over the long haul and in the face of heightened state repression. Among United Front members, the phrase *building the wall* was common parlance for their own efforts to redeem Cairo through the construction of just and equitable institutions. This scriptural representation of the power of collective self-help and racial unity functioned as an important rhetorical device in the United Front's efforts to mobilize all segments of the black community behind a new strategic agenda.[48]

United Front leaders also marshaled the Nehemiah story as an interpretative frame for white civic elite's opposition to their work. Koen reminded United Front members that when the people of Jerusalem unified to rebuild the city's walls, they inevitably drew the indignation of colonial administrators who mocked, manipulated, and terrorized the people in an effort to undermine their progress. In a departure from his earlier emphasis on racial reconciliation, Koen discouraged negotiations, frequently cautioning black Cairoites not to fall for the "tricks" and "shenanigans" of city administrators who, like their scriptural counterparts, were the natural enemies of God's work. "Nehemiah did not have time to leave the wall to sip coffee and eat donuts with the King," Koen explained. "He knew the King wasn't about 'sho-nuf' business." Similarly, black Cairoites did not "have time for donuts and coffee when lying [Mayor] Pete Thomas doesn't mean business about the problems of Cairo. When he gets ready to sit down and talk about our demands and meet our demands then we can talk. In the meantime, we will build the wall." In drawing such parallels, United Front leaders demonstrated their disillusionment with the politics of liberal integrationism and reinforced their commitment to self-determination and autonomous institution building. Earlier appeals to tear down walls of segregation and discrimination were now supplanted by the United Front's call to build walls of self-preservation, security, and protection.[49]

Building walls of protection that would insulate the black community from racial violence was a primary goal of the United Front's leaders. As in earlier periods, opposition to the black freedom movement often took on violent forms. The United Front's primary opposition came in the shape of a two-thousand-strong chapter of the White Citizen's Council, known locally as the United Citizens for Community Action (UCCA), which was established in 1969 by some of the city's leading retail merchants. The UCCA functioned at once as a vigilante organization and political-interest group, its members employing a combination of legal and extralegal strategies to undermine the work of the United Front and protect white supremacy, a fact made clear by the large sign hanging outside of the organization's offices on Washington Avenue, which was emblazoned with a Confederate flag and the motto "States' Rights—Racial Integrity." White citizens firebombed black churches, shot into the homes of activists, and burned the United Front's prefabricated housing factory to the ground.[50] In this context, United Front leaders also called upon the Nehemiah story to make a moral case for their adoption of armed self-defense. One of the most popular scriptures among local activists was Nehemiah 4:16–18 in which the Jewish official, plagued by rumors of a pending assault at the hands of neighboring colonial administrators, calls upon the people to work under the cover of night carrying weapons to protect them. For many, Nehemiah's instructions offered a scriptural mandate for the use of armed self-defense by those commissioned in the Lord's work. This sentiment was best captured by the United Front's symbol of a gun placed atop a King James Bible, which proudly adorned the altar at St. Columba's Church and was displayed in the homes of many members.[51] "Like Nehemiah," Koen declared, "we will carry the Bible in one hand and the gun to protect us in the other."[52] According to United Front member Clarence Dossie, "That gun was for our sure-enough protection, and that Bible was for your direction."[53]

The forging of "a whole new economic order" through the creation of parallel institutions was the United Front's primary strategy for counteracting the effects of capital flight, deindustrialization, and racial discrimination. However, the organization's radical leadership was also cognizant of the potential for black-owned and -operated institutions to reproduce the exploitative class dynamics of the dominant society. United Front leaders frequently voiced fears that "black people [might] supplant white exploitation with black exploitation."[54] Such statements reflected the organization's working-class base as well as broader concerns circulating within the radical wing of the Black Power Movement and other national liberation movements of the era. Ghanaian revolutionary Kwame Nkrumah, reprints of whose writings influenced many of the United Front's leaders, warned of the dangers of promoting a narrow nationalism that promised little more than the replacement of white colonial authorities with black demagogues. "Merely to change masters," Nkrumah cautioned, "is no solution to colonial poverty or neocolonialist strangulation, even if exploitation is subsequently practiced in a more subtle way." Accordingly, Nkrumah advocated a conception of African unity rooted in a socialist vision of society that included common ownership of the means of production, democratic decision making, and a state-planned economy.[55] Inspired by Nkrumah's philosophy, Koen advocated that the United Front's parallel institutions not only be black-owned and -operated but also be established on "a cooperative principal [sic]," allowing for wealth and decision-making power to be broadly and equitably distributed.[56]

While radical theorists such as Nkrumah informed the conception of economic justice held by United Front leaders, they also found "a righteous exemplar of godly political economy" in the Nehemiah story.[57] During the rebuilding of the wall, Jerusalem's impoverished peasantry cried out against the imposition of high mortgages, interest rates, and taxes by Jewish officials. Angered by the report, Nehemiah went before the city's ruling class, condemning the nobles for extracting usury from their own people and insisting that they restore a "covenant of brotherhood" by forgiving all debts and lending money and materials, interest free, to the poor (Neh. 5:1–13). For United Front leaders, the restoration of this covenant between the people of Jerusalem reflected God's privileging of human value and connectedness over profits. This ethic stood in stark contrast to what they defined as the "white value system" of "dollarbillism" that placed more emphasis on "me and mine" than on "we and ours." It was this value system, United Front leaders argued, that had fueled the exploitation of Cairo's black workers and their subsequent exclusion from the labor force.[58] Accordingly, Koen insisted that in developing their own parallel institutions, the United Front replace the ethic of "dollarbillism" with an alternative value system that emphasized mutuality, cooperation, and brotherhood. Referred to by United Front leaders as "Soulism," this religious ethic was operationalized through the practice of collective ownership and profit sharing, which allowed the "whole of the community [to] profit and not simply a few people."[59]

Conclusion

During the late 1960s and early 1970s, the United Front was responsible for spearheading the only substantive local initiatives designed to counteract the effects of plant closures, job losses, and economic discrimination. While modest, the organization's community-development programs bore fruit, providing much-needed services and employment to the city's struggling working class. Some programs, such as the cooperative grocery and clothing store, were short-lived and struggled to overcome white opposition and the comparative weakness of black consumer power in an already depressed regional marketplace. Others, like the United Front's housing program, the Egyptian Housing Development Corporation, achieved greater success by partnering with state and federal agencies to train local African American workers in construction and carpentry, building more than one hundred homes for low-income families in the city. In turn, the organization's law office, operated by the Lawyers' Committee for Civil Rights Under Law, provided free legal services to poor residents and mounted a successful campaign against employment discrimination through the courts, opening up municipal and county positions to black workers. In February 1976, under pressure from the federal Equal Economic Opportunity Commission (EEOC), city leaders agreed to maintain a black workforce of 17 percent as well as employ two African Americans on the fire department and three on the police department. Other legal suits filed by the Lawyers' Committee culminated in a number of county agencies, including the Department of Corrections, the Housing Authority, the Highway Department, and the public-aid office, hiring black workers in skilled and semiskilled positions.[60] Former United Front activist Clarence Dossie pointed to the significance of these gains for black workers: "If it wasn't for the movement . . . a lot of brothers that were around here they wouldn't have gotten jobs . . . because we were instrumental in helping them get jobs on the highway department and the prison jobs."[61] The United Front was able to make these gains in large part due to the skill of grassroots organizers in marshaling the resources of the city's black churches at a moment when political and economic opportunities were rapidly constricting. Repudiating traditional narratives of Black Power's de-Christianization, Cairo's homegrown activists forged a powerful mass movement under the banner of a new spiritual philosophy rooted in Nehemiah's call for the oppressed to rebuild fallen cities.

During the past forty years, Cairo's story has in many ways become America's story. Following in the river city's footsteps, black urban communities across the nation have faced the deleterious effects of economic restructuring, leading to unemployment, out-migration, and the collapse of institutions that provided the foundation for a robust black public sphere.[62] In the aftermath, black churches have emerged as vital "survival institutions" and potential vehicles for black working-class and cross-class protest.[63] Since the late 1980s, black inner-city congregations have been at the forefront of a new wave of faith-based community and economic development, building affordable housing for low-income residents, providing job-training and referral programs, and establishing a variety of cooperative enterprises.[64] In their efforts to rebuild distressed urban communities, many of these church-led initiatives have also invoked the postexilic story of Nehemiah as scriptural legitimation for a politics of black self-help and institution building. In Brooklyn, the East Brooklyn Churches (EBC) coalition established the Nehemiah Homes, a program aimed at addressing the shortage of affordable housing in the wake of urban renewal. Inspired by the EBC's work, faith-based coalitions in Baltimore, Philadelphia, and Sacramento launched their own Nehemiah housing developments based on the scriptural mandate to "arise and build." In this sense, the Cairo story also provides an important window into the possibilities of black working-class agency and protest in postindustrial cities, foreshadowing recent developments across the Rust Belt.[65]

Notes

I want to thank the editors of this volume as well as Darrell Jackson, Tracey Owens Patton, and Marcus Watson for their comments and suggestions. Earlier versions of this chapter were presented as conference papers in 2013 at the National Council of Black Studies (NCBS) in Indianapolis and the Association for the Study of the Worldwide African Diaspora (ASWAD) in Santo Domingo, Dominican Republic.

1. "Longest March of the Year Held," *East St. Louis Monitor*, 20 March 1970.

2. On the role of black churches in the Civil Rights Movement, see Aldon D. Morris, *The Origins of the Civil Rights Movement: Black Communities Organizing for Change* (New York: Free Press, 1984); Doug McAdam, *Political Process and the Development of Black Insurgency* (Chicago: University of Chicago Press, 1982); Aldon Morris, "The Black Church in the Civil Rights Movement: The SCLC as the Decentralized, Radical Arm of the Black Church," in *Disruptive Religion: The Force of Faith in Social-Movement Activism*, ed. Christian Smith (New York: Routledge, 1996), 29–46; Andrew Billingsley, *Mighty Like a River: The Black Church and Social Reform* (New York: Oxford University Press, 1999); Johnny E. Williams, "Linking Beliefs to Collective Action: Politicized Religious Beliefs and the Civil Rights Movement," *Sociological Forum* 17, no. 2 (June 2002): 203–22; Johnny E. Williams, *African American Religion and the Civil Rights Movement in Arkansas* (Jackson: University Press of Mississippi, 2003); David L. Chappell, *A Stone of Hope: Religion and the*

Death of Jim Crow (Chapel Hill: University of North Carolina Press, 2004); Charles Marsh, *The Beloved Community: How Faith Shapes Social Justice, from the Civil Rights Movement to Today* (New York: Basic Books, 2005); Paul Harvey, *Freedom's Coming: Religious Culture and the Shaping of the South from the Civil War through the Civil Rights Era* (Chapel Hill: University of North Carolina Press, 2005), esp. 169–217; Barbara Dianne Savage, *Your Spirits Walk beside Us: The Politics of Black Religion* (Cambridge, MA: Belknap Press, 2008).

3. For accounts that characterize the shift from civil rights to Black Power as the de-Christianization of the movement, see Marsh, *Beloved Community*; J. L. Jeffries, *Black Power in the Belly of the Beast* (Urbana: University of Illinois Press, 2006), 8; Charles Marsh, *God's Long Summer: Stories of Faith and Civil Rights* (Princeton, NJ: Princeton University Press, 1997); Steve McCutcheon, Judson L. Jeffries, and Omari L. Dyson, "The Black Panther Party and the Black Church," in *From Every Mountainside: Black Churches and the Broad Terrain of Civil Rights*, ed. R. Drew Smith (New York: SUNY Press, 2013), 127–28.

4. For studies that provide a more substantive discussion of the role of black churches and Christianity in the Black Power Movement, see Angela D. Dillard, *Faith in the City: Preaching Radical Social Change in Detroit* (Ann Arbor, MI: University of Michigan Press, 2007), and Kerry Pimblott, "Soul Power: The Black Church and the Black Power Movement in Cairo, Illinois, 1969–74" (PhD thesis, University of Illinois, 2012).

5. On the early settlement of Cairo, see John Asa Beadles, *A History of Southernmost Illinois* (Karnak, IL: Shawnee Development Council, 1990); Darrel E. Bigham, *Towns and Villages of the Lower Ohio* (Lexington: University Press of Kentucky, 1998); Arthur Clinton Boggess, *The Settlement of Illinois, 1778–1830* (Chicago: Chicago Historical Society, 1908); H. C. Bradsby, "History of Cairo," in *History of Alexander, Union and Pulaski Counties, Illinois,* ed. William Henry Perrin (Chicago: O. L. Baskin, 1883); Federal Writers' Project (Illinois), *Cairo Guide* (Cairo, IL: Cairo Public Library, 1938); Christopher K. Hays, "Way Down in Egypt Land: Conflict and Community in Cairo, Illinois, 1850–1910" (PhD thesis, University of Missouri–Columbia, 1996); Larry Heid, *River City: A Home-Town Remembrance of Cairo, Illinois* (New York: Exposition Press, 1966); John McMurray Lansden, *A History of the City of Cairo, Illinois* (Chicago: R. R. Donnelley and Sons, 1910); Herman R. Lantz, *A Community in Search of Itself: A Case History of Cairo, Illinois* (Carbondale, IL: Southern Illinois University Press, 1972), 7–40; Pimblott, "Soul Power," 29–76; Terri K. Wright, "The Upper Circle: The History, Society and Architecture of Nineteenth-Century Cairo, Illinois" (PhD thesis, Southern Illinois University at Carbondale, 1995).

6. Darrel E. Bigham, *On Jordan's Banks: Emancipation and Its Aftermath in the Ohio River Valley* (Lexington: University Press of Kentucky, 2006), 84–85, 220–21; Edward Noyes, "The Contraband Camp at Cairo, Illinois," in Historical Papers: *Selected Proceedings of the Sixth Northern Great Plains History Conference,* ed. Lysle E. Meyer (Moorhead, MN: n.p., 1972): 203–17; US Census Bureau, *Ninth Census of the United*

States, vol. 1, *Population of the United States* (Washington, DC: Government Printing Office, 1872), 108, 110; U.S. Census Bureau, *Twelfth Census of the United States: 1900*, vol. 1, *Population of the United States*, pt. 1 (Washington, D.C.: Government Printing Office, 1901), 651; Hays, "Way Down in Egypt Land," 238–44, 292–363; Christopher Hays, "The African American Struggle for Equality and Justice in Cairo, Illinois, 1865–1900," *Illinois Historical Journal* 90, no. 4 (Winter 1997): 267–71, 273–75, 278; Pimblott, "Soul Power," 41–43; Shirley J. Portwood, "African American Politics and Community in Cairo and Vicinity, 1863–1900," *Illinois History Teacher* 3 (1996): 14–15; Joanne Wheeler, "Together in Egypt: A Pattern of Race Relations in Cairo, Illinois, 1865–1915," in *Toward a New South? Studies in Post–Civil War Southern Communities*, ed. Orville Vernon Burton and Robert C. McMath (Westport, CT: Greenwood Press, 1982), 102–34.

7. On the concept of counterpublics, see Nancy Fraser, "Rethinking the Public Sphere: A Contribution to the Critique of Actually Existing Democracy," in *Habermas and the Public Sphere*, ed. Craig Calhoun (Cambridge: MIT Press, 1989), 109–42. On the concept of the black counterpublic, see Michael C. Dawson, "A Black Counterpublic? Economic Earthquakes, Racial Agenda(s), and Black Politics," *Public Culture* 7 (1994): 195–223; Michael C. Dawson, *Black Visions: The Roots of Contemporary African American Political Ideologies* (Chicago: University of Chicago Press, 2001), 23–29.

8. Joe William Trotter, *River Jordan: African American Urban Life in the Ohio River Valley* (Lexington: University Press of Kentucky, 1998), 78–80; Bigham, *On Jordan's Banks*, 249; Pimblott, "Soul Power," 43–51; "Notes on Morning Star Free Will Baptist and Ward Chapel A.M.E. Churches in Cairo, Illinois," Illinois Writers Project, "Negro in Illinois" Papers (hereafter IWP), box 17, folder 2, Vivian Harsh Research Collection of Afro-American History and Literature, Chicago Public Library; "Notes of Mt. Moriah Missionary Baptist Church in Cairo," IWP, box 17, folder 5; "Notes on early Baptist churches in Cairo, 1869–73," IWP, box 17, folder 4; Hays, "Way Down in Egypt Land," 327–29. On the theology and practices of the African Methodist Episcopal Church, see James T. Campbell, *Songs of Zion: The African Methodist Episcopal Church in the United States and South Africa* (New York: Oxford University Press, 1995).

9. Pimblott, "Soul Power," 43–51, 59–65; Hays, "Way Down in Egypt Land," 327–28, 353; "Notes on education in Cairo, Illinois, 1867–92," IWP, box 14, folder 4; "Notes on Cairo, Illinois," IWP, box 26, folders 22 and 23; "The NAACP of Cairo, Illinois," IWP, box 38, folder 2; Illinois Woman's Exposition Board, *Illinois Women's Work* (Springfield, IL: State Register Print, 1893), 7; "Cairo's Women's Clubs Meet," *Chicago Defender*, 19 June 1915; "What the People Are Doing in Cairo," *Chicago Defender*, 21 November 1914; "New Hospital Is Planned for Cairo, Ill.," *Chicago Defender*, 15 May 1915. For more on black churchwomen's activism during this period, see Bettye-Collier Thomas, *Jesus, Jobs, and Justice: African American Women and Religion* (New York: Alfred A. Knopf, 2010), and Evelyn Brooks Higginbotham, *Righteous Discontent:*

The Women's Movement in the Black Baptist Church, 1880–1920 (Cambridge, MA: Harvard University Press, 1993).

10. Quote from Illinois Interracial Commission, *Special Report on Employment Opportunities in Illinois* (Chicago, 1948), 8–9. Pimblott, "Soul Power," 51–53, 65–70; U.S. Census Bureau, *Fourteenth Census of the United States: 1920*, vol. 9, *Manufactures, 1919* (Washington, D.C.: Government Printing Office, 1928), 311; U.S. Census Bureau, *Fifteenth Census of the United States, Manufactures: 1929*, vol. 3, *Reports by States* (Washington, D.C.: Government Printing Office, 1933), 139, 141; "G.O.P. Chief Hails Tuesday Vote as New Deal Blow," *Chicago Daily Tribune*, 7 November 1935; Lantz, *Community in Search of Itself*, 42–46, 53–58, 113–14, 143–44; Illinois Interracial Commission, *First Annual Report of the Illinois Inter-Racial Commission* (1944), 62; U.S. Bureau of the Census, *Fourteenth Census of the United States*, vol. 3, *Population, 1920* (Washington, D.C.: Government Printing Office, 1922), 262; U.S. Bureau of the Census, *Sixteenth Census of the United States*, vol. 2, *Characteristics of the Population, 1940* (Washington, D.C.: Government Printing Office, 1943), 527, 613; U.S. Bureau of the Census, *Seventeenth Decennial Census of the United States*, vol. 2, *Population, 1950*, pt. 13 (Washington, D.C.: Government Printing Office, 1952), 9; U.S. Bureau of the Census, *U.S. Census of Population: 1960*, vol. 1, *Characteristics of the Population*, pt. 15 (Washington, D.C.: Government Printing Office, 1963), 31, 116, 135.

11. "Notes on Cairo, Illinois," IWP, box 26, folders 22 and 23; "The NAACP of Cairo, Illinois," IWP, box 38, folder 2; "The Beginning and Ending of the Colored Newspaper in Alexander County," IWP, box 42, folder 7; *Negro City Directory of Cairo, Illinois* (1936), Manuscript, Archives, and Rare Book Library, Emory University; Pimblott, "Soul Power," 70–71.

12. On the growing diversity of black religious traditions in northern urban communities during the interwar years, see Hans A. Baer and Merrill Singer, "Religious Diversification during the Era of Advanced Industrial Capitalism," in *African American Religious Thought: An Anthology*, ed. Cornel West and Eddie S. Glaude Jr. (Louisville, KY: Westminster John Knox Press, 2003), 495–533; Wallace D. Best, *Passionately Human, No Less Divine: Religion and Culture in Black Chicago* (Princeton, NJ: Princeton University Press, 2005); Arthur Huff Fauset, *Black Gods of the Metropolis: Negro Religious Cults of the Urban North* (New York: Octagon Books, 1974 [1944]); Joseph J. Washington Jr., *Black Sects and Cults* (Garden City, NY: Doubleday, 1973).

13. Cairo Community Development Association, "Report of the Population Committee," August 1957, Ephemera Collection, Special Collections Research Center, Morris Library, Southern Illinois University (hereafter SCRC), reel 4.

14. Religious studies scholar Eddie Glaude argues that the diversification of black religious traditions in northern urban communities after World War I necessitated that secular discourses supplant religious ones in black politics. Eddie S. Glaude Jr., "Babel in the North: Black Migration, Moral Community, and the Ethics of Racial Authenticity," in *A Companion to African-American Studies*, ed. Lewis R. Gordon and Jane Anna Gordon (Malden, MA: Blackwell Publishing, 2006), 494–511.

15. "Notes on Mt. Moriah Missionary Baptist Church in Cairo," IWP, box 17, folder 5; "Notes of First Missionary Baptist Church in Cairo, Illinois," IWP, box 17, folder 7; "Notes on Church of God in Christ in Cairo," IWP, box 17, folder 10; "The History of Everdale Missionary Baptist Church of Cairo, Illinois," IWP, box 45, folder 23; "First Central Baptist Church of Cairo, Illinois," IWP, box 45, folder 24; Cairo Community Development Program, "Report of the Church Committee," January 1957, Community Study and Development Program Reports, 1953–1962, SCRC, reel 4; Pimblott, "Soul Power," 70–74.

16. Quoted from "Notes on Morning Star Free Will Baptist and Ward Chapel A.M.E. Churches in Cairo, Illinois," IWP, box 17, folder 2;

17. On the political power of black Cairoites during the late nineteenth century and its restriction during the Progressive Era, see Bigham, *On Jordan's Banks,* 181, 189–91, 310; Hays, "African American Struggle for Equality and Justice," 274–77; Hays, "Way Down in Egypt Land," 348–51, 359, 380, 446–48, 450; Illinois Advisory Committee to the United States Commission on Civil Rights, *A Decade of Waiting in Cairo* (June 1975), 310; Lantz, *Community in Search of Itself,* 98; Pimblott, "Soul Power," 47–51, 57–58; Portwood, "African American Politics and Community," 14–15; Wheeler, "Together in Egypt," 122–28.

18. Quoted from "Militant Leader Pledges Fight against Bias," *Indianapolis Recorder,* 22 March 1958. Later in life, Jelks participated in Civil Rights campaigns in Baton Rouge, Louisiana; see Adam Fairclough, *Race and Democracy: The Civil Rights Struggle in Louisiana, 1915–1972* (Athens: University of Georgia Press, 1999), 333–34.

19. The central role of churches and church-based leaders to the post-WWII activities of the Cairo branch of the NAACP is widely documented in newspapers, personal papers, and organizational records; see Hattie Kendrick, untitled history of Ward Chapel A.M.E. Church, 18 March 1976, Kendrick-Brooks Family Papers, Library of Congress, Washington D.C. (hereafter KBFP-LOC), box 21, folder 15; Hattie Kendrick handwritten note, n.d., KBFP-LOC, box 22, folder 4; Report of Branch Activities in Cairo, Illinois, 1941, *Papers of the NAACP,* part 25, Branch Department Files, series A, Regional Fields, Special Projects, 1941–1955 (Bethesda, MD: University Publications of America, 1994), microform, reel 16, 0096, 0100; draft manuscript by Kathryn Ward, KBFP-LOC, box 22, folder 2; "Mass Meeting to Launch NAACP Membership Drive," *Cairo Evening Citizen,* 5 January 1952; "Mass Meeting under NAACP Sponsorship," *Cairo Evening Citizen,* 16 January 1952; Pimblott, "Soul Power," 65, 77–84.

20. On the Cairo school desegregation campaign of 1952, see Pimblott, "Soul Power," 84–99; June Shagaloff and Lester P. Bailey, "Cairo—Illinois Southern Exposure," *Crisis* 59 (April 1952); Len Schroeter, "Force and Violence in Illinois," *The Nation,* 9 February 1952; June Shagaloff, "A Study of Community Acceptance of Desegregation in Two Selected Areas," *Journal of Negro Education* 23, no. 3 (Summer 1954): 330–38; Bonita H. Valien, "Racial Desegregation of the Public Schools in Southern Illinois," *Journal of Negro Education* 23, no. 3 (Summer 1954): 303–9.

21. White citizens' use of legal and extralegal forms of repression to halt the desegregation campaign was widely reported in both the local and national press. For

example, see "Crosses Burn in Cairo, Ill. Negro Areas," *Southern Illinoisan,* 28 January 1952; "Bomb Blasts Illinois Negro Doctor's Home," *Washington Post,* 1 February 1952; "Cairo Quiet after Three Hectic Nights," *Cairo Evening Citizen,* 1 February 1952; "Negro Pupils Change Schools, Crosses Burn," *Jet,* 7 February 1952; "Charged with Conspiracy," *Cairo Evening Citizen,* 9 February 1952; "Grand Jury to Hear 4 in Bombing," *New York Amsterdam News,* 9 February 1952; "Racial Violence Flares in Cairo, Ill.," *Jet,* 14 February 1952; "Grand Jury Is Dismissed after Report," *Cairo Evening Citizen,* 22 February 1952; "NAACP Assigns Top Defense for Cairo Parents," *Jet,* 28 February 1952; "Cairo School Situation," *Crisis* 59 (March 1952): 143–45; "Dynamite Arrow: Neighbor Points Out Foe of Segregation," *Life,* 1 February 1954; Langston Hughes, "A Sentimental Journey to Cairo, Illinois," *Chicago Defender,* 15 May 1954. For a secondary account of this campaign of terror and its participants, see Pimblott, "Soul Power," 94–96.

22. Hattie Kendrick, untitled history of Ward Chapel A.M.E. Church, 18 March 1976, KBFP-LOC, box 21, folder 15.

23. Hattie Kendrick handwritten note, n.d., KBFP-LOC, box 22, folder 4.

24. W. A. Fingal to Thurgood Marshall, 10 September 1953, *Papers of the NAACP,* part 3: The Campaign for Educational Equality, series C: Legal Department and Central Office Records, reel 1, 0476–0479.

25. Hattie Kendrick, untitled history of Ward Chapel A.M.E. Church, 18 March 1976, KBFP-LOC, box 21, folder 15; Charles E. Koen, *The Cairo Story: And the Round-Up of Black Leadership* (Cairo, Ill., n.d.), 47–49; transcripts of audiotapes 3 and 4 made by Hattie Kendrick, n.d., KBFP-LOC, box 19, folder 2.

26. Koen, *Cairo Story,* 49–51; "20 SIU Students Attend Sit-In Meeting in Cairo," *Egyptian* (Carbondale, IL), 29 June 1962; "Anti-Bias Group Formed," *Southern Illinoisan,* 21 July 1962; Newsletter of the Cairo Non-Violent Freedom Committee, July 1962, James Forman Papers, Library of Congress (hereafter JFP-LOC), box 69, folder 9; Student Nonviolent Freedom Committee, "Report on Student Nonviolent Activities in Southern Illinois," 29 September 1962, David Ibata Collection of Racial Strife, SCRC, box 1, folder 6; John Lewis and Michael D'Orso, *Walking with the Wind: A Memoir of the Movement* (New York: Simon and Schuster, 1998), 190–91; "Here's Why Southern Illinois Has Earned the Sad Title of 'Little Mississippi,'" *Chicago Daily Defender,* 7 July 1962; "Cairo Committee Tells 11-Point Freedom Plan," *Chicago Daily Defender,* 5 July 1962; Pimblott, "Soul Power," 99–116.

27. James Peake Jr., "Freedom Fight Spreads to Cairo, Ill.," *Guardian,* July 1962.

28. Quotes from "John O'Neal Explains Non-Violence Committee," *Egyptian,* 24 July 1962; untitled speech given by the Cairo Non-Violent Freedom Committee, July 1962, JFP-LOC, box 69, folder 9.

29. "No Quitting, Negro Says," 1962, JFP-LOC, box 69, folder 9.

30. Transcripts of audiotape 3 made by Hattie Kendrick, n.d., KBFP-LOC, box 19, folder 2.

31. Untitled speech given by the Cairo Non-Violent Freedom Committee, July 1962, JFP-LOC, box 69, folder 9.

32. Koen, *Cairo Story*, 50–51.

33. U.S. Department of Commerce, *The Social and Economic Status of the Black Population in the United States: An Historical View, 1970–1978* (Washington, D.C.: U.S. Department of Commerce, Bureau of the Census, 1979), 41; United States Commission on Civil Rights, *Cairo, Illinois: A Symbol of Racial Polarization* (Washington, D.C., February 1973), 6. On the Cairo urban rebellion of 1967, see Pimblott, "Soul Power," 123–34.

34. Hattie Kendrick handwritten note, n.d., KBFP-LOC, box 22, folder 4; "Mayor and City Council Members Issue Statement," *Cairo Evening Citizen*, 21 July 1967; "Meeting on Cairo Job Opportunities Apparently Produces Positive Results," *Cairo Evening Citizen*, 26 July 1967; "Negroes Seek Jobs as Test of Promise by Plant in Cairo," *Post-Dispatch* (St. Louis, MO), 24 July 1967; Jerome P. Curry, "Merchant Drive to Hire More Cairo Negroes," *Post-Dispatch* (St. Louis, MO), 21 July 1967; "Human Relations Commission Brings Cairo City Council, Negroes Together on Jobs," *Illinois Commission on Human Relations Newsletter* 2, no. 1 (October 1967): 3.

35. "Chapter of Committee of 10 Million Formed in Cairo," *Cairo Evening Citizen*, 31 July 1967; "Cairo Whites Urge Arrests of Arsonists and Snipers," *Post-Dispatch* (St. Louis, MO), 22 July 1967; "Cairo Organizes Unit to Control Disorders," *Southern Illinoisan*, 31 July 1967; "Cairo Residents Arming for Summer," *FOCUS/Midwest* 6, no. 40 (1968): 27; "Another Group Asks Peaceful Cairo Settlement," *Cairo Evening Citizen*, 24 July 1967; Koen, *Cairo Story*, 54.

36. On the broader efforts of black workers to address job discrimination and the early effects of economic restructuring during the postwar era, see Thomas J. Sugrue, "Affirmative Action from Below: Civil Rights, the Building Trades, and the Politics of Racial Equality in the Urban North, 1945–1969," *Journal of American History* 91, no. 1 (June 2004): 145–73; Trevor Griffey and David Goldberg, eds., *Black Power at Work: Community Control, Affirmative Action, and the Construction Industry* (Ithaca, NY: ILR Press, 2010).

37. Benjamin Looker, *Point from Which Creation Begins: The Black Artists' Group of St. Louis* (Columbia: University of Missouri Press, 2004), 43–44; Koen, *Cairo Story*, 55; "Southern Illinois Co-Operative Assn. Teaches 'Importance of the Dollar,'" *East St. Louis Monitor*, 18 January 1968; "Buying Club Grosses $700," *East St. Louis Monitor*, 15 February 1968; "S.I.C.A. Forms Credit Union," *East St. Louis Monitor*, 1 February 1968; "S.I.C.A. Begins Operations in Carbondale," *East St. Louis Monitor*, 9 February 1968; Minutes of the Special Task Force Committee, 29 April 1968, Illinois Conference of Churches (hereafter ICC) Records (1880–1997), box 10, folder 31, Abraham Lincoln Presidential Library (hereafter ALPL); Harold R. Piety, "Revolution Comes to East St. Louis," *FOCUS/Midwest* 68 (1968): 13–17; Clarence Lang, *Grassroots at the Gateway: Class Politics and the Black Freedom Struggle in St. Louis, 1936–75* (Ann Arbor: University of Michigan Press, 2009), 208; Kenneth Jolly, *Black Liberation in the Midwest: The Struggle in St. Louis, Missouri, 1964–1970* (New York: Routledge, 2006), 63–65; and Clayborne Carson, *In Struggle: SNCC and the Black Awakening of the 1960s* (Cambridge, MA: Harvard University Press, 1995), 190–91.

38. For discussion of the transformative effect of Black Power on the black church, see C. Eric Lincoln and Lawrence H. Mamiya, *The Black Church in the African American Experience* (Durham, NC: Duke University Press, 1990); Gayraud S. Wilmore and James H. Cone, *Black Theology: A Documentary History, 1966–1979* (Maryknoll, NY: Orbis Books, 1979); Gayraud S. Wilmore, *Black Religion and Black Radicalism: An Interpretation of the Religious History of African Americans,* 3rd ed. (Maryknoll, NY: Orbis Books, 1998), 222–52.

39. "Races: War in Little Egypt," *Time,* 26 September 1969; "History of Struggle," *Chicago Daily Defender,* 10 December 1970; Koen, *Cairo Story,* 57; Charles E. Koen, *United Front Philosophy* (Cairo, IL: United Front, 1970), 7; Pimblott, "Soul Power," 156–58.

40. Quote taken from Preston Ewing Jr., and Jan Peterson Roddy, *Let My People Go: Cairo, Illinois, 1967–1973* (Carbondale: Southern Illinois University Press, 1996), 19.

41. For a detailed study of the United Front's relationship with local black congregations as well as the religious dynamics of its distinctive movement culture, see Pimblott, "Soul Power."

42. Allen Dwight Callahan, *The Talking Book: African Americans and the Bible* (New Haven, CT: Yale University Press, 2006), 80–81; and Allen Dwight Callahan, "Remembering Nehemiah: A Note on Biblical Theology," in *Black Zion: African American Religious Encounters with Judaism,* ed. Yvonne Chireau and Nathaniel Deutsch (New York: Oxford University Press, 2000), 153–59.

43. "Cairo Will Die!," *East St. Louis Monitor,* 14 March 1968; "Cairo," *East St. Louis Monitor,* 29 February 1968; "Longest March of the Year Held" and "Progress Report from the United Front," 1969, ICC Records, box 11, folder 8.

44. For a detailed examination of the United Front's institution-building activities, see Pimblott, "Soul Power," esp. 206–61.

45. "Struggle Reaches New Levels," *United Front News,* 13 March 1971; "Progress Report from the United Front," 1969, ICC Records, box 11, folder 8.

46. "Blacks Vote Boycott On," *United Front News,* 26 September 1970, ICC Records, box 19, folder 23.

47. J. N. K. Mugambi, *Christian Theology and Social Reconstruction* (Nairobi: Action, 2003), 172–73.

48. "Longest March of the Year Held," 1969, ICC Records, box 11, folder 8.

49. "Blacks Vote Boycott On," *United Front News,* 26 September 1970.

50. Pimblott, "Soul Power," 270–71; "White Citizens Council Founder to Speak in Cairo," *East St. Louis Monitor,* 28 May 1970.

51. For examples of the United Front mobilizing the Nehemiah story in support of armed self-defense, see Koen, *United Front Philosophy;* Bernard Gavzer, "Fear and Hate Abound; Gap Is Widening," *Chronicle Telegram* (Elyria, OH), 15 March 1970; J. Anthony Lukas, "Bad Day at Cairo, Ill.," *New York Times Magazine,* 21 February 1971.

52. "United Front Explains Curfew," *East St. Louis Monitor,* 5 February 1970.

53. Quote taken from Ewing and Roddy, *Let My People Go,* 21. .

54. Michael Watson, "Cairo," *PROUD*, October 1971. For more on the United Front's economic program, see Koen, *United Front Philosophy.*

55. Kwame Nkrumah, *Handbook of Revolutionary Warfare: A Guide to the Armed Phase of the African Revolution* (New York: International, 1969), 28.

56. "Progress Report from the United Front," 1969, ICC Records, box 11, folder 8.

57. Callahan, "Remembering Nehemiah," 161.

58. "Black Congress Supports Cairo Blacks," *United Front News*, 12 September 1970; "How Long Must We Wait?," *United Front News*, 12 September 1970; "Capitalism Is Compared to Cooperatives," *United Front News*, 3 October 1970.

59. Koen, *United Front Philosophy.*

60. Pimblott, "Soul Power," 328–30; "Cairo: The Legacy of Racism," *Washington Post*, 22 March 1987; Michael P. Seng, "The Cairo Experience: Civil Rights Litigation in a Racial Powder Keg," *Oregon Law Review* 61, no. 285 (1982): 301–4; Illinois Advisory Committee to the United States Commission on Civil Rights, *A Decade of Waiting in Cairo* (June 1975), 16–17.

61. Clarence Dossie interview with the author, Cairo, Illinois, 5 February 2010;

62. For a discussion of the effects of economic restructuring on the black working class at the end of the twentieth century, see Manning Marable, *How Capitalism Underdeveloped Black America: Problems in Race, Political Economy, and Society* (Cambridge, MA: South End Press, 1983 [2000]), 53–68; Sundiata Keita Cha-Jua, "The New Nadir: The Contemporary Black Racial Formation," *Black Scholar* 40, no. 1 (2010): 38–58. On the pernicious effects of economic restructuring on the black counterpublic, see Dawson, "Black Counterpublic?"

63. Meredith Ramsay, "Redeeming the City: Exploring the Relationship between Church and Metropolis," *Urban Affairs Review* 33 (May 1998): 595–628; C. J. Green, ed., *Churches, Cities, and Human Community: Urban Ministry in the United States 1945–1985* (Grand Rapids, MI: Eerdmans, 1996); June Manning Thomas and Reynard N. Blake Jr., "Faith-Based Community Development and African American Neighborhoods," in *Revitalizing Urban Neighborhoods*, ed. W. D. Keating, N. Krumholz, and P. Star (Lawrence: University Press of Kansas, 1996), 131–43; and Michael W. Foley, John D. McCarthy, and Mark Chaves, "Social Capital, Religious Institutions and Poor Communities," in *Social Capital and Poor Communities*, ed. Susan Saegert, J. Phillip Thompson, and Mark R. Warren (New York: Russell Sage Foundation Press, 2001), 215–45.

64. Laura E. Reese, "Economic Development Activities of Urban Religious Institutions," *International Journal of Economic Development* 1, no. 2 (1999): 166–200; Mark R. Warren, *Dry Bones Rattling: Community Building to Revitalize American Democracy* (Princeton, NJ: Princeton University Press, 2001); and Thomas and Blake, "Faith-Based Development and African American Neighborhoods," 131–43.

65. "New York's Nehemiah Plan," *Washington Post*, 6 July 1968; Erik Brady, "A Beacon of Hope," *USA Today*, 14 April 1995; and Sherry Stone, "Interfaith Community Helps Rebuild Neighborhoods," *Philadelphia Tribune*, 6 August 1993.

PART II

Christianizing Capitalism

6

Emma Tenayuca, Religious Elites, and the 1938 Pecan-Shellers' Strike

ARLENE SÁNCHEZ-WALSH

Life was bleak in 1930s San Antonio for most Mexicanos who were not middle-class Tejanos or part of the Mexican immigrant class. By nearly every measure—employment, health care, education—Mexican workers and working-class Tejanos were treated as an expendable workforce who, because of the dual-wage labor system, constant threat of job loss, and eventual deportation, were powerless to contend against the entrenched interests of San Antonio's business, political, and religious elite. Life for workers in particular industries was particularly harsh. Cigar workers grew tired of their poor working conditions and organized and struck in 1934, led by Emma Tenayuca. Four years later, Tenayuca would play a pivotal role in organizing another, more successful strike against the San Antonio pecan industry. This chapter explores Tenayuca's role in organizing the pecan-shellers' strike, specifically with reference to the role of San Antonio's religious communities, some of whom supported the strike and many of whom did not because of Tenayuca's Communist activism.

The largest single player in the religious marketplace in which Mexican workers were situated was the Roman Catholic Church. Around 90 percent of the pecan shellers were Catholic, but support from the archdiocese for the strikers was mixed. Although Mexicanos did not typically attend the Reform Temple Beth-El, its rabbi, Ephraim Frisch, spoke out on behalf of the strikers. Temple Beth-El was in a prime position to exert some influence on Southern Pecan Shelling Company owner Julius Seligmann, who was himself a member. Also in the mix was a small group of Pentecostal women who worked as pecan shellers. Their voices have largely been lost, buried under the auspices of Assemblies of God missionary Henry C. Ball. Ball took it upon himself to speak for these women. Yet on the rare occasions that he mentioned women workers at all, he cast them as lost to Romanism, poverty, and potentially forever to Communism.

Given Ball's distaste for the Catholic Church, it was ironic that he found himself on the same side of the dispute as the archdiocese. Both argued that the strikers should not be supported if they were going to be led by the likes of Emma Tenayuca, a local labor organizer whose Communist sympathies posed a mortal threat to their souls. The Roman Catholic Church did not view the Assemblies of God as viable competition in the 1930s. Protestant conversion was annoying and something to be avoided, but not a real demographic threat. One place where all these varied forces—the vested political, legal, business, and religious interests—found common cause was in undermining perceived Communist influence within Mexicano unions.

This chapter places Mexican workers at the center of a contest for religious and social control over their lives. Only by working outside dominant religious institutions, as Tenayuca did, were any of these religious activists able to support the striking pecan shellers. Born and raised culturally Catholic herself, Tenayuca fit the profile of a Catholic dedicated to social-justice causes and less concerned with the institutional teachings and programs that bishops would have wanted the Mexican population to utilize as a way of becoming better Catholics and better citizens. Unfortunately, we do not have her story, let alone those of the less heralded Pentecostal women pecan shellers; all we have are the words of their overseer, Henry Ball. In this essay I strive to decolonize those words, restoring the voices of these women, who created their own space of activist popular religion despite the opposition of religious institutions and their gatekeepers.

San Antonio was a conservative city. It maintained some of its Old South ties to a racist hierarchy that guided public policy. As historian Karl Preuss put it, "Most whites did not consider Mexicans white, they also treated blacks poorly and kept both minorities 'in their place' and out of civic life." In fact, "During the 1930s, overt discrimination against blacks and Mexicans (unlike more covert discrimination in Northern states) was taken for granted and so entrenched that it went unchallenged even by the city's most progressive citizens."[1]

Since the early 1920s, pecans were one of Texas's most lucrative crops, with groves running all around the Red, Trinity, Brazos, Colorado, Nueces, and Guadalupe Rivers. From 1927 to 1936, the state grew twenty-two million pounds, comprising 48 percent of the total US crop. In 1926, with an initial investment of $50,000, Julius Seligmann opened the Southern Pecan Shelling Company (SPSC). By 1936, the company made three million dollars in profits.[2] The SPSC would be making nearly fifty million dollars a year in today's currency. Seligmann is important to the story in several ways. He was the owner of one of the companies who most fiercely resisted the reforms of the Fair Labor Standards Act. He also chose not to mechanize his factory when most of the others did, instead relying on cheap and abundant Mexican labor to crack the nuts by hand through the late 1930s. His approach to management would later provoke Rabbi Frisch to denounce him as one who promoted the "soulless" acquisition of profits.[3]

When Seligmann not only refused to mechanize but also took advantage of the contracting system in which large companies "sold" pecans to independent contractors, who in turn had Mexican subcontractors do the work at home, he created an economic and workplace environment in which Mexican workers would never be able to contend for a fair wage. This was especially true given the excess of Mexican workers willing to do the work for much lower piecework wages.[4] The pecan workers were mostly young, single, Tejana and Mexicana women, and they made up 79 percent of low-paid workers in the garment, cigar, and pecan-shelling industries. Historian Zaragosa Vargas notes that "regardless of their skills or occupations, women of color were generally classified as unskilled by the National Recovery Administration (NRA), and hence received the lowest wage rates."[5] In fact, when the NRA wanted to change the wage structure for pecan workers to $6.50 per week, Julius Seligmann walked out of the negotiations and formed his own Southwestern Pecan Shellers Association, with the express purpose of ignoring the NRA codes.[6]

Working conditions for pecan shellers were deplorable. No better were the overall conditions of most San Antonio Tejanos who lived on the west side of the city in cramped, shack-like conditions with minimal sanitation, little indoor plumbing, pestilential levels of diseases such as tuberculosis, and shocking rates of infant mortality.[7] Workers shelled pecans between November and March. For those who worked at home, conditions for the entire west side were bad. As historian Matthew Keyworth writes,

> [A] lack of water inside the home meant that most Tejanos neither bathed nor washed their hands regularly, further compounding health problems and reinforcing the stereotype of "dirty" Mexicans. . . . One study of living conditions in the late 1920s found private toilets nonexistent in the tenements. In some instances, outhouses sat in courtyards for use by up to fifty families. A

government report in 1940 demonstrated that the situation improved only marginally during the 1930s. By that date, more than ninety percent of homes in the barrio still lacked private toilets.[8]

Among the myriad illnesses that plagued the city's Mexicanos, however, tuberculosis proved the most fatal. Thirteen percent of Mexicans who died on the west side in 1938 succumbed to the disease—more than double the rate for Anglos.[9]

Things were not much better for those who did not work at home but instead shelled nuts in the shops. Conditions were poor. Natural ventilation was inadequate, and historian Gabriela González writes that, in addition to the lack of ventilation, the brown dust from the pecans contributed to respiratory problems, with tuberculosis rates already high.[10] The tables where the shells were cracked were long and backless, with poor lighting; as such, workers were forced to hunch over to ensure no nuts were broken, as broken nuts were worthless. Sanitation was nearly nonexistent; there was one toilet for all the workers.[11]

Numbers vary, but workers were paid between $2.50 and $2.73 a week.[12] There were attempts at unionizing before 1938: a local independent union called El Nogal organized four thousand workers from 1933 to 1936 but had relatively few dues-paying members, and therefore little success at work actions. The Pecan Shelling Workers Union of San Antonio organized by Magdaleno Rodriguez, but effectively run by benefactor Julius Seligmann, organized thousands of workers to make sure they did not cause the company trouble.[13] The United Cannery, Agricultural, Packing, and Allied Workers of America (UCAPAWA) issued a charter to yet another iteration of a pecan-shellers' union in 1937 with the purpose of eventually bringing them into the CIO (Congress of Industrial Organizations). It would be the CIO representatives that would end up negotiating an end to the 1938 strike. Although there had been strikes against the pecan companies in 1934 and 1935,[14] those did not render a victory on behalf of workers. The 1938 strike, organized and initially led by Emma Tenayuca, was successful even as it relegated Tenayuca to exile after several years of being blacklisted as a Communist in the San Antonio area.

In January 1938, responding to a reduction in the per-pound wages from seven cents per pound to five to six cents per pound, thousands of shellers went on strike. Between six to eight thousand workers went on strike, demanding an end to the wage cut, better working conditions, and the elimination of the piecework-at-home regimen that undercut their ability to earn a decent wage. This strike, opposed by Seligmann and the San Antonio business elite as well as local law enforcement, was also opposed by nearly all the religious leaders of San Antonio, who saw the strike as a Communist threat. This anti-Communist zeal masked the serious issues workers brought to the table simply because of the people who brought them. Tenayuca was, perhaps naively, a Communist, which nullified her participation in the strike almost immediately, giving the opposition the excuse they needed to consider the strike illegal and illegitimate. Barely beneath the surface of anti-Communist fervor was a tangle of anti-Mexican sentiment as well as sentiments against Tenayuca's gender and her choice to marry a white man, Homer Brooks, in a time when mixed marriages were met with disdain. This seemed as though Tenayuca was intent on breaking as many taboos as possible; certainly, she did not appear to consider the consequences of these actions and how they would be used against her as the strike progressed.

Historians suggest that Tenayuca's activism was rooted in her upbringing by a politically aware grandfather, who exposed her to San Antonio's open-air political soapboxes, where speakers touted and debated the latest revolutionary ideas from Mexico and those US cities that had a significant Mexican population. In an interview with historian Jerry Poyo, Tenayuca described a typical weekend with her grandfather: "Well, yes, when I was growing up . . . San Antonio was in a unique position here, because you had Carranzistas, you had followers of Obregón, Maderistas and then you had followers of the Magón brothers."[15] Tenayuca spent her youth listening to speeches advocating all manner of ideologies and political actions—and the ones that seemed to stick were ones that advocated worker's rights.

What historians have not done as well as documenting her upbringing is to examine Tenayuca's religious life. They have assumed that because she joined the Communist Party at the young age of twenty and did not tie her work to her Catholicism, her motivations to act on behalf of dispossessed Mexicanos/as was motivated by everything other than religion. This view of Tenayuca is shortsighted, particularly because it does not take into account the fact that most Mexican Catholics lived their faith lives outside the confines of the institutional church, where folk beliefs and practices—and certainly political causes considered at odds with the Church—would only find life in a robust investment in popular religious expressions. Thus, Tenayuca, a lifelong Catholic, was viewed in her death as a quasi-religious figure by her admirers, as someone who had some sense that she was doing the morally correct thing by being an activist. One need not use religious language to mark oneself as a Catholic; in fact, one did not even have to be a "practicing" Catholic to consider themselves Catholic. Although this runs against the standards of belonging within Roman Catholic orthodoxy, this is, of course, the point. Working-class Mexican Catholics sought out the refuge of their popular religious faith more so than their attachment to an institutional American church, which for decades did not have their interests in mind. Church officials were committed to training Mexican Catholics to be good institutional Catholics as well as good Americans. Tenayuca's religious biography is discussed later, but for now, a brief sketch of the strike and Tenayuca's role in bringing that action to pass is warranted.

Historian Zaragosa Vargas's argument regarding Tenayuca's Communist sympathies is that they were minimal, and what historians should be looking at was her desire to help the Mexicano/Mexicana community of San Antonio. He writes that "the Marxist ideology motivated the Tejana less than did her strong attachment to her working-class community."[16] He concludes that she joined the Communist Party because there was no one else helping the Mexicano community. "Driven by anti-communist obsession, San Antonio city bosses and the Catholic Church condemned Emma Tenayuca and launched a Red-baiting campaign to discredit her."[17] Despite the attempts to discredit her by her own church, Tenayuca did not renounce her Catholicism—but neither did she believe they were in any way an option for worker's rights in 1930s San Antonio. Tenayuca's first foray into labor strikes came in 1933 at the age of sixteen, when she walked a picket line on behalf of the cigar workers from the Finck Cigar company—the majority of whom were women, many threatened with deportation for striking by San Antonio police chief Owen Kilday.

Tenayuca's complicated relationship with her Catholicism may have begun with the cigar strike, since the owner of the cigar company was Catholic. Moreover, Catholic priests mobilized against Communism. As one historian has noted, San Antonio's Father Clem Casey and others "expressed an attitude that every union is a communist union. They backed Finck to the hilt. I was told that even in the confessional box they had been advised not to join."[18] This pattern seemed to tilt Tenayuca away from the Church and toward labor organizing. The anti-Communist fervor that controlled the Church's response to the cigar-worker's strike would also control San Antonio's civic, business, and religious elite's response to the pecan strike a few years later. The animus against Socialism for churches had historic roots going back to the Russian Revolution, where churches warned against the coming Bolshevik Revolution if loyalty to God and country were not made of prime importance in American's public schools and governmental agencies as well as its churches.

The continued animus toward Communism in the 1930s, particularly regarding Mexico and ensuring that Mexicans became good Americans, was part of the work in which the Church found no stronger advocate than the small but zealous Pentecostal movement along the borderlands. In operation in Kingsville, Texas, since 1915 under the leadership of Henry C. Ball, the Assemblies of God—a denomination founded in 1914 in Hot Springs, Arkansas—began targeting the San Antonio area in the 1920s and settled in Saspamco on a ranch where they ran a Bible school and a farm. Mexicano/Mexicana converts were offered the opportunity to work for their tuition in the Bible school, and training converts began in earnest. One of the reasons for the urgency in training Mexicanos and Mexicanas was the ongoing political revolutions in Mexico that made proselytizing in Mexico untenable, so training Mexicana/Mexicano converts in the United States with the express purpose of sending them back to counter the "Communism" taking over their country was never far from the mind of Henry Ball or his fellow missionaries. By examining the work of Ball and his associates in Texas, one can discern some of the ways that religious elites viewed Mexicans: they were uncivilized; they required supervision; they were easily swayed and therefore required supervision; and, ironically, they were considered both objects of pity, because of their poverty, and politically very dangerous, because of their ability to be radicalized into movements like Communism. For the religious elite of San Antonio, especially the Assemblies of God, the answer to Mexican poverty was for them to leave Catholicism and their political radicalism behind and become devout Pentecostals. They also thought all Mexicans should return to Mexico if they did not choose to assimilate as Americans and leave behind the taint of Mexican Communism.

Ball rarely if ever used the actual words of his charges when writing to the Assemblies of God headquarters in Springfield, Missouri. Most of the letters and articles printed in their weekly magazine, the *Pentecostal Evangel*, are Ball's interpretations of what Mexican converts were thinking and feeling. Rarely is there an authentic voice from Mexicans themselves. Coloring Ball's narration was his vociferous anti-Catholicism and his racist attitudes toward Mexicans. These attitudes as well as his political predilection toward conservatism meant that Ball simply could not see beyond his biases. He did not exhibit any self-reflection about them and was so convinced of the certainty of his religious convictions that he seemed to believe that those religious convictions carried over to his racial and political views. Although Ball noticed that the conditions for Mexicans living on the west side of San Antonio in the 1930s were clearly substandard and in fact were verging on criminally negligent, he was incapable of tying the dire poverty of Mexicans to anything other than their Catholicism. When he wandered into the dangerous territory of blaming the United States, he quickly backtracked so as not to offend potential donors. But there were times when he did not self-censor his feelings for Mexicans in San Antonio. In 1936, Ball wrote, "As a matter of fact I despised them [Mexicans] for their poverty and degradation. . . . The Mexican people do not seem to prosper in the United States. They have always been poor and they are still poor. Mexico seems to me a very pathetic nation . . . the American people hold them down as much as they possibly can. They will not give them a real chance to prosper. The Mexican people have to take the work, poorly paid work."[19]

Some of Ball's congregants were pecan shellers, so we can infer that Ball knew of their poor pay as well as the general poor pay for Mexican workers. By the mid-1930s, Ball blamed Mexican poverty on the stranglehold the Roman Catholic Church had on their money as well as the fact that the Church did not help them out. Even as Catholicism preoccupied Ball's proselytizing among Mexicans, Communist infiltration in San Antonio began to bother other Pentecostal missionaries in the area. Several months earlier, in July 1935, Ball's unnamed missions assistant wrote to Assemblies of God headquarters that San Antonio was perilously close to Communism's dangerous wiles. In his communication, he said, "The activities of the representatives of Communism are very manifest in many of the Latin American countries, and now the door to Mexico has been closed to future foreign missionary effort. . . . Let us remind our readers that our primary object is the evangelization of Old Mexico. We have to do our work from the American side . . . they would now both be property of the government and likely used to teach socialism & atheism, the favorite hobbies of the godless rulers of Mexico at the present time."[20]

Ball's secretary, writing on his behalf, is plainly making the case that converting Mexicans is a politically sound anti-Communist strategy, and that potential donors and readers of the *Evangel* do not have to worry because Ball's mission never intended for the Mexicans to stay in the United States. They fully expected them to go back as anti-Communists, inoculated against the socialist leanings of the Cardenas government, ready to take Mexico back both from the godless followers of Cardenas and the Romanist followers of the "false" church.

While traveling through San Angelo, Texas, in 1937, Ball mentioned how the Mexican pastors of the area were suffering under the Depression, with most of them on government relief.[21] In what would become a typical response to their depleted economic circumstances, Ball created a narration of the pastors' lives that found the answers to their material deficiencies solely in spiritual goals. This time, attending a missions conference, Ball concluded that poverty would be helped with a renewed zeal "for lost souls."[22] Ball informed his readers that most of his "trainees" worked in the cotton fields and had little or no formal education, adding that this was balanced by their experience of the baptism of the Holy Spirit.[23] However, in another letter, Ball acknowledged that his own pastors got cheated but did not have any remedy for that treatment.

If fellow missionary A. L. Branch's report in the Pentecostal magazine *Latter Rain Evangel* is credible, Ball's efforts at shaping the religious and political worldviews of his trainees paid off. Branch was impressed with the efforts of the pastors to raise Sunday school attendance, reflecting, "They settled like trained horses into the harness and pulled the Sunday School attendance from 292 to 434 in one week."[24] Branch, like Ball, narrates on behalf of the congregants of Templo Christiano, pastored by Rev. Josue Cruz, saying that all the hard work the Mexican saints have done has been done with the "hearty co-operation of many of the AG churches," adding that this ensured that they would be "traveling the glory road instead of the downward trail of Communism, as so many of the Mexicans are doing."[25] Again, what is important here is the agenda of both Branch and Ball to narrate an account of a sacrificial Mexican population, working through economic downtimes, zealously reaching out to their fellow Mexicans living in the deplorable conditions on San Antonio's west side, all the while accepting being mistreated by unscrupulous landlords.

This idealized portrait that Ball and others created about the long-suffering but compliant Mexican Pentecostal convert accomplished several things. For one, it made the "sell" to readers of the *Pentecostal Evangel* easier, since whatever monies they gave would surely be well spent with a group of people in such dire need because, presumably, they would be grateful for whatever they received. It also shored up the idea that the Assemblies of God held about their spiritual superiority over a supposedly "degraded" Catholic population, equating their Pentecostalism with thrift, sobriety, success, and progress. Finally, for the purposes of attempting to put some of these historical voices of workers—particularly pecan shellers—back into the story, what this imaginary did was turn their piecework, low wages, and substandard working conditions into places of potential spiritual victory to the exclusion of political success.

Ball's column about the pecan shellers steers clear of any potential labor strife (since there were strikes in 1935), does not side with the workers, and never mentions them by name. His column, titled "Revival Work among the Mexicans," has little in the way of news about revivals; rather, it contains a lot of his interpretations of Mexican poverty and working conditions for shellers. Beginning his piece with a comparison of the poverty he has seen among Mexicans in California and Mexicans in Texas, Ball expresses surprise that Mexicans are as bad off in both states, assuming that Texas would be much worse.

Ball's only comments about pecan shellers are worth quoting in their entirety:

> Many of our Mexican women work all week long shelling pecan nuts, making only 70 cents a week, some make a dollar and a quarter. Also many of our Mexican women sew, making the garments that are sold cheaply in the East and elsewhere. . . . We thank God we are working among these poor people who for centuries have been under the yoke of Romanism, who for centuries have been held down and degraded. But when the gospel of Christ comes to them, even though they live in such poverty, they have something in their lives, they have never had before. They can now shell pecan nuts and at the same time be singing "Glory To His Name." They have something now that fills the vacancy in their homes. Something that seems to drive out the extreme poverty. It does not always fill their stomachs, but at least it fills their hearts with joy.[26]

This imaginary Ball paints for his readers supports the contention that these creative narrations intended to promote the idea that Catholicism was to blame for the shellers' problems. Therefore, any sheller wanting to go on strike would have been pressured not to do so because they would no doubt be going out with Catholic strikers. In the 1930s Assemblies of God world, especially among Latino/Latina converts, part of the strategy for conversion was to turn them away from institutional Catholicism, which was corrupting, and from popular Catholicism, which was idolatrous.

This narration also succeeds in laying blame for low wages on that same Catholic Church. Ball claimed that their newfound faith could act as an antidote to the misery of shelling pecans. Yet he was less sure about whether their faith would be sufficient to counter their poverty. Only this last imaginary is directly contradicted by the labor strikes of 1934, 1935, and especially 1938. Because Ball did not mention the labor issues, let alone whether any of his congregants was a striker, one has to enter the realm of the imaginary and deduce that Mexican Pentecostal women would have been discouraged from striking. Not only were they taught that their working situation was a result of the lingering effects of Catholicism, but they were also told that they suffered from anti-Christian, Communist ideas. Perhaps the most pressing influence on Pentecostal shellers was echoed by Ball himself: there was no longer any need to view their temporal, material lives as indicators of happiness or success. Their conversion ensured salvation.

In one of many ironies, neither Ball's Assemblies of God nor the Archdiocese of San Antonio had political ideologies or theologies suited for systemic social action. The early years of the Assemblies were marked by the immediacy of the eschaton, making involvement in politics unnecessary. The Catholic Church, unburdened by the premillennial schema for centuries, reverted to the "contamination" thesis—simply working alongside Communists led to moral corruption. What the Catholic Church of 1930s San Antonio failed to see was that Tenayuca's moral imperative to better the lives of pecan shellers was based on her Catholicism. Communism was a vehicle to live out deeply held beliefs about social justice. Henry C. Ball, on the other hand, would not only have had difficulty with Tenayuca's Communism, which would have made her an object of scorn, but also her Catholicism, which would have made her a subject of conversion.

Another parallel working in Ball's imaginary was the idea that shellers were not suffering as much as people were led to believe. Seligmann's conflicts with his Judaism and his work as an entrepreneur again were not played out by him, but rather by his rabbi, who tried, ultimately unsuccessfully, to get Seligmann to play fairly.

Seligmann, like Ball, saw it was in his best interest to narrate the pecan-shellers' experience and downplay their lack. As he put it, "The Mexicans don't want much money, the Mexicans have no business here anyway . . . they flock into San Antonio with their kind and then they cause labor troubles or go on relief at the expense of the tax payer."[27] Seligmann repeated some of the more common tropes about Mexican working life in the United States—that they did not belong here, that they came in large numbers when they did migrate, and that they were a drain on government resources. What he did not mention was that by refusing to mechanize his plant in the early 1930s, instead choosing to rely on cheap Mexican labor, he created the situation for more workers to move to San Antonio to take work as shellers. Seligmann also wanted to make the point that shellers received adequate compensation because, in addition to the five cents they earned per pound, they ate the product as they worked.[28]

Historian Karl Preuss contextualizes the small Jewish population of less than seven thousand. Within Preuss's framework, Seligmann was part of the industrialist class, inclined toward Reformed Judaism and largely from German roots that set up shop in San Antonio specifically to take advantage of the Mexican labor force. In this case, Seligmann was doing what others had done before. For example, Charles Schwartz moved his shirt- and dressmaking company from Chicago to San Antonio in 1918. In 1934, the International Ladies Garment Worker's Union sent organizers to San Antonio to unionize the Mexicanas who dominated that industry. When fifty Mexicanas went on strike in 1936, there were violent clashes on the picket lines.[29]

Preuss has argued that Reform rabbis had a different social context than their counterparts in large urban areas. For these rabbis in the South, many of them found themselves with congregations composed of conservative business and civic leaders. These Southern Jews, aware of their difference in San Antonio, tried their best to blend into the community without arousing suspicion that they were sympathetic to leftist causes, especially those that included African Americans.[30] For Jews in San Antonio, other worries included localized aspects of national issues: the rise of nativism, religious fundamentalism, and anti-Semitism. When Temple Beth-El rabbi Ephraim Frisch responded to a controversial police raid of Worker's Alliance headquarters by calling that action on par with the likes of "Mussolini, Stalin or Hitler," he set off a firestorm of controversy among his congregation, and especially his board, of which Julius Seligmann was a member. The raid was conducted at the behest of police chief Owen Kilday, who rarely tolerated union activities and took it upon himself to use the power of his office to root out Communist influences—either real or perceived. Frisch's language precipitated some in his congregation to brand him as "radical," even though he had a history of liberal social activism for over a decade before the 1937 raid.[31] Kilday was looking for evidence that the labor unrest and organizing attempts by the Worker's Alliance stemmed from Communist influences. Since Tenayuca was the chief organizer of the Worker's Alliance and had joined the Communist Party in 1937, what Kilday found was enough to begin his watch of Tenayuca. With the shellers' strike occurring months later, Tenayuca's Communist membership was enough to make her leadership of the strike in February 1938 a very short reign.

Before Frisch made his comments about the police raid, he had already run afoul of many of the business and civic leaders who worshipped at Temple Beth-El. According to Preuss, Frisch delivered several sermons excoriating the businessmen's lack of ethics and their brazen profiteering without regard to their ethical commitments as Jews.

Frisch disapproved of Seligmann's treatment of the shellers. Some of Frisch's messages were cautionary tales about the immorality of unfettered capitalism. He accused the business community of predatory practices and he denounced the profit motive as soulless. The successful business leaders in his congregation disliked his sermons.[32] Weary of the labor strikes that seemed to occur with regularity in San Antonio, Frisch's support of strikers and a host of worker causes made him unpopular, although, as Preuss notes, Frisch was already unpopular with conservatives in his congregation, the business community, and Archbishop Arthur J. Droessarts.

Droessarts was the main reason the Catholic Church did not support workers in 1930s San Antonio; he viewed any capitulation to Communist influences as unacceptable. Droessarts was suspicious of Frisch early on, after Frisch let it be known that he had supported the Republicans in the Spanish Civil War (1936–39). This animosity toward Frisch did not result in him leaving voluntarily. The board, opined Preuss, tried to diminish his influence by hiring a younger, more personable, and non-Communist rabbi, David Jacobsen. Frisch, though, was convinced that Jacobsen's hiring meant his tenure was near an end and decided to retire in 1942 rather than risk being fired.

Frisch, never an easy person to get along with, seemed to lack the political awareness and self-control that often comes with religious leadership. As such, his support of workers and comments about the San Antonio police bearing resemblances to Stalin, Mussolini, and Hitler were controversial for two reasons. First, it was feared that Frisch's perceived disloyalty would fuel a growing anti-Semitism in the United States. Second, it allowed detractors outside the temple to question whether Frisch was so unstable that perhaps it was time for him to retire. Preuss adds that the larger question in San Antonio, where the Jewish population was never very high, became the overwhelming drive toward assimilation. Particularly prone to rapid assimilation were German Jews who "had become so assimilated into the non-Jewish community, they had lost sight of the ethical precepts of social justice that undergirded the Reform movement."[33]

In terms of the shellers' strike, there did not appear to be any view that Seligmann's intransigence as the owner at offering workers a decent wage or better working conditions had anything to do with the other stereotype—that of Jewish businessmen who had no other interests than making money. In fact, Tenayuca appears to be very grateful that Frisch supported the shellers' strike. She wrote him a thank-you note that was appreciative of his efforts on their behalf and for his earlier stand on the police raid.[34] Moreover, Preuss has suggested that the religious elite in Reform Judaism thus diminished their ability to promote Judaism's ethical component. In fact, this move toward assimilation for both Mexicans and Jews tended to be what anti-Communist activists sought with their attempts to purge any hint of Communist influence in the lives of Americans.

Soon after the strike began, police chief Kilday organized a raid on Tenayuca and the Worker's Alliance. He was looking for incriminating evidence that the head of organizing for the Worker's Alliance was "nothing but a paid agitator sent here to stir up trouble among the ignorant Mexicans."[35] Like Ball, Kilday and Droessarts narrated their own view of Mexican workers, almost always beginning with the idea that they were intellectually incapable of independent thought. The difference was that Kilday's political agenda did not include a religious component. There was, however, an explicit religious agenda behind the archdiocese's attempts to smear Tenayuca. In a curious attempt to portray her as disloyal and somehow treacherous to her own people, the official Catholic newspaper, La Voz, wrote, "In the midst of this community exists a woman by the name of Emma Tenayuca who wants to spread disorder and hatred. . . . Mrs. Teneyuca [sic] de Brooks is not a Mexican, she is a Rusofile, sold out to Russia, communist. If she was a Mexican, she should not be doing that type of work."[36] Hoping to capitalize not only on anti-Communism but also on the idea that Tenayuca was a traitor to her Mexican-ness by marrying a white man, this approach seems to be meant to cast doubt on Tenayuca's political as well as ethnic loyalty. Capitalizing on their monopoly over the religious life of San Antonio's Mexican community, their attempts to portray Tenayuca as disloyal did not extend to her own Catholicism, which by all accounts she retained for the rest of her life.

In an interview with historian Jerry Poyo, Tenayuca reflects on the importance of the Church in her young life: "What really kept us together was the church—St. Agnes. I made my first communion there, I attended catechism classes. I stayed through . . . 12 years old."[37] Raised by her grandparents, her grandfather was not a regular churchgoer, but her grandmother was. As such, the institutional church was not a large part of her life past the age where she would have made her confirmation. In terms of her attitudes toward the Church, she seemed to have great admiration for priests who sacrificed for their faith, such as those who were being "thrown out" of Mexico during the revolution. She notes with some sadness that there was not one Mexican priest who came to St. Agnes in the time she was regularly attending; all her priests were Spaniards.[38] However, she did mention to Poyo that the Irish priest who helped her through her catechism class regaled her with stories of Irish resistance to poor treatment in parts of non-Republican Ireland. She was inspired by Irish Catholics' fight for civil rights against Northern Irish Protestants.[39]

When it came to her own sense of what being a "good" Catholic meant, Tenayuca is more circumspect, offering this example of what a bad Catholic might look like. "And this guy, Finch, FINCK, this guy here was a devout Catholic. I don't know where his father is whether he's up above or down below somewhere, but he was close." Tenayuca laughed at her depiction of the owner of the Finck Cigar company as being in hell. As one of the organizers and sympathizers of the cigar worker's striker of 1933, Tenayuca judged the Catholic owner of the company based on his treatment of workers—which, by her account, was deplorable enough to earn him an eternity of endless torment.

The San Antonio Archdiocese within which Tenayuca grew up was already under the control of conservative archbishop Droessarts. He wanted to ensure rapid Americanization of his large Mexican congregations. Droessarts erected separate churches for Mexican Catholics because they were "strangers among strange people." David Badillo adds, "Mexicans and Mexican Americans in San Antonio did not have much say in allocating priests and overseeing pastoral work, partly due to the absence of a genuine immigrant clergy capable of bridging the gap between the increasingly diverse lay community and the episcopacy. Frequently they found themselves besieged [by] patterns of labor exploitation and and a pervasive anti-Mexican racial animus."[40] As such, Catholic instruction played a dual role in the archdiocese; it provided both traditional religious instruction and pedagogies for effective Americanization education. Droessarts's goal was to "acquire some knowledge of our English language . . . and perhaps even some thin veneer of American ways and manners."[41] The goals, then, of the religious elite of the Catholic Church were to secure Catholic identity through the practice of institutional Catholicism and continued patterns of Americanization. For Mexicanos though, as Badillo writes, their Catholic identity, played out as vibrant popular devotions, primarily among women towards the Virgen de Guadalupe, secured their identity as Catholics even when access to priests remained scarce.[42]

When it came to the shellers' strike, although more than 90 percent of them were Catholics, the Church opposed the strike because of the Communist influence. Along with Droessarts, Father Juan Lopez of the National Catholic Welfare Council acted as the spokesperson for the shellers during the first days of the strike. His agenda included rooting out the Communists from the CIO. The CIO assumed control of the strike days later and Tenayuca had by that time voluntarily removed herself from the strike because her Communist membership was neutralizing her ability to organize workers. Lopez supported the workers, but opposed the strike even though he found conditions for the shellers among "the most disgraceful among Mexicans in the United States."[43] Historian Matthew Keyworth describes Lopez's politicking on behalf of the strikers, promoting the idea that they charter with the CIO rather than the UCAPAWA, whom Lopez viewed as hopelessly tainted by Communist influence. When having to answer critics' charge that the Church failed the strikers, Lopez's retort is similar to Ball's response for why Mexican shellers were better off converting to Pentecostalism. Lopez and Droessarts both resorted to the trope that Catholicism brought Mexicans out of their pagan indigenous religions and in doing so, brought them civilization. Droessarts, echoing Ball's sentiments about how much better off the pecan shellers were even though they were living in miserable conditions earning terrible wages, responded that "the public must support the police department's fight to exterminate the most dangerous of all doctrines: atheist Communism."[44]

Nearly every major organization chose not to support the strike. The more conservative Latino and/or civil rights organizations—the League of United Latin American Citizens (LULAC), the Mexican Chamber of Commerce, the normally sympathetic San Antonio Ministerial Association, and even the International Ladies Garment Worker's Union—refused to support the strike because of the Communist influence they all saw as represented by Tenayuca's initial organization and leadership of the strike.[45] Lopez added that the Communist influence could not be allowed to stand, since it would bring from within the "corruption of the morals of the Catholic workers."[46]

All this opposition leads to speculation about what kind of threat, if any, Tenayuca posed. What were her actions around the strike that might have caused alarm? It is to the strike itself and the aftermath of Tenayuca's blacklisting and exile that we turn next.

Laura Cannon Dixon shows that the drive to paint Tenayuca as a dangerous and orthodox Communist began immediately. When the strike occurred in the winter of 1938, Chief Kilday refused to acknowledge the legal rights of strikers to picket and trotted out many obscure laws about the holding of signs in an attempt to crush the strike through legal maneuvering. While that went on, strikers by the hundreds were arrested for these arcane infractions. When officers were brought to court to answer to why these laws were being enforced when they had not been observed in years, they changed the subject, noting that their work was critical because it involved exposing the fact that Tenayuca, despite her "resignation," was still working with the union. One officer claimed he had overheard her saying that once the Communists got control, they were going to "burn the churches and murder the priests like they do in Russia."[47] Given Tenayuca's being a lifelong Catholic who had expressed her admiration for priests and knew they were suffering persecution in Mexico, one seriously doubts the police officer's claim. No matter; when it came to Red-baiting, anything and everything was fair game.

Tenayuca never denied being a Communist. She and her husband Homer did try to tell workers about the positive effects of Communist worker revolt, but San Antonio's Tejano and Mexican workers did not join the party in large numbers.[48] Looking back at her relationship with Brooks, Tenayuca admitted that it was Brooks who was a more uncompromising and inflexible orthodox Communist than she was, telling historian Poyo that "[Brooks] would not make compromises for anything. He didn't have a sense of humor; my background was absolutely different from his."[49] They divorced shortly after marrying in 1937 and she left the Communist Party, due in large part to the Soviet/Nazi alliance. Historian Zaragosa Vargas suggests that Tenayuca's lack of organizing after the shellers' strike was directly tied to the vested interest of San Antonio Red-baiting her out of public life.

Tenayuca's organizing began earlier than her work with the pecan shellers. When she was twenty, she organized the Workers Alliance, expanding it to fifteen branches with about three thousand members each. This became her base when she continued to organize and support the pecan shellers. Every major civic organization was against the strike and nearly all of them chose to Red-bait Tenayuca. Even her own Catholic Church was fearful that this union strike would inspire more Communist insurgency. Vargas writes, "The Catholic Archdiocese's responses to the strike grew out of its paternalism towards Mexicans, but it was also driven by the desire to battle communist influences that threatened to seize union leadership. The 1937 Papal Encyclical, "Divini Redemptoris," made the case that it was up to the Church to prevent the spread of communism among 100,000 Spanish-speaking parishioners."[50]

The strike lasted three months. One thousand picketers were arrested, tear gas was used, and the police and fire departments were drafted for riot duty. Both mayor C. K. Quin and police chief Kilday refused to acknowledge the strike. Historian Gabriela González analyzed Tenayuca's activism as compared to a contemporary activist, Carolina Munguía, with an eye toward the gender and class differences between the two.

Carolina Munguía was a teacher from San Antonio's middle class, born in Mexico. Her focus was on training Mexican women to be proper Mexican women. Tenayuca was born in San Antonio; she organized both male and female workers. Munguía's activism followed a familiar trajectory. Even though she was Catholic, she did most of her work under the auspices of the Methodist Church and the mainline Protestant commitment to service. Tenayuca's social and political involvement, formed by her exposure to the politically charged surroundings of San Antonio in the 1920s, did not attach her political activism to any prevailing institutional Catholic influence but it would seem that Tenayuca's sense of fairness and justice foreshadowed the turn the Catholic Church made in the mid-twentieth century toward liberation and a vibrant social-justice agenda.[51] Tenayuca was also affected by the specter of race. Tenayuca's father was ostracized from his family because he was *puro Indio*: in the complicated race politics of Mexico, dark-skinned Mexicans of "pure" Indian stock rank lowest in the racial hierarchy; mestizos (mixed-blood Spanish and Indian stock) are in the middle; and the lightest-skinned, mostly European-blood stock, are at the top. Tenayuca kept that in mind and part of her organizing strategy was not to leave the immigrant Mexicanos behind. She had no patience for organizations like LULAC, a conservative civil rights organization that distanced themselves from organizing immigrant Mexicans. Tenayuca's brief stint with LULAC began and ended in high school, when they refused to help her organize Mexicanos.

Tenayuca's marriage, along with much of her personal life after her organizing years were over, is not well known. What is known is that she married fellow Communist organizer Homer Brooks in October 18, 1937, and divorced him in April 1941. According to González, "though married during the height of her political activism, [Tenayuca] did not organize around the mantle of domesticity."[52] Quite the iconoclastic public figure, when Tenayuca was forced to leave Texas in the 1950s and headed to San Francisco to go to college, she had a son and apparently raised him on her own while establishing a life in California. Tenayuca's personal life beyond her organizing is largely cordoned off by her heir and niece Sharyll Soto Tenayuca, who donated her aunt's papers to Texas Women's University but sealed all her private correspondences, which might have given more insight into Tenayuca's post-organizing California years.

We know much more about what led to her exile first to Houston and then to San Francisco, her college years there, and her teaching career both in San Francisco and in San Antonio, where she finally returned. It is difficult to see how Tenayuca and Brooks used their Communist organizing and advocacy to profoundly affect the political and religious elite around them. At the time, perhaps it was naïveté and a lack of understanding about the ferocious anti-Communism they were subjected to; it is only with the benefit of decades separating us from the events that we can even begin to understand the collective anxiety that looking for Communist influences in every aspect of mundane life must have wrought on a public who had been prepared by incessant political propaganda to believe that there may indeed have been a Communist under every bed.

Tenayuca's organizing of the shellers' strike ended when other unions refused to help the strikers while she was in charge. She took her activities underground and a year later resurfaced when the Worker's Alliance, at that time dominated by Communist Party members, requested and secured a permit to hold a rally at the San Antonio Municipal Auditorium. When rumors spread that the progressive and newly elected mayor of San Antonio, Maury Maverick—elected with the help of the Mexican vote, to the consternation of the archdiocese—had allowed Communists to hold meetings, anti-Communists became highly agitated. Arriving at the auditorium with hopes of stopping Tenayuca and Brooks from speaking were, among others, a local Catholic priest and the American Legion; their arrival helped spark a riot at the auditorium when Tenayuca, Brooks, and other members of the Worker's Alliance began singing the national anthem. The KKK also joined the riot, which caused Tenayuca and her husband to be rushed off stage out of the auditorium via an alternative exit; the KKK threatened more than the mere rampage of bottle throwing and subsequent chaos that would ensue if they got their hands on either one of them.[53]

Unable to continue organizing and blacklisted by employers in the San Antonio area, Tenayuca first went to Houston where she struggled to find work and engaged in some sporadic organizing activity throughout the 1940s. The FBI began a file on her during that time, even though when she divorced Brooks in 1941, she also left the Communist Party, disillusioned by its activities in Europe during World War II. In 1942, she applied to join the WAAC (Women's Army Auxiliary Corps); they initially accepted her, but then upon a second pass rejected her application without comment, no doubt influenced by a standard background check, which would have meant a review of her FBI file.[54]

In the 1950s, raising her son, she received a degree from San Francisco State University and became a teacher. She did not return to San Antonio until 1968, where she continued her teaching career. She spent some of her retirement being rediscovered by a cadre of aspiring academics and literary types who found inspiration in her life story. She herself discovered, by the time she retired in the late 1980s, that she was an iconic figure in Texas labor and Latina history. When she died in 1999, several well-known literary figures, including Carmen Tafolla and Maria Antonietta Berriozábal, contributed pieces to her eulogy that encapsulated her political life and in the process turned her into a religious figure. Of particular note is Berriozábal's take on the traditional Catholic rosary. Said the day before the funeral at the wake, the rosary was a retelling of the traditional mysteries of the rosary, with Tenayuca and the Virgin Mary sharing equal space as revered figures of Mexican religious life.

For Berriozábal, Emma was like the Mary in her willingness to sacrifice for her people, to endure long suffering on behalf of all Mexicans—immigrant and those born in the United States. Like Mary, Tenayuca answered her call and said yes, even though there would be difficult challenges in answering that call. "A woman of great faith, she did not question how things would be accomplished or who would listen or if her work would be fruitful."[55]

Tenayuca, as historian Vargas and poet Tafolla conclude, was much more driven by her love of her Mexican community than by ideology. At her funeral, Tafolla shared a short quote from one of Tenayuca's last interviews with her; when asked whether she had any bitterness or resentment toward those forces who forced her into exile, Tenayuca responded, "If I had any hatred in those years, I wouldn't have lasted at all. Hatred is self-destructive . . . you have to love for a cause."[56]

It took at least another generation for American and US Latino/Latina Catholicism to see its way toward an embrace of an active social-justice agenda. In many ways, Tenayuca's agenda for justice would not have come from an institutional Catholic upbringing, where she would have been taught under the auspices of Archbishop Droessarts that the most important thing good Catholics should have been doing in the 1930s was helping to weed out Communism. One doubts that Tenayuca would have heard anything about justice and advocacy for the Mexican community until the arrival of Archbishop Robert E. Lucey, who succeeded Droessarts in 1941. By then, Tenayuca was divorced, no longer a Communist, and trying to cobble together a living in Houston. It was only by living outside the boundaries of institutional Catholicism that Tenayuca was able to put any of her activism to work. As she told another interviewer about her approach to issues, "You see a problem, and if you have any morality, you take up the issue."[57] I share Vargas's contention that Tenayuca's activism was driven much more by her love for the Mexican community and less by her husband's doctrinaire Communism. I further suggest that much of Tenayuca's ethics derive not from churchgoing or the administration of the sacraments, but from her deinstitutionalized Catholicism—and ethic of self-sacrifice and justice toward the less fortunate. Her reaction to the Finck Cigar owner's hypocrisy and her interviews later in life lead one to conclude that the Catholicism Tenayuca was raised in was insufficient in its social-justice component and therefore, as Vargas notes, Tenayuca gravitated to the only group that was doing anything for the working Mexican communities of San Antonio: the Communist Party. In short, the Catholicism that Tenayuca could have drawn from explicitly and, I suggest, that she drew from implicitly, did not exist in 1930s San Antonio.

Notes

1. Karl Preuss, "Personality, Politics and the Price of Justice: Ephraim Frisch, San Antonio's 'Radical' Rabbi," *American Jewish History* 85, no. 3 (1997): 270.

2. Kenneth P. Walker, "The Pecan Shellers of San Antonio and Mechanization," *Southwestern Historical Quarterly* 69, no. 1 (July 1965): 45.

3. Preuss, "Personality, Politics, and the Price of Justice," 272.

4. Walker, "Pecan Shellers of San Antonio," 46.

5. Zaragosa Vargas, "Radical: Emma Tenayuca and the San Antonio Labor Movement during the Great Depression," *Pacific Historical Review* 66, no. 4 (1997): 558.

6. Walker, "Pecan Shellers of San Antonio," 47.

7. Vargas, "Radical," 560.

8. Matthew Keyworth, "Poverty, Solidarity and Opportunity: The 1938 San Antonio Pecan Shellers Strike" (master's thesis, Texas A&M University, 2007), 55.

9. Ibid., 57.

10. Gabriela González, "Carolina Munguía and Emma Tenayuca: The Politics of Benevolence and Radical Reform," *Frontiers: A Journal of Women Studies* 24, nos. 2–3 (2003): 213.

11. Ibid.

12. Walker, "Pecan Shellers of San Antonio," 47; González, "Carolina Munguía and Emma Tenayuca," 213.

13. Walker, "Pecan Shellers of San Antonio," 49.

14. Patricia E. Gower, "Unintended Consequences: The San Antonio Pecan Shellers Strike of 1938," *Journal of the Life and Culture of San Antonio,* available at www.uiw.edu/sanantonio/gower.html.

15. Jerry Poyo, interview with Emma Tenayuca, Oral History Project, University of Texas–San Antonio, Libraries Digital Collections, transcript, 1987, 9.

16. Vargas, "Radical," 556.

17. Ibid., 557.

18. González, "Carolina Munguía and Emma Tenayuca," 211.

19. Henry C. Ball, "What God Hath Wrought," *Pentecostal Evangel (PE)*, March 14, 1939, 1, 5–6.

20. "A Visit among Our Latin American Brethren," *PE,* 13 July 1935, 9.

21. Henry C. Ball, "Our Latin American Work," *PE,* 20 November 1937, 8.

22. Ibid., 8.

23. Ibid., 10.

24. A. L. Branch, "A Mexican Pentecostal Church," *Latter Rain Evangel,* April 1938, 22.

25. Ibid.

26. Henry C. Ball, "Revival Work among the Mexicans," *PE,* 26 October 1935, 3.

27. Preuss, "Personality, Politics, and the Price of Justice," 270.

28. Ibid., 270.

29. "Encyclopedia of Southern Jewish Communities: San Antonio," Goldring/ Woldenberg Institute of Southern Jewish Life, www.isjl.org/history/archive/tx/san-antonio.html, accessed 1 September 2013.

30. Preuss, "Personality, Politics, and the Price of Justice," 267.

31. Ibid., 263.

32. Ibid., 272.

33. Ibid., 288.

34. Ibid., 288.

35. Ibid., 272.

36. Vargas, "Radical," 569.

37. Poyo, interview with Emma Tenayuca, Oral History Project, University of Texas–San Antonio, Libraries Digital Collections, transcript, 1987, 9.

38. Ibid., 12.

39. Ibid., 37.

40. David A. Badillo, "Between Alienation and Ethnicity: The Evolution of Mexican-American Catholicism in San Antonio," *Journal of American Ethnic History* 16, no. 4 (Summer 1997): 62. Academic Search Premier, EBSCOhost, accessed 8 June 2015.

41. Ibid., 24.

42. Ibid., 26.

43. Keyworth, "Poverty, Solidarity and Opportunity," 130.

44. Ibid., 130.

45. Ibid., 112–13.

46. Gower, "Unintended Consequences," 3.

47. Laura Cannon Dixon, "Police Brutality Makes Headlines: Retelling the Story of the 1938 Pecan Shellers Strike" (master's thesis, Indiana State University, 2010), 36.

48. Ibid., 10.

49. Poyo, interview with Emma Tenayuca, Oral History Project, University of Texas–San Antonio, Libraries Digital Collections, transcript, 1987, 39; Vargas, "Radical," 553–80.

50. Vargas, "Radical," 568.

51. González, "Carolina Munguía and Emma Tenayuca," 209.

52. Ibid., 201.

53. Vargas, "Radical," 217.

54. Ibid., 219.

55. Maria Antonietta Berriozábal, "Emma and Maria," *Frontiers: A Journal of Women Studies* 24, nos. 2–3 (2003): 230.

56. Carmen Tafolla, "La Pasionera," *Frontiers: A Journal of Women Studies* 24, nos. 2–3 (2003): 234.

57. Quote taken from the cover of a play performed in Tenayuca's honor: "Altar 4 Emma," by Beva Sánchez-Padilla, Our Lady of the Lake University, Center for Mexican American Studies, 2008.

7

Radical Christianity and Cooperative Economics in the Postwar South

ALISON COLLIS GREENE

The story could begin at the beginning:

It is January 1939. A crowd gathered at the Tyrrell County Training School quiets as eighty-year-old Eliza Jones rises slowly to her feet to speak: "I got five cents as says there ought to be a savings club in this here community." Six months of study clubs among farmers and teachers culminate in this moment. Jones's five-cent investment launches the Light of Tyrrell Credit Union in Tyrrell County, a remote coastal swampland in northeastern North Carolina.[1]

The credit union's name reflects the troubles, the effort, and the hopes of its members. Scattered across the small townships of Columbia, Alligator, Scuppernong, and Gum Neck, African Americans compose 36 percent of Tyrrell County's 5,500 souls but own less than 10 percent of its farmland. Most farm someone else's land. Tyrrell's sparse population is nonetheless too large for the islands of dry ground between the swamps and the fields of corn, beans, and potatoes. Many citizens reside in the swamps, in unpainted houses that teeter on rotting stilts sunk into soggy ground. Cardboard covers the windows, and burlap keeps flies and mosquitoes from the open doorways. In summer, the air sits hot and thick; in winter, it gusts with a biting chill. For a black farmer, credit is about as hard to find as dry ground. The founders of the Light of Tyrrell plan to provide an alternative to usurious lending rates, help black farmers save their land and their homes, and offer loans to fill the swamps and build livable houses with electricity. They envision improvements to health care, education, farming, community life—all the result of a local, grassroots effort.[2]

The story could also start at the beginning of the end:

It is just past nightfall on Monday, August 11, 1947. A young couple hud-dles together in a swampy ditch that stretches between green rows of corn. Nearby, two young men flatten themselves on the ground beneath the corn-stalks; one more clings to the trunk of a tree on the field's edge. On a typical summer evening, these students would sit together in the twilight and talk over the din of croaking frogs in the nearby swamp. As they ended a day of hard work with group Bible study and prayer, they would swat occasionally at the mosquitoes that buzzed around them. But not tonight. Tonight, they do not hear the frogs and they dare not swat the mosquitoes. Tonight, they pray more fervently, more quietly. Tonight, they hide.[3]

Seven weeks earlier, a multiracial group of nine college and divinity stu-dents representing the Fellowship of Southern Churchmen arrived in rural Tyrrell County to construct a new store for the Light of Tyrrell, a success-ful African American farming cooperative and credit union. They planned to provide a Christian model of interracial cooperation and cohabitation to the county's white inhabitants. Ultimately, the camp's leader explained, they hoped to help "[burst] the bonds of race and culture that divide the human family." The campers' ongoing struggle to find adequate lodging, meals, worksite, tools, and transportation would have driven most people away—and were intended to do just that. But the students were determined to stay. It would take a moonlit mob of three hundred men to scatter them to the cornfields, and it would take a midnight chat with the local sheriff to persuade them to leave town the next morning.[4]

This pair of stories—a grassroots beginning and a white backlash sparked by charges of outside agitation—suggests an all-too-familiar civil rights nar-rative. Yet, in 1940s North Carolina, two communities—the black farmers and professionals in Tyrrell County and the multiracial network of leftist Protestants who applauded and supported their work—open up a new kind of civil rights story. Theirs is a story of interaction, interdependence, and partnerships built on a shared belief in the inseparability of economic and racial justice.

Historians have long emphasized the turn from a Depression-era empha-sis on economic and racial justice as two parts of a greater whole to a Cold War–era focus on civil rights and racial integration. The anti-Communism of the postwar years, they contend, crippled the economic critique and forced activists in a new direction.[5] Jarod Roll, Erik Gellman, and others have begun to complicate this narrative by describing the ongoing economic activism among radical Protestants, while civil rights historians like Hassan Jeffries and

Françoise Hamlin have emphasized the revival of the economic critique—or "freedom rights"—when civil rights and voting rights achievements of the 1950s and 1960s failed to produce true equality.[6]

If the "classic phase" of the civil rights movement still appears to be a story of rights divorced from economics, that story is already frayed at the edges.[7] This is a story of two of those edges—a swampy outpost on North Carolina's eastern fringe and a prophetic movement on Protestantism's left periphery. Together, activists and everyday people at these edges imagined a world where equal opportunity grew from mutual respect and shared responsibility. Together, they concluded that racial equality required economic equality. Together, they fought for both.

Before they joined forces, the Light of Tyrrell and the Fellowship of Southern Churchmen fought separate battles, beginning a few years and a few hundred miles apart.

"A New Economic Life"[8]

The principal of the Tyrrell County Training School, Simpson P. (S. P.) Dean, organized the meeting that prompted Eliza Jones to lay down her nickel. Dean was neither native nor new to Tyrrell County. He had been principal of its black high school for ten years when he decided to quit the job, and the county. The oldest of eleven college-educated children born in New York, Dean had transformed Tyrrell County's four-room, unpainted shack for black students into a model rural school with a new building and seven faculty. He began the work himself in the midst of the Great Depression, taking out a personal loan to fill the swamp, construct a new building, and provide transportation for students. Then the state of North Carolina took over the busing, and the New Deal's National Youth Administration added a new vocational arts building. Private philanthropic funds followed to support new teachers and courses. Dean deemed his decade of service finished, and in the summer of 1937, he moved to New York City to take courses at Columbia University. He planned to finish his master's degree in education and leave rural North Carolina behind.[9]

Dean's summer course in rural education seemed an easy enough introduction to graduate school. The professor, Mabel Carney, had recently returned from a study of cooperatives among Nova Scotia's fishermen, and she argued that rural black schools could likewise introduce cooperative principles and teach their communities to combine resources and work toward economic independence.[10]

Cooperatives like those Carney described worked simply. Marginalized community members joined forces and resources to claim a measure of control over their own labor and finances. Workers might pool funds to make bulk purchases and avoid markups by local merchants; farmers might combine their harvests and hold them for bulk sale at better prices; community members might chip in monthly savings to create a fund for health or burial expenses. More elaborate cooperation could foster local credit unions that made small loans from collective investments. Cooperatives first appeared in early industrial Europe in the eighteenth century, and by the turn of the twentieth century had become a popular economic model among critics of modern capitalism. Some saw cooperatives as a way to ameliorate the ills of capitalism; others as a gradual and welcome shift toward socialism. Successful cooperative models thus proved irresistible to a range of reformers, from committed radicals to lukewarm progressives.[11]

Cooperatives held particular promise in the South, because they allowed local communities simultaneously to circumvent and to challenge segregation by disconnecting poor farmers from economic structures that served white elites and pushed black farmers off their land. A few Southern cooperative experiments were interracial; most were not. But because cooperatives sought to undermine the economic power of the white elite over the poor of both races, even segregated ones threatened a Jim Crow order dependent on a ready supply of divided, passive, and desperate workers. Carney argued that schools provided the ideal training ground for cooperative organizing, and this lesson resonated with Dean, who knew of just such a school not too far from his home in Tyrrell County.[12]

Brick Rural Life School in Edgecombe County operated a demonstration farm and rural life education center focused on teaching local families better farming practices. The school first opened in 1846 as an American Missionary Association junior high school, then became a junior college, and again changed course after 1925, when North Carolina invested in black colleges. Its higher-education programs now redundant, Brick School shut them down and reopened as a farm and adult education center. Soon, it helped community members organize a credit union that made small loans to farmers and a cooperative store that allowed locals to pool resources and buy in bulk. The school proved remarkably successful in its new mission to cultivate local leaders and instill in community members a commitment to racial uplift, economic cooperation, and adult education.[13]

Dean took what he knew of North Carolina and what he learned in New York, and he concluded that his work in Tyrrell County was not finished after all. His feet had scarcely hit North Carolina soil again at summer's end when he set to work. First, Dean enlisted a few of his teachers and a local minister to introduce cooperative ideals in the community and the school. English students wrote poetry about cooperatives, math students learned to calculate interest rates, and agriculture and home economics students arranged buying clubs. Dean also began to pull together study clubs in communities across Tyrrell County to gather and discuss the need for a credit union like the one at Brick School. That school's success had taught Dean about the importance of local buy-in, and Mabel Carney's course had given him some ideas about how to organize.[14]

Dean made no secret of his faith in education, and he cultivated the Light of Tyrrell in his school. Although he kept his religious ideas—or lack of them—to himself, Dean also understood the importance of local churches. Tyrrell County's only town, Columbia, boasted three established black churches: one missionary Baptist, one Disciples of Christ, and one African Methodist Episcopal Zion. Dean sought the support of those churches and their ministers, as well as of churches in surrounding communities. Dean and the Light of Tyrrell members embraced religious metaphors—even in the organization's name—and they relied on churches and religious leaders as organizers. One Columbia minister was so impressed with the Light of Tyrrell that he later helped organize what would become an even larger credit union in his nearby hometown of Edenton. Yet perhaps because of division in local churches or perhaps because of Dean's emphasis on the primacy of the schools and education, the Light of Tyrrell's leaders emphasized the economic and community aspects of its work and minimized its religious ties, even as they relied on local ministers and, later, outsiders with religious interests.[15]

With their own small churches and only recently consolidated schools, Tyrrell County's fractured, isolated black communities had little background of cooperative effort. Worse, some still smarted from the failure of a local fraternal order's insurance program. Dean meant to change all that. Soon, farmers, teachers, and preachers gathered to discuss local conditions and to evaluate what they might do to set black farmers on more even ground with white farmers in a rigged system in a Jim Crow state.[16]

Dean and his professional colleagues understood that farming mattered more than work of any other sort, because there wasn't much other work to be found in rural Tyrrell County. Labor on someone else's farm meant bowing to the owner's or manager's way of doing business and still ending most years with near-empty pockets. It also meant bowing to the owner's or manager's politics, because speaking out could jeopardize a family's place on the farm. Work on one's own farm, by contrast, meant a chance at a profit—with good weather, good luck, and good lenders. Farm ownership also allowed for relative economic and political independence.[17]

Yet for the first half of the twentieth century, farm ownership declined steadily as the result of wildly fluctuating prices, federal policies that favored larger farms, and astronomical lending rates. Tyrrell County was no exception. Small farmers generally had to borrow funds for seed and supplies, to be repaid after the harvest, and high interest rates could quickly absorb a farmer's profits. A single bad year could leave a farming family in debt, with the farm itself as collateral. Turned from their own land, many families had little choice but to work as tenants on someone else's. Dean often told the story of a farmer who borrowed $500 to rebuild his house after it burned to the ground. His lender granted a six-month loan at 6 percent interest with a $100 fee. When the loan came due, the farmer could pay only the interest, and he had to pay another $100 fee to extend the loan to a year. Soon, his $500 loan ballooned to an unpayable $900.[18]

Black farmers like the one Dean described suffered most. Between 1930 and 1940, Tyrrell County's population grew slightly, and its proportion of African Americans increased from 33 percent to 36 percent. At the same time, the proportion of farmland owned by African Americans dropped from an already abysmal 11.4 percent to 9.4 percent—or from 4,335 of 37,873 total acres to 3,768 of 39,896 acres. So as the black population of the county grew, its landholdings diminished.[19]

Black farmers had scarcely a chance at all in the hands of Tyrrell County's high-interest creditors, and reasonable bank loans were unattainable for most black Southerners. As they gathered with Dean and his colleagues to discuss the insurmountable odds facing them, many—like Eliza Jones—began to see that they could circumvent the creditors if they pooled their resources. Eliza Jones's symbolic nickel could not save anyone's farm. But when twenty-five founding members of the Light of Tyrrell each invested twenty-five dollars in the credit union, the organization could begin to support its members. Subsequent members could join for just five dollars per share, and each shareholder held one vote. Many farmers invested a few nickels and dimes each month until they reached the five-dollar threshold. In the meantime, those farmers who could joined the county's small black professional class in providing the funds necessary to bring their idea to life.[20]

It worked simply enough: members invested their own savings into the credit union, which used some of those savings to make loans approved by a committee composed of elected credit union members. Members could take out loans together for cooperative enterprises or bulk purchases that then allowed other members to purchase goods and services at lower rates. The credit union also provided programs to train members to manage their money. Because of their shared training and common economic interests, credit union members worked together to ensure that loans would be repaid.[21]

Credit unions represented the most popular form of economic cooperation in the United States. They addressed the widespread need for accessible savings and reasonable credit, and their outwardly conservative nature—built on a long-standing model of segregated self-help—meant that they gained widespread support. Black North Carolinians had begun to organize credit unions and cooperative purchasing groups during the 1910s as a way to circumvent discriminatory lending and pricing practices. A state credit union law passed in 1915 encouraged the growth of credit unions and even provided training and support for credit union organizers.[22]

The Light of Tyrrell obtained a state charter in January 1939, and by the end of the year, it had 187 members and had already made twenty-five small loans totaling just over $1,000. During World War II, when farmers benefited from the increased prices of a wartime economy and observed restrictions on purchasing, the credit union flourished. By 1945, the Light of Tyrrell had made 528 loans for a total of $67,461 and boasted assets of $43,456. One of those loans went to the farmer who owed $900 to his lender. He kept his farm and repaid the low interest credit union loan in three years.[23]

The study clubs that had formed the foundation of the credit union continued to meet in schoolhouses and churches across Tyrrell County. Soon, six families took out a group loan to purchase a farm and the machinery necessary to operate it. They built a cooperative sawmill on the farm, which then provided low-cost lumber and materials used to repair or rebuild housing for twenty-five more members of the credit union.[24] Credit union members used the sawdust from the mill to fill the swamps underneath their sturdy new houses, which boasted windows, doors, and firm foundations. The school's vocational agriculture teacher organized cooperative groups to purchase farm supplies, livestock, and machinery, again eliminating contact with creditors and allowing farm owners and sharecroppers access to equipment otherwise unavailable or cripplingly expensive. Several women headed up a health-care cooperative to cover hospitalization and maternity expenses. Dean began to investigate the possibility of a rural electrification program. Five Light of Tyrrell members, including a woman who had managed her own shop in the past and worked as credit union treasurer, started a cooperative grocery store. Just as Dean had hoped, the credit union provided the economic and social foundation for a host of new cooperative enterprises.[25]

Dean expanded the Light of Tyrrell's work outside the county as well. Almost as soon as it began operations, the Light of Tyrrell joined with Brick School to found the Eastern Carolina Cooperative Council, which in turn launched half a dozen local study clubs to begin new cooperatives in nearby counties, beginning with the one in Edenton. Like the Light of Tyrrell, these new credit unions continued to grow during World War II. When the war ended in 1945 and wartime restrictions on travel and consumption ceased, participation ballooned from just over 3,000 total members of black credit unions in North Carolina in 1944 to more than 9,500 in 1946.[26]

While he remained committed to the Light of Tyrrell, Dean's efforts to help other local people establish their own credit unions reflected credit union advocates' belief that theirs was a model that could transform the nation's economic system from the ground level. The Light of Tyrrell was important in part because it was replicable. That their remote county boasted a model all-black credit union and cooperative made locals of both races proud, particularly when the organization drew national attention. S. P. Dean and the Light of Tyrrell so impressed the nation's most prominent credit union advocate, Roy Bergengren, that he highlighted Dean's work at a national conference in Chicago and in a book that promoted credit unions as part of a cooperative economic model for postwar rebuilding around the world. He celebrated the farmers who learned "to build for themselves a new economic life," and who as a result told him, "We have learned to laugh when we would cry."[27]

If Roy Bergengren was the Light of Tyrrell's most renowned promoter, he was not in the end its most important. In early 1945, Nelle Morton, head of the Fellowship of Southern Churchmen, introduced herself to S. P. Dean as one of "a group of leaders in the South trying to interpret the Christian faith in action now in terms of some Southern problems and needs." She explained that she had known of the credit union for some time, but that Roy Bergengren had encouraged her to get in touch. Her introduction judiciously vague, Morton then asked if the Fellowship of Southern Churchmen might send some members to Tyrrell County to work and worship with members of the credit union on one of their new projects. So began a collaboration that would reshape the fortunes of S. P. Dean and the Light of Tyrrell.[28]

The "Holy Book Is Not a Stick of Candy but a Stick of Dynamite"[29]

The Fellowship of Southern Churchmen, like the Light of Tyrrell, emerged during the Great Depression to offer an alternative to a violent and broken

Southern capitalist economy. S. P. Dean stressed the local, the practical, and the immediate even as he imagined how his small project might provide a transformative economic model for African Americans in the postwar South. The founders of the Fellowship of Southern Churchmen began from the opposite end, and at their first meeting in 1934 proposed a sweeping theological and economic reinvention of America, with local visionaries and activists like Dean as its ground troops.[30]

Predominantly but not exclusively white and male, the Fellowship of Southern Churchmen pulled together southern Protestants who believed that the region's churches should take the lead in whittling away at Southern capitalism to make way for a more just racial and economic order. At their first meeting in May 1934, this gathering of Southern Christian radicals lamented the fundamentally conservative nature of Franklin Roosevelt's program for recovery. They expressed tepid approval of "the objectives of the New Deal, in so far as they seek to abolish poverty, end child labor, recognize the right of the workers to bargain collectively . . . and provide a more equitable distribution of wealth." But they also contended that "the objectives of the New Deal can not be achieved under the profit economy, and that these short-comings of the New Deal are inherent in the capitalistic system." In other words, they believed that Roosevelt's attempt to ameliorate capitalism's injustices but to save the system itself was doomed to fail.[31]

As their critique suggests, many fellowship members represented the robust Southern contingent of a national network of Christian socialists who understood the Great Depression to be an inevitable result of capitalism rather than anathema to it. All those gathered at that first meeting agreed on "the need of developing a radical political party of all races, composed of farmers, industrial workers, and members of the middle class" to remake the nation's economic system. This new party, they believed, must advocate for the "socialization of natural resources, the principal means of production and distribution, including the nationalization of land, with the clear understanding that the farmer retains possession of the land he uses."[32]

Fellowship members' emphasis on Christianity as the way toward revolution grew more from pessimism about politics than from optimism about religion. Several of the fellowship's founders had been students of Reinhold Niebuhr at Union Theological Seminary in the late 1920s and early 1930s, and others had been members of Niebuhr's Fellowship of Socialist Christians. The group called Niebuhr its "spiritual godfather," and although he could not join the organization because he was not Southern, he appeared regularly at its meetings. In part inspired by *Moral Man and Immoral Society*

(1932), the fellowship adopted Niebuhr's form of Christian realism. Members agreed with him that "human society will never escape the problem of the equitable distribution of the physical and cultural goods which provide for the preservation and fulfillment of human life." They believed that Christians must recognize that any political system was necessarily flawed. They should push nonetheless for "the most rational possible social goal, that of equal justice," which in the 1930s Niebuhr and most members of the fellowship deemed to be Marxian socialism. Yet they also believed that the revolution must begin with local people, in their own communities and their own congregations.[33]

Committed to the notion of a revolution based in local churches, fellowship members acted in the 1930s as support network for radical Christian experiments across the South. Members like labor advocate Lucy Randolph Mason, writer Lillian Smith, Highlander Folk School founders Myles Horton and James Dombrowski, Howard University president Mordecai Johnson, and the fellowship's executive secretary Howard Kester worked to connect those grassroots initiatives to one another and to supporters across the South. Many, like the Southern Tenant Farmers Union in the lower Mississippi Valley, the Delta and Providence Cooperative Farms in the Mississippi Delta, and Highlander Folk School in East Tennessee, worked to protect workers of both races through labor unions, worker education, and extensive cooperative enterprises. Such organizations often turned to the fellowship for connections to supporters such as Reinhold Niebuhr and Yale-based activist Sherwood Eddy, and for help in raising funds and public awareness.[34]

By the time the United States entered World War II, Niebuhr and many of his Southern admirers—like many Depression radicals—parted ways with socialism and moved rightward. Fellowship members now publicly disavowed many of their leftist colleagues, even as they acknowledged that those colleagues led the charge for racial and economic justice in the South.[35] Although the fellowship's rhetoric shifted from radical to liberal, its members' work continued to emphasize the church's place in supporting labor and challenging segregation. For the first half of the decade, however, this mattered little. World War II captured fellowship members' attention and their energy, and the organization's efforts languished.[36]

At the start of 1945, just as the Light of Tyrrell began to draw widespread attention, the fellowship welcomed a new leader and prepared to work in a transformed political and economic environment. Wartime manufacturing and employment, combined with the end of severe restrictions on domestic consumption and construction, made for a flush postwar economy. But that economy benefited some Americans more than others, particularly as anti-Communist fervor led to the repression of the broader left. The uneasy wartime alliance between the United States and the Soviet Union turned to bitter enmity as the two superpowers squabbled over the spoils of victory. Americans now lived in a world where capitalist heroes squared off against Communist villains. Even baseless charges of Communism stuck, and they stuck in particular to those who dared suggest that American capitalism had not created equal economic opportunity for all—or even that equal opportunity represented a worthy aim. Dissent was now treachery, and critics of capitalism could only be allies of Communism.[37]

Fellowship members hired Southern Presbyterian youth organizer Nelle Morton to help the organization navigate this postwar context. With a background in youth work rather than political or economic activism, Morton seemed a solidly liberal but relatively uncontroversial choice. Her record indicated a deep commitment to racial justice, but she expressed more interest in practical action than philosophical discussion. Like many white Southern liberals after World War II, she argued that interracial contact and conversation among youth provided a path toward gradual integration. Yet Morton's work, and that of her fellowship colleagues, was not so easy to categorize.[38]

During the postwar 1940s, Morton established Chapel Hill, North Carolina, as the fellowship's operational headquarters, and there she helped to organize student fellowship chapters on thirteen college campuses, developed a student newsletter, and held regular interracial and intercollegiate meetings. At those meetings, students learned to talk as much about economic as interracial cooperation as the foundation of a more just postwar world. Fellowship students and clergy began to work together to integrate their local churches, and at the same time they participated in interracial work camps to support economic and labor initiatives across the rural South. They continued to argue that land should belong to those who worked it rather than to absentee titleholders. In collaboration with the American Friends Service Committee, fellowship members took their interracial work abroad as they helped organize the first integrated relief trip to postwar Europe under the auspices of the United Nations Relief and Rehabilitation Administration (UNRRA).[39]

Rarely did fellowship members challenge the foundations of capitalism as directly as their 1930s predecessors had. They knew well the perils of anticapitalist language in the Cold War world. But they continued to imagine an economy built on economic cooperation and organized labor while they stressed more clearly than ever before the churches' responsibility to challenge

Southern segregation. They also continued to argue for the inextricability of racial and economic justice. "The labor movement in the South is serving the common man," one member observed. "Will the churches of the South, whose denominational roots are revolutionary and whose Holy Book is not a stick of candy but a stick of dynamite, do as much to bring to the farm and factory worker a good wage, a decent house, a free assembly, a brotherhood enfolding all races?" Their radical critique muted but by no means eviscerated, Morton and the Fellowship of Southern Churchmen sought new ways to promote racial and economic justice in a region that offered little of either.[40]

A "Very Orderly" Mob[41]

It is no surprise, then, that when Nelle Morton heard of S. P. Dean's work in Tyrrell County in early 1945 she began to imagine the possibilities of collaboration between the two organizations. Even though the Light of Tyrrell was not a religious organization, it modeled the principles of economic cooperation and racial justice that fellowship members embraced, and did so in a way palatable to local whites. A locally based, grassroots effort that seemed poised to spread across North Carolina, the Light of Tyrrell represented one possible way forward for Christian radicals and progressives in the postwar South, and Nelle Morton wanted to support its work.

Morton's brief introduction quickly led to a visit with Dean in Columbia, where she expressed astonishment at his grueling workload and talked with him about ways the fellowship might help. Dean remained principal of the black high school, he oversaw the Light of Tyrrell's operations, and he traveled across eastern North Carolina to train the growing number of community leaders now interested in establishing and expanding their own credit unions. Already, Dean was exhausted, but always the educator, he refused to turn away anyone who hoped to learn from his work in Tyrrell County.

Despite Dean's emphasis on the credit union's educational work, Morton came away impressed with its religious potential. She reported that local credit union members told her that the organization had "practically eliminated fights between church and school and the jealousies between various churches." More important, "The ministers now talk of co-ops from their pulpits and relate their sermons more to the daily living of the people." Perhaps Morton was overeager to find the religious value in the Light of Tyrrell, but its remarkable success undoubtedly created a new sense of unity across Tyrrell's black communities and the churches and schools at their center.[42]

Energized by their visit together, Morton and Dean decided to organize a summer workshop to host new credit union and cooperative organizers. The workshop would more directly connect the Light of Tyrrell to the small but vibrant Christian left in the South. It would allow Dean to cut back on his travel expenses and bring local organizers to Columbia, where he could showcase the Light of Tyrrell to influential outsiders like Roy Bergengren and his mentor, Mabel Carney. Although Dean had worked largely with black credit unions, this workshop would be interracial, and it would take place at his school.[43]

That summer, more than sixty black and white North Carolinians gathered at the Tyrrell County Training School for the Workshop on Cooperative Living. Attendees lodged separately but joined together for ten days of sessions led by Dean, Carney, Bergengren, representatives from the Credit Union National Association and the State Credit Union Division, a few prominent clergy and a representative from the Federal Council of Churches, and faculty of several North Carolina universities. Attendees also piled into cars to tour credit unions and cooperatives nearby. The ten-day interracial gathering resulted in the creation of a statewide credit union association. Dean soon accepted an appointment as its full-time promotional director. This job relieved Dean of his work at the high school and provided a small salary that allowed him to teach other communities how to follow Tyrrell's model. He continued to work with the Light of Tyrrell, but he also traveled the state to support new credit unions and cooperatives. Nelle Morton helped procure funding for Dean's work from the state's liberal Christians as well as from its economic progressives.[44]

Dean remained involved with the Light of Tyrrell, but his absence created gaps that he hoped the Fellowship of Southern Churchmen might help fill. In early 1947, he invited Nelle Morton to send some youth to help the credit union build a new cooperative store that summer. Following the example of the American Friends Service Committee, a Quaker service organization that worked all over the world to promote peace and racial justice, the fellowship had by that point conducted a number of successful multiracial work camps across the South, providing a small-scale model of integrated living both to the college-age participants and the communities in which they tilled farms, built churches, and nurtured relationships.[45]

Because of their successful work with the Light of Tyrrell and good relationship with local whites, fellowship members believed that Tyrrell County residents would welcome the student group they sent in the summer of 1947. Morton hand-selected a group of college and seminary students who would stay with S. P. Dean and his wife Lilly and prepare their shared meals next door in the kitchen of the Tyrrell County Training School. They planned for the students to spend their days constructing the new cooperative store, with additional space for a credit union office.[46]

Things began to fall apart almost as soon as they had come together. A month before the camp began, Morton reassigned the two white women headed to Tyrrell to a different work camp. "Someone has put the pressure on Mr. Dean," she explained vaguely. Roy Bergengren stepped in to suggest that the camp be stopped altogether because "Mr. Dean's work has progressed so well that I am anxious nothing should happen to develop any hostility to it." Morton reassured him that the students "have a wonderful opportunity to interpret Mr. Dean's work through the Negro and white churches there," and that he would "find the setup too natural to bring about any problems of antagonism, and the students of such high calibre [sic] that they will avoid any incidents which might lead to misunderstanding." The camp would also include a Japanese American student and a Lebanese student, who "will broaden the bi-racial aspect and tend to lessen any tension." Morton chose her words carefully. In direct response to white Southerners' claims that racial prejudice was innate and segregation necessary, Morton instead characterized integration as "natural." If segregation was not a biological imperative, then integration could be taught. Morton proposed to teach white Southerners by "loving them into understanding."[47]

The remaining participants arrived in Columbia at the end of June. Led by John and Garland Anderson—"Jack" was a white college professor at Alabama's historically black Talladega College—the group first included only young men: four white, one Lebanese, and two African American. Two young women, one African American and one Japanese American, arrived shortly after the camp began. All the students came from the South. Alexander "Zan" Harper was a Yale Divinity School student, but he had grown up in eastern North Carolina. Harper and Jack Anderson reported regularly to Nelle Morton, but otherwise the campers were on their own.[48]

They arrived at their worksite to discover an empty lot, with neither tools nor building supplies. They would have to get the lumber from a farmhouse eight miles away. The lumber *was* the farmhouse, though, and they would first have to tear it down. But the credit union's old truck—the crew's only form of transportation—wound up in the shop more than it was on the road. The planned summer of hard work became a summer of sporadic labor, odd jobs, and frequent frustration, but the students stayed and did what work they could. From the start, they worried over fractures among members of the credit union, which they traced to anger at Dean's frequent absences and full work schedule.[49]

The students noted that the Light of Tyrrell was more controversial in Columbia than they had realized, particularly among whites who increasingly understood the credit union as an expression of black economic independence. On Sundays, the campers attended churches of their own traditions. The black students made no attempt to cross the Sunday-morning color line. Still, the outsiders' presence in their small churches proved unsettling to white Columbians, whose welcome, as Jack Anderson reported, "was not exactly what I'd call cordial." Anderson warned by mid-July that "everywhere around here there seems to be plotting, intrigue, mistrust." Twice, the campers made plans to leave, and twice credit union members helped them find the equipment and supplies necessary for them to stay. The credit union's board of managers joined in the construction work as they could.[50]

When the work stalled, the campers assigned themselves readings on cooperatives and planned programs to provide both education and recreation in Columbia. They hosted games of softball, met with local community members of both races, and in the evenings gathered on the Deans' screened porch to discuss "cooperatives and the freedom of man."[51]

Despite the swirling rumors—or perhaps because of them—the students also made friends. By mid-summer, local youth, curious about the new young people they had seen in their churches, grew bolder. Black and white high schoolers and college students home for the summer began to stop by the Deans' house to sit together on the porch and chat with the students. Some came early to help with the work, and many stayed late into the evenings, finding their hometown far more interesting than it had ever been before.[52]

But construction of the store proceeded slowly, their kids came home talking about economics and justice, and some local whites began to murmur that the students must be up to no good. The sheriff and other white community members also began to visit regularly to warn that "general public sentiment" was against the campers. In part at Zan Harper's insistence, the group decided to stay. A month into the project, the young men moved from the Deans' house in Columbia to the credit union farm in an attempt to defuse tensions. Since they had torn down the farmhouse, they spruced up the farm's old chicken house and moved in. The two young women remained with the Deans.[53]

Then, that weekend, the students hosted a fellowship work group from nearby Phoebus, Virginia. This one included white women, and all the campers and some of their local friends picnicked and worshipped and played together.[54] The next night, several visitors—some angry, some anxious—visited the Deans to warn the campers that they were in trouble. The Deans asked them to segregate for just one night. The white campers and their leaders retired to the farm, while the remaining campers stayed at the Deans' house.[55]

The white campers arrived at the farm without incident, but soon "noticed the whole road ablaze with headlights." The campers fled for the cornfields and dropped to the ground as men armed with knives, guns, and farm tools jumped out of their cars and gave chase. There were nearly three hundred men in all, many of them World War II veterans from Tyrrell and surrounding counties.[56]

All five students and their two leaders escaped, and for three hours they lay motionless as the men shouted, cursed, and threatened them in the darkness. Finally the local sheriff arrived at the farm. He dispersed the mob before calling the students out of the fields, as he "was worried, the place being full of rattlesnakes." He instructed the students to pack their bags, and they agreed to take the first bus out of Columbia the following morning. They lined up together under the bus entrance labeled "colored" and waved good-bye to Columbia from their seats against the back window of the bus.[57]

The reporting in the aftermath of the camp focused on the campers' racial message rather than their economic advocacy. The sheriff who had gathered the campers from the cornfields told reporters, "I don't know of any law preventing white folks from living with Negroes, but I do know people here don't think much of it." The *New York Times* picked up the story, with the sheriff's added declaration that the mob was "very orderly and I don't believe any of them were armed." Accusations of Communist organizing and orgies at the Deans' house quickly spread, and a local columnist applauded the "level-headed citizens at Columbia who rid their town and community of a bunch of 'academic idiots' . . . who were defying all conventions, practices, and customs of our bi-racial East."[58]

But other responses demonstrated that the real threat to white Columbians was as much economic as racial. Will Norcum, the leader and spokesperson of the mob, just so happened to operate a local sawmill, which would have operated in direct—and losing—competition with the Light of Tyrrell's cooperative sawmill. One white resident of Columbia accused both the Deans and the campers of "trying to make niggers independent," while others defended the accusers' real target: the credit union. One man shrugged and said, "I believe colored folks have a right to anything I have a right to," and mentioned a black family who had recently bought a farm with the credit union's help. The man said little more, but his commentary makes clear that he understood the controversy to be as much about the economic independence the credit union offered African Americans as about integration—the two efforts together a far more effective threat to white supremacy than either alone.[59]

The organizers of the Light of Tyrrell and the Deans remained largely quiet in the aftermath of the incident, apart from a brief interview Lilly Dean granted a local white paper. She matter-of-factly outlined the summer's events and distanced herself from them as much as possible. Otherwise, only the white perspective on the camp and its breakup survives in the historical record. But the black residents of Tyrrell County paid for the work camp's dissolution. After months of harassment and phone calls warning them to leave town, the Deans finally did. The following year, S. P. Dean also resigned his position with the statewide credit union organization, his health failing after years of overwork and months of mistreatment. He and Lilly Dean left North Carolina altogether.[60]

Without his leadership, and in the face of hostility where there had once been accord with local whites, the Light of Tyrrell faltered. Local whites who had once celebrated the credit union as a model of self-help now condemned it as a threat to racial harmony, and the credit union's new leaders missed Dean's talent for placating whites while unifying the county's African American communities. Within two years, the credit union liquidated, the store relocated and then shuttered, and all cooperative efforts except the health program ended. The credit unions and cooperatives modeled on the Light of Tyrrell thrived, as did the network Dean had helped to organize. But the people Dean cared for most, those among whom he had lived and worked for two decades, watched the Light of Tyrrell wink out.[61]

Nelle Morton and the fellowship now understood the hard reality that local people would invariably face the worst fallout from the long fight for economic and racial justice. The youth who participated in the work camp endured some harassment after local papers published their names, colleges, and addresses—a well-worn tactic that would become common practice among supposedly genteel white supremacist groups like the Mississippi-based Citizens Councils. But the youth could return to their lives outside Columbia. Morton, the campers, and other fellowship leaders tried to control the wildest rumors and bear the brunt of the rage themselves in a futile effort to spare the Deans and other African American allies. Aware of the dangers of talking about economic justice in Cold War America, they spoke only of the camp as a Christian interracial experiment and mentioned the Light of Tyrrell as little as possible. In a sharp rebuke to the vast majority of white Southern churchgoers, Morton told reporters, "Segregation is a sin and as we begin living as Christians, segregation lines will dissolve."[62]

Morton was wrong, and she probably knew it. White Southern churches had not only made peace with Jim Crow but worked actively to maintain it. Many even provided theological justification for racial violence and white supremacy. Black Southern church members remained central to protest movements, but their churches and clergy often lagged behind in open advocacy for justice. They rarely formed the kind of alliances with white churches or white activists that Dean formed with Morton. The Fellowship of Southern Churchmen's radical prophetic vision faded, though the organization survived. That the Fellowship of Southern Churchmen has no real contemporary counterpart is testament not only to the forces of oppression that persist in white Southern Christianity but also to the seemingly unassailable power of large-scale capitalism in the post–Cold War world.[63]

Morton's response to the work in Tyrrell County gave those powers an easy weapon to dismiss both radical Southern Christianity and local economic organization. When Morton took responsibility for the work in Tyrrell County, she meant to spare Dean and the Light of Tyrrell. But she unwittingly validated the outside-agitator accusations that demeaned local, grassroots efforts and disparaged the fight for economic and racial justice as a misguided and dangerous effort to stir up black Southerners. Her emphasis on the racial, rather than the economic, efforts in Columbia further distanced the rights-based efforts that would come to characterize civil rights leadership from the economic efforts that often grew organically from local people. This response reflected a common strategy to counter the accusations—of Communist conspiracies and interracial sex—that civil rights activists and their supporters would face for the next two decades. But local people, from S. P. Dean in Columbia to Vera Pigee in Clarksdale, Mississippi, to Alice Moore in Alabama, also understood that rights could not be divorced from opportunity, that racial justice without economic justice would mean a hollow victory.[64] And from North Carolina to Mississippi to California, local people continue to fight for both.

Notes

1. Elsie N. Danenberg, *Get Your Own Home the Cooperative Way* (New York: Greenberg, 1949), 137; Nathan Alvin Pitts, *The Cooperative Movement in Negro Communities of North Carolina* (Washington, DC: Catholic University of America, 1950), 26–31, 103. "Tyrrell" is pronounced with a short *y* and emphasis on the first syllable: *teer*-ul.

2. Danenberg, *Get Your Own Home the Cooperative Way*, 137; Pitts, *Cooperative Movement*, 26–31, 103; "Lights of Tyrrell: A Credit Union Lights the Way to a Better Life,"

Virginia Extension Division Publication, *New Dominion Series* 57 (1 October 1944): 2; U.S. Bureau of the Census, *Sixteenth Census of the United States,* 1940, 382.

3. Jack Anderson to Nelle Morton, 17 August 1947, folder 93, box 9, Fellowship of Southern Churchmen Records #3479, Southern Historical Collection, Wilson Library, University of North Carolina at Chapel Hill (hereafter FSC Papers); Mounir Khouri to Nelle Morton, 19 September 1947, folder 97, box 9, FSC Papers; Kay Kaneda to Nelle Morton, 16 September 1947, folder 97, box 9, FSC Papers; Cornelia Lively to Charles Jones, 18 August 1947, folder 94, box 9, FSC Papers; Fellowship of Southern Churchmen Newsletter, November 1947, box 10, folder 105, FSC Papers; "Mob Runs Mixed Student Group Out of Town," *Pittsburgh Courier,* 30 August 1947, 1, 4. This story is pieced together from several sources, which sometimes offer contradictory details. I have compiled a version of the story as close as possible to that described by fellowship members and work campers in their private and public reports on the incident.

4. John Anderson, "A Study in Reconversion," *Prophetic Religion* 6, no. 3 (Winter 1945): 85–87 (quotation at end of first paragraph on 85); Fellowship of Southern Churchmen Newsletter, November 1947, folder 105, box 10, FSC Papers; Cornelia Lively to Charles Jones, 18 August 1947, folder 94, box 9, FSC Papers; "Columbia Mob Orders Students from Negro Home," *Daily Advance* (Elizabeth City, NC), 18 August 1947, 1.

5. For a few examples of this argument, see Robert Korstad and Nelson Lichtenstein, "Opportunities Found and Lost: Labor, Radicals, and the Early Civil Rights Movement," *Journal of American History* 75 (December 1988): 786–811; Alan Brinkley, *The End of Reform: New Deal Liberalism in Recession and War* (New York: Vintage, 1995); Ellen Schrecker, *Many Are the Crimes: McCarthyism in America* (Princeton, NJ: Princeton University Press, 1998); and Glenda Elizabeth Gilmore, *Defying Dixie: The Radical Roots of Civil Rights, 1919–1950* (New York: W. W. Norton, 2008).

6. Jarod H. Roll, *Spirit of Rebellion: Labor and Religion in the New Cotton South* (Urbana: University of Illinois Press, 2010); Erik S. Gellman and Jarod H. Roll, *The Gospel of the Working Class: Labor's Southern Prophets in New Deal America* (Urbana: University of Illinois Press, 2011); Françoise Hamlin, *Crossroads at Clarksdale: The Black Freedom Struggle in the Mississippi Delta after World War II* (Chapel Hill: University of North Carolina Press, 2013); Hassan Kwame Jeffries, *Bloody Lowndes: Civil Rights and Black Power in Alabama's Black Belt* (New York: New York University Press, 2009); Robert Rodgers Korstad and James L. Leloudis, *To Right These Wrongs: The North Carolina Fund and the Battle to End Poverty and Inequality in 1960s America* (Chapel Hill: University of North Carolina Press, 2010); Danielle McGuire and John Dittmer, eds., *Freedom Rights: New Perspectives on the Civil Rights Movement* (Lexington: University Press of Kentucky, 2011).

7. For a recent encapsulation of the development of, and debates regarding, the "classic" periodization of the modern civil rights movement, see Steven F. Lawson's introduction to McGuire and Dittmer's *Freedom Rights,* 9–38.

8. Nelle Morton, "The Light of Tyrrell," *Prophetic Religion* 6, no. 1 (Summer 1945): 23.

9. "Saga of Simpson Dean," *Chicago Defender*, 1 June 1946, 13; Morton, "Light of Tyrrell," 23–25; "Lights of Tyrrell," 2–3.

10. On Carney, see Richard Glotzer, "The Career of Mabel Carney: The Study of Race and Rural Development in the United States and South Africa," *International Journal of African Historical Studies* 29, no. 2 (1996): 309–36; Mabel Carney, "Desirable Rural Adaptations in the Education of Negroes," *Journal of Negro Education* 3, no. 3 (July 1936): 448–54.

11. Gilbert C. Fite, *Farm to Factory: A History of the Consumers Cooperative Association* (Columbia: University of Missouri Press, 1965); and Benson Y. Landis, *A Cooperative Economy: A Study of Democratic Economic Movements* (New York: Harper and Brothers, 1946).

12. Ibid. On the importance of both race and class to Jim Crow, see Stephen Kantrowitz, *Ben Tillman and the Reconstruction of White Supremacy* (Chapel Hill: University of North Carolina Press, 2000).

13. Pitts, *Cooperative Movement*, 26–28, 86; Morton, "Light of Tyrrell," 23–25. On Brick Rural Life School, see Ruth A. Morton, *Men of the Soil: Brick Rural Life School* (New York: American Missionary Association, 1945); Neill A. McLean, *Brick Rural Life School*, undated (1938?) pamphlet available at Internet Archive, https://archive.org/stream/brickrurallifescoobrow/brickrurallifescoobrow_djvu.txt, accessed 7 August 2013.

14. Pitts, *Cooperative Movement*, 86–87, 101–2; Morton, "Light of Tyrrell," 23–25; "Lights of Tyrrell," 4–5.

15. David E. Davis, *The History of Tyrrell County* (Norfolk, VA: James Christopher, 1963), 50, 61; Pitts, *Cooperative Movement*, 40. On the Edenton credit union, see "So Shines a Good Deed: Cooperatives in Edenton Inspired by Success of Tyrrell," *Virginia Extension Division Bulletin*, *New Dominion Series* 81 (1 June 1946): 2.

16. Pitts, *Cooperative Movement*, 27–28; Davis, *History of Tyrrell County*, 80–81.

17. Recent works on black farming and land ownership in the South include Pete Daniel, *Dispossession: Discrimination against African American Farmers in the Age of Civil Rights* (Chapel Hill: University of North Carolina Press, 2013), and Debra A. Reid and Evan P. Bennett, eds., *Beyond Forty Acres and a Mule: African American Landowning Families since Reconstruction* (Gainesville: University Press of Florida, 2012).

18. Morton, "Light of Tyrrell," 24; Roy Bergengren, *I Speak for Joe Doakes: For Co-Operation at Home and among Nations* (New York: Harper and Brothers, 1945), 106–7.

19. U.S. Bureau of the Census, *Census of Agriculture, North Carolina* (Washington, D.C.: Government Printing Office, 1930 and 1940), 309.

20. Pitts, *Cooperative Movement*, 27–28; "Lights of Tyrrell," 2–7.

21. Pitts, *Cooperative Movement*, 21–23, 36–39.

22. Ibid., 21–23. On the broader history of credit unions in the United States, see J. Carroll Moody and Gilbert C. Fite, *The Credit Union Movement: Origins and Development, 1850–1980* (Lincoln: University of Nebraska Press, 1971).

23. Pitts, *Cooperative Movement*, 29–30; Bergengren, *I Speak for Joe Doakes*, 93–95; Morton, "Light of Tyrrell," 24.

24. Pitts, *Cooperative Movement*, 29–30.

25. Ibid., 28–31; "Lights of Tyrrell," 1–4.

26. Pitts, *Cooperative Movement*, 39–40, 43; S. I. Hayakawa, "Story from Edenton, N.C.," *Chicago Defender*, 23 November 1946, 15.

27. Morton, "Light of Tyrrell," 23, 25; Bergengren, *I Speak for Joe Doakes*, 95; S. I. Hayakawa, "That Credit Union Man Is Here," *Chicago Defender*, 31 March 1945.

28. Nelle Morton to S. P. Dean, 24 February 1945, folder 8, box 1, FSC Papers.

29. David Burgess, "Preachers Beware!," *Prophetic Religion* 6, no. 2 (Fall 1945): 38.

30. On the broader history and mission of the Fellowship of Southern Churchmen and its most involved leaders, see Paul Harvey, *Freedom's Coming: Religious Culture and the Shaping of the South from the Civil War through the Civil Rights Era* (Chapel Hill: University of North Carolina Press, 2007), 92–106; John A. Salmond, "The Fellowship of Southern Churchmen and Interracial Change in the South," *North Carolina Historical Review* 69, no. 2 (April 1992): 179–99; Robert Francis Martin, *Howard Kester and the Struggle for Social Justice in the South, 1904–77* (Charlottesville: University of Virginia Press, 1991); Robert Francis Martin, "Critique of Southern Society and Vision of a New Order: The Fellowship of Southern Churchmen, 1934–1957," *Church History* 52, no. 1 (March 1983): 66–80; Robert Francis Martin, "A Prophet's Pilgrimage: The Religious Radicalism of Howard Anderson Kester, 1921–1941," *Journal of Southern History* 48, no. 4 (November 1982): 511–30; Anthony P. Dunbar, *Against the Grain: Southern Radicals and Prophets, 1929–1959* (Charlottesville: University of Virginia Press, 1982).

31. "Findings, Conference of Younger Churchmen of the South," Monteagle, Tennessee, 27–29 May 1934, folder 328, box 9, Howard Anderson Kester Papers, SHC; David Burgess, "The Fellowship of Southern Churchmen: Its History and Promise," n.d., 1–3, folder 40, box 3, Charles M. Jones Papers #5168, SHC. The Fellowship of Southern Churchmen was initially called the Conference of Younger Churchmen of the South. It adopted the new name when the organization expanded beyond the group of young male clergy who founded it.

32. "Findings, Conference of Younger Churchmen," Monteagle, Tennessee, 27–29 May 1934, folder 328, box 9, Howard Anderson Kester Papers, SHC. A number of historians have stressed the possibilities for a radical critique in the early 1930s, even in the South. See, for instance, Ira Katznelson, *Fear Itself: The New Deal and the Origins of Our Time* (New York: Liveright Press, 2013); Roll, *Spirit of Rebellion*; Gilmore, *Defying Dixie*; Robin D. G. Kelley, *Hammer and Hoe: Alabama Communists during the Great Depression* (Chapel Hill: University of North Carolina Press, 1990); Alan Brinkley, *Voices of Protest: Huey Long, Father Coughlin, and the Great Depression* (New York: Vintage, 1983).

33. Burgess, "Fellowship of Southern Churchmen," 1; Reinhold Niebuhr, *Moral Man and Immoral Society: A Study in Ethics and Politics* (New York: Charles Scribner's Sons, 1932), 82, 169–74 (quotations on 170–71); Fox, *Reinhold Niebuhr*, 111–66. See also Reinhold Niebuhr, "Is Peace or Justice the Goal?," *World Tomorrow*, 21 September 1932, 275–77. On Christian socialism in this period, see Janine Giordano Drake, "The Church Outside the Church: The Working-Class Religious Left, 1886–1936" (PhD diss., University of Illinois, 2012); Roll and Gellman, *Gospel of the Working Class*; Joseph Kosek, *Acts of Conscience: Christian Nonviolence and Modern American Democracy* (New York: Columbia University Press, 2011); and Mark Fannin, *Labor's Promised Land: Radical Visions of Gender, Race, and Religion in the South* (Knoxville: University of Tennessee Press, 2003). A classic in the field, by a founder of the FSC, is James Dombrowski, *The Early Days of Christian Socialism in America* (New York: Columbia University Press, 1936).

34. The most accessible source on the fellowship's theology and work in the 1930s is its journal, *Prophetic Religion*, published quarterly. See also Burgess, "Fellowship of Southern Churchmen," and Salmond, "Fellowship of Southern Churchmen and Interracial Change in the South."

35. On this general shift, see Fox, *Reinhold Niebuhr*; and Gellman and Roll, *Gospel of the Working Class*.

36. A careful reading of *Prophetic Religion* and fellowship meeting notes indicates a clear survival of economic activism and support for organized labor among many fellowship members, particularly during Howard Kester's absence from the organization in the postwar 1940s.

37. The historiography of the wartime economy and spurning of postwar economic critique is extensive. Particularly relevant are James T. Sparrow, *Warfare State: World War II Americans and the Age of Big Government* (New York: Oxford University Press, 2011); Ellen Schrecker, *Many Are the Crimes: McCarthyism in America* (Princeton, NJ: Princeton University Press, 1999); and Alan Brinkley, *The End of Reform: New Deal Liberalism in Recession and War* (New York: Vintage Books, 1996).

38. Despite her emphasis on action during her fellowship years, Morton later became a noted feminist theologian; see Nelle Morton, *The Journey Is Home* (Boston: Beacon Press, 1986).

39. Salmond, "Fellowship of Southern Churchmen and Interracial Change in the South," 180–84; Martin, "Critique of Southern Society and Vision of a New Order," 76–78; Martin, *Howard Kester and the Struggle for Social Justice in the South*, 1432–43; Nelle Morton to Tony Dunbar, 3 January 1978, FSC Papers, box 24, folder 277; interview with Nelle Morton by Dallas Blanchard, 25 June 1983, F-0034, transcript, 17, Southern Oral History Project; Charles M. Brashares to Nelle Morton, 26 April 1946, folder 29, box 3, FSC Papers; William Howard Deihl, "Heifers for Europe," folder 276, box 9, Howard Anderson Kester Papers, SHC.

40. David Burgess, "Preachers Beware!," *Prophetic Religion* 6, no. 2 (Fall 1945): 36–38. An exception to the 1940s' silence regarding capitalism as a system appeared

in the Winter 1947 issue of *Prophetic Religion*: "Christianity Challenges Capitalism," 99, 111.

41. "Columbia Mob Orders Students from Negro Home," *Daily Advance* (Elizabeth City, NC), 18 August 1947, 1; "Ordered to Leave Town," *New York Times*, 19 August 1947.

42. Morton, "Light of Tyrell," 25.

43. Fellowship newsletter, November 1947, 3; Hayakawa, "Story from Edenton, N.C."

44. Pitts, *Cooperative Movement*, 31–34, 89–91, 109–10, 135–38; fellowship newsletter, November 1947, 3.

45. Fellowship newsletter, November 1947, 3; Eugene Smathers, "Lessons for the Future," *Prophetic Religion* (Winter 1947): 98–99; Salmond, "Fellowship of Southern Churchmen and Interracial Change in the South," 185–91. See also Allan W. Austin, *Quaker Brotherhood: Interracial Activism and the American Friends Service Committee, 1917–1950* (Urbana: University of Illinois Press, 2012).

46. Fellowship newsletter, November 1947, 2–4. Even this project was a backup plan after an earlier project to build a cannery in Columbia fell through.

47. Nelle Morton to Gertrude Bullock, 7 June 1947, folder 81, box 8, FSC Papers; Roy Bergengren to Nelle Morton, 11 June 1947, folder 82, box 8, FSC Papers; Nelle Morton to Roy Bergengren, 13 June 1947, folder 83, box 8, FSC Papers; Zan Harper to Nelle Morton, 26 June 1947, folder 85, box 8, FSC Papers.

48. Fellowship newsletter, November 1947, 2, 4–5; Mounir Khouri to Nelle Morton, 19 September 1947, folder 97, box 9, FSC Papers; Kay Kaneda to Nelle Morton, 9 September 1947, folder 97, box 9, FSC Papers; Evangeline Royall to Nelle Morton, 5 September 1947, folder 96, box 9, FSC Papers; "Six Living with Negro Are Ousted," *Charlotte Observer*, 19 August 1947.

49. Fellowship newsletter, November 1947, 4–5; Jack Anderson to Nelle Morton, 1 July 1947, folder 86, box 8, FSC Papers.

50. Fellowship newsletter, November 1947, 4–5; Jack Anderson to Nelle Morton, 14 July 1947, folder 88, box 8, FSC Papers.

51. Jack Anderson to Nelle Morton, 19 July 1947, folder 89, box 8, FSC Papers; Bob Wherritt to Nelle Morton, 16 July 1947, folder 88, box 8, FSC Papers.

52. Jack Anderson to Nelle Morton, 14 July 1947, folder 88, box 8, FSC Papers; Garland Anderson to Nelle Morton, 24 July 1947, folder 90, box 8, FSC Papers; Garland Anderson to Nelle Morton, 3 August 1947, folder 91, box 8, FSC Papers; Garland Anderson to Nelle Morton, 10 August 1947, folder 92, box 9, FSC Papers.

53. Fellowship newsletter, November 1947, 5–6; Garland Anderson to Nelle Morton, 3 August 1947, folder 91, box 8, FSC Papers; Kay Kaneda to Nelle Morton, 16 September 1947, folder 19, box 9, FSC Papers.

54. Fellowship newsletter, November 1947, 6; John Anderson to Nelle Morton, 10 August 1947, folder 94, box 9, FSC Papers.

55. Kay Kaneda to Nelle Morton, 16 September 1947, folder 97, box 9, FSC Papers; A. M. Rivera Jr., "Mob Runs Mixed Student Group Out of Town," *Pittsburgh Courier*,

30 August 1947, 1, 4. It is unclear whether the Lebanese student was still with the group at this point—he may have left early. If he remained, he was classified "white" and sent to the farm. The Japanese student may have been designated as "colored" because she was a young woman and the Deans believed she would be safer with them, or because of anti-Japanese sentiment in town.

56. Kay Kaneda to Nelle Morton, 16 September 1947, folder 97, box 9, FSC Papers; Rivera, "Mob Runs Mixed Student Group Out of Town," 1, 4; fellowship newsletter, November 1947, 6–7. Estimates ranged from two to four hundred men. Some reports say they were armed; others insist they were not. The first report, from the local sheriff, counted three hundred men, some of whom he claimed to have disarmed at the Deans' house. He would later report that none of the men had been armed.

57. Kay Kaneda to Nelle Morton, 16 September 1947, folder 97, box 9, FSC Papers; Rivera, "Mob Runs Mixed Student Group Out of Town," 1, 4.

58. "Columbia Mob Orders Students from Negro Home," *Daily Advance* (Elizabeth City, NC), 18 August 1947, 1; "Ordered to Leave Town," *New York Times*, 19 August 1947; Roy Parker, "Roy Parker's Column: The Tyrrell Way," *Jackson (NC) News*, 28 August 1947, 12; "Six Living with Negro Are Ousted," *Charlotte Observer*, 19 August 1947; "Roy Parker's Column," *Jackson (NC) News*, 29 August 1947; "Students' Ouster Said Unfortunate," *Daily Advance* (Elizabeth City, NC), 20 August 1947; Cornelia Lively to Nelle Morton (two letters), 19 August 1947, folder 94, box 9, FSC Papers.

59. Fellowship newsletter, November 1947, 2; "Speaking Out from the New South," *Chicago Defender*, 6 September 1947, 14.

60. "Wife of Tyrrell Negro Tells How Inter-Race Student Group Came to and Left Columbia," *Daily Advance* (Elizabeth City, NC), 19 August 1947; Zan Harper to Cornelia Lively, August 1947, folder 92, box 9, FSC Papers; Cornelia Lively to Nelle Morton, 19 August 1947, folder 94, box 9, FSC Papers; "Prominent Carolinian Asked to Leave Town," *Atlanta Daily World*, 10 September 1947, 3; Pitts, *Cooperative Movement*, 34.

61. The exact reasons for the credit union's rapid dissolution remain difficult to unravel. Certainly, Dean's leadership was important, as were his connections with other communities around the state. His departure itself was somewhat mysterious, and the fellowship letters as well as local commentary hinted that his health had suffered even before the work camp began, in ways that affected his leadership. Nathan Pitts attributed the credit union's collapse entirely to Dean's departure and "the failure to develop local leaders"; Pitts, *Cooperative Movement*, 87. At the same time, the sudden hostility of local whites surely made it very hard for credit union members, many of whom still had white employers or creditors, to move forward; Pitts, *Cooperative Movement*, 30, 33–34, 87–88, 116.

62. "Students' Ouster Said Unfortunate," *Daily Advance* (Elizabeth City, NC), 20 August 1947, 1; "Wife of Tyrrell Negro Tells How Inter-Race Student Group Came to and Left Columbia," *Daily Advance* (Elizabeth City, NC), 19 August 1947; "Six Living with Negro Are Ousted," *Charlotte Observer*, 19 August 1947; fellowship newsletter,

November 1947, 1–6; Nelle Morton to Cornelia Lively, 12 August 1947, folder 93, box 9, FSC Papers.

63. On the range of white Southern Christian responses to segregation, see Gellman and Roll, *Gospel of the Working Class*; Joseph Crespino, *In Search of Another Country: Mississippi and the Conservative Counterrevolution* (Princeton, NJ: Princeton University Press, 2009); Harvey, *Freedom's Coming*; David L. Chappell, *A Stone of Hope: Prophetic Religion and the Death of Jim Crow* (Chapel Hill: University of North Carolina Press, 2005); and Jane Dailey, "Sex, Segregation, and the Sacred after Brown," *Journal of American History* 91, no. 1 (June 2004): 119–44.

64. On Vera Pigee, Alice Moore, and the ongoing fight, see Hamlin, *Crossroads at Clarksdale*, and Jeffries, *Bloody Lowndes*.

8

Catholic Social Policy and Resistance to the Bracero Program

BRETT HENDRICKSON

In the fall of 1959, Archbishop Robert E. Lucey of San Antonio stood before the National Catholic Welfare Council to address the Church's hierarchy. Never one for mincing words, Lucey reported that US agriculture had become "a sacred cow, feeding fat on the exhaustive work of an underpaid, semi-captive labor force." He called on his fellow bishops to do all in their power to alleviate the current labor situation, which he called "a national scandal and an international crime."[1] The situation that Lucey condemned was the imported labor force known popularly as the "bracero program." The name referred to the mighty arms, "*brazos*," of the Mexican men who worked stoop labor in the fields of the American West and Southwest. The program, which ran from 1942 to 1964, allowed American industries—mostly agribusiness—to employ hundreds of thousands of temporary Mexican workers.

The synecdoche in the program's name—workers as "arms"—underscored the fact that the imported Mexican laborers were principally valued for the power their bodies produced. For a select group of American Catholic clergy familiar with the experiences and needs of the mostly Catholic braceros, there was ample reason to condemn this elision of the human person not only out of pastoral concern but also on doctrinal grounds. More than fifty years before the inception of the bracero program, Pope Leo XIII published his famous encyclical *Rerum Novarum*, a touchstone of modern Catholic social doctrine. In it, he declared, "it is shameful and inhuman to treat men like chattels to make money by, or to look upon them merely as so much muscle or physical power."[2] A handful of US priests, bishops, and even archbishops—sometimes in contention with many of their peers—were some of the most vocal and successful opponents of the bracero program. Instructed and empowered by official Catholic social policies regarding labor, union organizing, and workers' dignity, these Catholic leaders implored American Catholics to hold true to Catholic values of solidarity, subsidiarity, and the importance of stable family life. This essay demonstrates how Catholic social doctrine sanctioned the activities of American Catholic clergy to provide pastoral care to braceros even while militating against the bracero program itself. While the priests who protested against the injustices of the program were in the ecclesiastical minority and occasionally clashed with their clerical brethren, they nevertheless benefited from and were supported by papal teaching.

Moreover, this essay highlights the legacy of Catholic critiques of the bracero program. As discussed in more detail later, labor leader and civil rights activist César Chávez got his start as an organizer alongside Catholic priests who were working against the bracero program. Likewise, the United Farm Workers (UFW) was born in part from Catholic community organizations, which were rooted in the social teachings of the Catholic Church. These early relationships between activist priests, braceros, and citizen farmworkers created the context for later, more nationally visible official Catholic support for Chávez and the UFW. A number of important books and articles have been published in the past ten years concerning the role religion took in Chávez's life and career.[3] In a sense, this essay's story of Catholic clergy and lay opposition to the bracero program can be understood as a prequel to Catholic collaboration with the UFW and its various tactics and labor-organizing efforts.

The Bracero Program

During World War II, powerful growers in the vast fields of California lamented acute labor shortages. The mobilization for the war had exhausted their supply of young men willing to do seasonal work at low wages. Under pressure from agribusiness lobbies, the US and Mexican governments signed the Emergency Labor Program, which was funded and codified in the United States as Public Law 45. The binational accord and subsequent US law authorized the import of Mexican contract labor. This workforce—the so-called braceros—was intended to alleviate wartime labor shortages and ostensibly offered Mexican laborers legal, safe, and dependable work. From 1942 to 1947, around 220,000 braceros participated in the program. Despite the end of the war, the program grew steadily and was renewed in 1947, the year in which

Mexico also began to allow braceros to work in Texas. In 1951, the program was once again renewed with the passage of Public Law 78, and more workers than ever before were imported to work throughout the American West. In the latter half of the 1950s, more than 400,000 braceros came across the border every year. The numbers decreased somewhat in the early 1960s, but the program still attracted hundreds of thousands of migrant workers until its final year in 1964. By the time the program ended, over 4.6 million working Mexican men had left their country to work seasonally in the United States. During the decades of the program, these imported workers made up one-fifth of all migratory farmworkers in the United States and dominated stoop-labor crops such as cotton, melon, citrus, lettuce, and truck vegetables.[4]

An early issue with the program was the large numbers of Mexicans in the United States illegally. The legalized and documented importation of Mexican laborers within the bracero program had intended to stabilize wages and ensure a semblance of safe working and living conditions for laborers. However, growers regularly hired undocumented Mexicans alongside bracero counterparts because even the growing numbers of the latter group were often unable to meet demand for fieldwork. But the undocumented workers, referred to at the time as "wetbacks," could often expect wages even lower than those of the braceros since they enjoyed none of the braceros' limited legal protections. Even though lower wages was a potential drawback from working without a legal contract, some braceros jumped their contracts on the US side of the border for a variety of factors, including insufficient work in the limited geographic zone of their contract, a desire to remain in a specific region, or to escape poor or abusive conditions.

In her important study of the bracero program, Mae Ngai discovered "how fluid was the line between 'wetback' and bracero." Whereas some growers preferred to hire illegal workers, most of the workers understandably wanted to work under a contract, but this was not always possible or sufficiently flexible.[5] Eventually, government oversight caught up with the discrepancies between bracero and "wetback." First, immigration officials and the border patrol began to legalize undocumented workers, either on paper alone or by allowing them to take one step onto Mexican soil and one step back with a bracero contract. These legalized workers were known as "specials," or in some cases, as "dried out" or "dehydrated Wetbacks."[6] Along with the legalization effort, the Immigration and Naturalization Service also instituted "Operation Wetback" in 1954. In this operation, officials deported hundreds of thousands of undocumented Mexicans. At best a short-term success, "drying out" the undocumented workers and sending many others back to Mexico did little to improve wages or working conditions. As union organizer Ernesto Galarza commented, both braceros and illegal workers were "two sides of the same phony coin," and both groups depressed wages, broke strikes and unionization efforts, and decreased employment opportunities for American citizens.[7]

In addition to these problems, the braceros who were legally in the United States experienced many well-documented abuses. Because of the braceros' limited mobility and evidence that their contracts were regularly broken, many contemporary critics of the program lamented its "slave-labor camp conditions."[8] One of the most damning exposés of the program was written by the aforementioned Galarza, an organizer who worked for various unions and farm-labor associations. In 1956, commissioned by the Joint United States–Mexico Trade Union Committee, Galarza published a widely circulated pamphlet titled *Strangers in Our Fields*, which systematically listed the various degradations the braceros endured, starting with their application process in Mexico and moving through mismanaged wages, inhumane housing, shortcomings in health care and transportation, and the social isolation that braceros suffered. As one bracero explained to Galarza, "These things have to be tolerated in silence because there is no one to defend our guarantees. In a strange country you feel timid—like a chicken in another rooster's yard."[9]

But for Galarza and other organizers, the ultimate problem, which compounded the abuses frequently suffered by the imported workers, was the inability to organize. Closely related to this problem was the bracero program itself. With its seemingly endless supply of low-wage, low-demand workers, the program basically guaranteed that citizen farmworkers lacked any sort of leverage against the growers. As Rodolfo Acuña put it, the bracero program was the growers' "lethal weapon" against organization.[10] Although not the only factor in Catholic critiques of the bracero program, the pronounced assault on unionization that the bracero program represented was of serious concern for Catholics cognizant of papal social teaching. In response, Catholic actions emerged from Texas to California to minister to Spanish-speaking migrant farm laborers. Those priests who had opportunity to work side by side with braceros often ended up criticizing the ways in which the program weakened worker organization efforts. And while these priests were rarely in the majority in their dioceses or in the national Catholic hierarchy, they did benefit from the support of papal social teaching. This teaching allowed their militancy against the bracero program to take on a doctrinal character.

Catholic Social Teaching and Archbishop Lucey

Even prior to the vast influx of Mexican workers under the auspices of the bracero program, Mexican and Mexican American Catholics in the United States
had prompted what many leaders in the Church called the "Mexican problem." For most of the American Catholic hierarchy, this problem was characterized principally by the perceived religious illiteracy of Mexican-origin
Catholics and by the oft-expressed fear that a lack of Catholic priests, religious
instruction, and regular mass would result in losses to Protestant proselytism.
An important exception to this assessment came from the archbishop of San
Antonio, Robert E. Lucey. As a young priest in his native California, Lucey
had headed the Catholic Charities Bureau and had proved himself to be an
important interpreter of Catholic social teaching and a proponent of social
justice for migrants and Spanish-speaking Catholics. Presaging the analysis
of Chicano civil rights leaders, Lucey insisted that, besides religious needs,
the "Mexican problem" also included troubling statistics about Mexican and
Mexican Americans' family incomes, mortality rates, political enfranchise-
ment, inclusion in labor unions, and their access to health care.[11]

In 1943, Lucey and Raymond McGowan, director of the Catholic Church's
Social Action Department, organized a conference in San Antonio to discuss
the needs of Spanish-speaking Catholics in the Southwest. In the wake of this
meeting and other such gatherings, it was decided that this growing Catholic
constituency deserved and required some sort of institutionalized ongoing
support.[12] With his track record of outspoken advocacy, Lucey became the
first executive chairman of the Bishops' Committee for the Spanish-Speaking
(BCSS), which formed early in 1945.[13] The purpose of the BCSS was to provide pastoral care, education, and other forms of assistance both to Mexican
Americans and to newly arrived Mexican laborers inside and out of the bracero program.

For Lucey, the job of caring for Spanish-speaking Catholics was complicated by the fact that this group was economically divided between nonbra-
cero legal residents and Mexican American citizens on the one hand, and
braceros and undocumented migrants on the other. While all of these groups
were employed in large numbers in migrant farm labor, Lucey believed that,
for citizens and legal residents (nonbraceros with green cards), unionization
represented the best hope for improving their situation because labor unions
could best help them learn "how to protect their job and defend their rights,
[learn] how to secure a contract and how to keep others from violating that
contract." Further, Lucey felt that local parish pastors, under episcopal tute-

lage and in concert with papal teachings, ought to facilitate meetings between union organizers and citizen or legal resident migrant workers. To be sure, the BCSS under Lucey never asked priests to organize unions themselves, and it is not clear that many priests actually followed the bishops' admonition that they introduce migrant workers to union officials.[14] Even so, the impulse to support workers associations was clearly part of the BCSS's vision for Spanish-speaking Catholics. Unfortunately, and Lucey knew this fact all to well, such a strategy was not realistic for braceros or undocumented workers, who could easily be deported if their employers suspected them of organizing.[15]

One of the challenges facing Lucey and the BCSS was that many Catholics were unaware of the Church's official doctrines concerning labor organizing and workers' rights. A series of papal encyclicals had provided Church leaders with a clear mandate to support workers in situations such as the one confronting Mexican American, bracero, and undocumented farmworkers in US fields. Despite this doctrinal support for clergy involvement in labor issues, most priests did little to educate their parishioners about papal social teaching. One Catholic reported in the early 1950s: "I go to mass every Sunday and I have never once heard anyone mention in Church anything about these encyclicals. If the Church wants to get anything done as they are taught in the encyclicals, why don't they tell the people?"[16] In what follows, I provide a profile of Catholic social teaching in order to contextualize the BCSS's opposition to the bracero program and to show that those clergy closest to Mexican and Mexican American farmworkers were quite prepared to draw on these encyclicals both to guide and defend their activities.

The key Vatican document, which would be the anchor for all later social teaching, was Pope Leo XIII's 1891 encyclical *Rerum Novarum*. The impetus for *Rerum Novarum* came from the perceived threat of European socialism and Marxist calls for revolutionary political and economic change. Leo XIII, pope from 1878 to 1903, issued his famous encyclical in part to answer socialist trade-union challenges to Catholic ideals for a just society. The trade unions generally proposed secular plans for worker organizations and economic power in class conflict with the capitalist owners and industrialists. Even before Leo XIII's pontificate, European bishops had condemned the secular unionists' notion of the proletariat in revolt against capitalism in crisis and instead promoted social change based on spiritual renewal and social relationships among all people guided by biblical ethics.[17] At stake was the Church's ability to articulate a social vision and sustain a relevant ministry to workers and their families that could rival the actions of both liberal social reformers and socialist organizers. *Rerum Novarum* offered a middle way between what Leo XIII perceived as the hyperindividualism of capitalism and the dehumanizing collectivism of socialism. In so doing, he maintained the Church's long-standing commitment to bring reason and moral theology to bear on social problems, an orientation that stood in sharp contrast to Marxist materialist critiques.

To wit, *Rerum Novarum* articulates ideal Catholic social relationships in explicit religious and biblical terms. After a defense of private property as a God-given right, the encyclical moves into what would become one of the central features of Catholic social thought: the contention that the family is the basic unit of society. As the encyclical declared, this social structure was decreed by God both in the Bible and "in the laws of nature. . . . No human law can abolish the natural and primitive right of marriage, ordained by God's authority from the beginning. 'Increase and multiply.' Thus we have the family; the 'society' of a man's own household; a society limited indeed by numbers, but a true 'society,' anterior to every kind of State or nation, with rights and duties of its own, totally independent of the commonwealth."[18] This basic unit of social organization, the family, is held up throughout *Rerum Novarum* as the essential and sacrosanct body that all other social polities and organizations must defend and support. As discussed later, the bracero program's stress on families was, indeed, one of the principal motivators for Catholic opposition to the program.

Much of the remainder of the encyclical is dedicated to prescribing how labor practices should contribute to this original and central objective. To this end, a call for a just wage is key in Leo XIII's formulation:

> Let it be granted, then that, as a rule, workman and employer should make free agreements, and in particular should freely agree as to wages; nevertheless, there is a dictate of nature more imperious and more ancient than any bargain between man and man, that the remuneration must be enough to support the wage earner [and by extension, his family] in reasonable and frugal comfort.[19]

But if workers do not achieve a living wage through agreement with their employers, *Rerum Novarum* advocates that they unionize to protect and defend this right. Indeed, the encyclical calls on bishops and other clergy to be active in the organization of workers. In Leo XIII's terms, Catholics ought to "strive to unite working people of various kinds into associations, help them with their advice and their means, and enable them to obtain honest and profitable work. The bishops, on their part, bestow their ready good will and support; and with their approval and guidance many members of the clergy, both secular and religious, labor assiduously on behalf of the spiritual and mental interests of the members of associations."[20]

These papal calls for fair wages, familial integrity, and the right to organize would have a powerful impact on all subsequent Catholic social policy both at the level of the Vatican and in regional episcopal councils.

On the heels of the Great Depression, Pope Pius XI published in 1931 his encyclical *Quadragesimo Anno* ("After Forty Years") to celebrate *Rerum Novarum's* fortieth anniversary and to expand upon its teachings for the middle of the twentieth century. Its issuance had the effect of solidifying the central importance of *Rerum Novarum*, which *Quadragesimo Anno* refers to as the "Magna Charta on which all Christian activities in social matters are ultimately based."[21] Pius XI's encyclical is probably best known for its articulation of the concept of subsidiarity—that basic social units like the individual or the family should not be superseded by larger units, and that the larger units should exist to assist the smaller ones. In such an arrangement, the intrinsic human ability to self-govern is not unduly eliminated even while the need for the support of social relationships is clearly recognized. This notion naturally sustained *Rerum Novarum's* support of workers' associations and collective bargaining because as legal scholar Thomas Kohler explains in his commentary on *Quadragesimo Anno*, "Subsidiarity emphasizes that humans can achieve self-realization only in and through relations with others. Unions reflect this aspect of human character."[22] However, the encyclical is also quite clear that collective bargaining for unions should remain focused on the dignity of the person and the centrality of the family instead of on class divisions or conflict. In this way, faithful workers and employers are expected not to clash as enemies but to engage as "well-ordered members of the social body . . . [thus] binding men together not according to their position in the labor market, but according to the diverse functions which they exercise in society."[23]

This last statement demonstrates a key element of Catholic social teaching: namely, all human beings belong to a natural created order that sometimes finds itself in conflict due to human sinfulness. *Rerum Novarum* and the other social encyclicals admonish Christians to hold fast to the inherent dignity in each person and both to recognize and work against hurtful divisions in society. The inhumane living and working conditions of many bracero camps, the forced separation of families, and the social divisions that arose around competing claims of legality and citizenship among farmworkers all represented grave concerns for Lucey, the BCSS, and other clergy in ministry to Spanish-speaking migrant workers.[24]

For several years, the BCSS focused the bulk of its efforts on providing the sacraments and sufficient pastoral care to Spanish-speaking populations, including the braceros. But after witnessing firsthand the degradation and family separation caused by the bracero program, the BCSS in 1953 began to issue repeated calls for the discontinuance of the entire program as completely incompatible with the holistic health of families and detrimental to all migrant workers, both citizen and bracero. Similar resolutions were passed by the committee in ensuing years as well as more widespread calls for all Catholics to get involved in the cause. For instance, in 1955, bishops and laypeople together resolved, "That since migratory farm labor is often voteless, unorganized, and poorly protected by law, the Catholic Council for the Spanish Speaking urges its members to form local citizens' committees to represent the interests of its citizens who are farm laborers."[25] The following year's meeting in Grand Rapids, Michigan, by virtue of its location, gave a clear message to Catholics and government officials that the problem of migrant labor and abuses against the braceros had become a national issue. It must be noted that caring for the workers' religious needs lest they fall prey to "different religious sects" remained a central concern for the BCSS. But by the late 1950s, it was evident that Lucey's guidance of the committee had led them toward consistent and robust expressions of concern for the worker that went far beyond fears of Protestant proselytism. These expressions included appeals to the government, explicit support of unionization, and a public-education campaign about the bracero program's serious shortcomings. The 1956 meeting combined these preoccupations with the recommendation that Public Law 78, which governed bracero importation, be terminated.[26]

In his personal statements, Archbishop Lucey declared his own condemnation of the program in no uncertain terms, and he shared his feelings with various groups. Ten years before the bracero program would be discontinued, Lucey addressed a national readership to condemn imported labor, injustices committed against "wetbacks," and the moral morass in which growers and employers found themselves:

> The growers who like foreign slave labor, even when their own fellow citizens are unemployed, can concoct a rather persuasive argument for their iniquity. After all [say the growers], these illegal aliens are human beings and children of God. . . . Plenty of people in our country do not see the sophistry of these excuses which are offered to hide crimes of greed and injustice.[27]

In 1960, he used the precise words of *Rerum Novarum* when he announced, "We owe it to them [farmworkers] to give them a chance to lead their lives *in decent and frugal comfort.*"[28] He also addressed his Mexican counterparts to whom he wrote concerning the braceros that "they generally do not receive the sacraments and at times the moral conditions in the labor camps are bad." He continued that the Mexican bishops ought to "explain to the *braceros* how difficult it is to work in the United States and persuade them not to come."[29]

Lucey worked tirelessly, and often contentiously, for Spanish-speaking Catholics and migrant workers until his retirement in 1969. Besides his denunciation of the excesses and inherent injustices he saw in the bracero program, Lucey also spent considerable effort on education and welfare support for Mexicans and Mexican American parishioners under his purview. One example of his activities is the Confraternity of Christian Doctrine, an organization committed to catechetical education for all Catholics in his area. To this end, he recruited Latin American missionaries to help catechize the Spanish-speaking residents and migrant workers in the region, and he insisted for years that every priest in the archdiocese become proficient in Spanish, going so far as to inspect personally the attendance records for the biweekly Spanish lessons priests were required to take. In addition to religious education, he also established a successful social welfare agency through the diocese, which earned him accolades in both the national press and as far away as Mexico City.[30] On the way, he inspired several clergy, especially in California, who would play an important role in the eventual end of the bracero program.

California's Spanish Mission Band and Growing Calls for Unionization

In California's rich fields, the agricultural economy had long relied on seasonal workers. Consequently, the bracero program found its greatest utilization in California; during the years of the program, braceros constituted between 12 and 28 percent of the Californian seasonal hired labor force.[31] This concentration of bracero workers created an obvious focus for the BCSS and related Catholic groups. The most important such group to arise in California was the Spanish Mission Band. First conceived in 1948 after Fathers Donald McDonnell and Ralph Duggan attended a conference sponsored by the BCSS, the Spanish Mission Band was a novel approach to ministry to the Spanish speaking in the northern area of the San Joaquin Valley. Four young priests—McDonnell, Duggan, Thomas McCullough, and John Garcia—with the blessing and oversight of Archbishop John Mitty of San Francisco, were freed from parish responsibilities so that they could dedicate all their time to serving Spanish-speaking Catholic farmworkers in the rural areas of the archdiocese. Beginning in 1950 and extending until 1961, the Mission Band organized community centers, celebrated masses in the fields, led Catholic education for migrant families, and, perhaps more than any other Catholic body at the time, advocated for the unionization of farm laborers.[32]

Like Archbishop Lucey in Texas, the priests of the Mission Band found definitive guidance in the social encyclicals. Soon after the band was formed, they were presented with an opportunity to share papal teachings on workers' organizations when they came into contact with Ernesto Galarza and Hank Hasiwar, organizers for the National Farm Labor Union (NFLU). The union representatives worked closely with the priests, especially when the latter group proved themselves to be well versed in Catholic teaching concerning workers' rights. As early as 1950, the Mission Band counseled braceros and Mexican Americans of their God-given right to organize and to strike if necessary. When he was later asked how they got started collaborating with unionization efforts, Father McCullough recalled,

> Well, the historical event was the organization of the strike of Tracy tomato workers by Ernesto Galarza. We were just in the process of going in to arrange for a mass the next day, when there was this disturbance. People were running around hollering, "Huelga, huelga!!" [Strike, strike!!] . . . so we began following this thing . . . and going to the union meetings and listening to them.
>
> This was all done with ecclesiastical approval. Father McDonnell wrote . . . to the Bishop to ask if we could attend the meetings of the union workers, and if we could say anything. The reply was yes. We couldn't take sides, but we certainly could read the social encyclicals and present the teachings of the social encyclicals . . . that was the thing to do.[33]

In addition, the band had specific criteria that they demanded any workers' organizations meet before the priests would lend their support. Echoing concepts in *Rerum Novarum*, these included requirements that the organization base its program on human dignity before all else, that it recognize the right to private property, and that it operate by emphasizing cooperation between management and labor.[34]

Papal social teaching also aided the Mission Band in their interactions with other similarly oriented religious organizations. During the years of the bracero program, Catholics at times worked with ecumenical partners in the mainline Protestant–dominated National Council of Churches (NCC), which had long had a presence among farmworkers with its Migrant Ministry. This group, like the Spanish Mission Band, ultimately saw worker organization as a necessary step to alleviate misery and injustice for citizen and bracero migrants. Unlike their Catholic counterparts, however, the Protestant NCC did not have doctrinal and hierarchical backing for their attitudes about workers' associations. As the Migrant Ministry director Rev. Wayne Hartmire wrote, for many Protestant ministers, asking their congregations to support unions was *"institutionally* impossible" and could result in "institutional chaos."[35] This meant, at least in the case of the Mission Band, that the priests could sustain talk of unionization much more stridently than their Protestant peers. Nevertheless, it is notable that the members of the Spanish Mission Band, despite their institutional mandate to promote worker organization, had to seek allies with like-minded Protestants rather than with other Catholics.[36]

The overt prounion stance of the Mission Band led them into unique supporting roles in the formation of community and workers' groups. One was an organization of their own creation: the Agricultural Workers Association (AWA). Father McCullough was the architect of the AWA, which functioned as a mutual-aid society to help farmworkers. Dolores Huerta, who would go on to build the United Farm Workers, helped him write AWA's constitution.[37] The band also collaborated with an organization out of San Jose called the Community Service Organization (CSO), a group that organized migrant workers along the principles of Saul Alinsky's community organizing Industrial Areas Foundation. Father McDonnell worked closely with the CSO and its leader, Fred Ross. McDonnell introduced a young César Chávez to Ross, and Chávez would go on to become the CSO's lead organizer.[38] The efforts of the AWA and CSO eventually got the notice of national labor organizers, and in 1959, the AFL-CIO created the Agricultural Workers Organizing Committee (AWOC) to see to the bargaining needs of agricultural seasonal workers. The AWOC absorbed the AWA and eventually was one of the constituent units of the United Farm Workers union.[39]

In addition to promoting worker organization, the priests of the Spanish Mission Band worked vociferously to denounce the injustices they perceived in the bracero program. Joining their voice with Archbishop Lucey and the rest of the BCSS, they spoke repeatedly in front of governmental committees calling for the repeal of Public Law 78, the legislation that had extended the import of braceros well past the end of World War II. In 1958, Father McCullough spoke before the House Committee on Agriculture to condemn the importation of Mexican labor and its deleterious effects on citizen employment.[40] Soon after the bracero program officially ended in 1964, Father McDonnell addressed the Department of Labor to ensure that there would be no quick replacement under new legislation. First, he noted that the bracero program had "caused a fearful number of broken homes in Mexico, something the Mexican bishops have long protested." Then, to drive home his point, he quoted *Rerum Novarum* to the gathered officials: "Rich men and masters should remember this—that to exercise pressure for the sake of gain, upon the indigent and destitute, and to make one's profit out of the need of another, is condemned by all laws, human and divine."[41]

The Legacy of Catholic Teaching upon Latino Migrant Labor Organizing

The bracero program came to an end in 1964 when pressure from organized labor, religious groups, and shifting public opinion, combined with the mechanization of farmwork, made continuation of the program untenable.[42] The stridency and consistency of Catholic protests had an impact on its demise, though the actions and statements of Archbishop Lucey, the BCSS, and the Spanish Mission Band were not universally accepted by all Catholics. Critiques made by fellow priests as well as laypeople in the Church accused the activist clergy of meddling outside of their ecclesiastical jurisdiction, of focusing on political instead of spiritual matters, of taking sides against the (sometimes Catholic) growers, and even of being Communists. Criticisms like these and growing outrage from growers, including the threat of a lawsuit that demanded that the Church's tax-exempt status be revoked, led to the Spanish Mission Band's termination in 1961.[43] If these members of the clergy crossed a line into organizing, it was not only out of personal political persuasion but was also always rooted, often quite explicitly, in Catholic social teaching and in the pastoral vision that grew from that doctrine. Father James Vizzard, the director of the National Catholic Rural Life Conference (NCRLC) during the bracero years, said, "To some it may seem strange that the NCRLC and the other church organizations . . . have such a strong and continuing concern with matters of social and economic policy when the final objective justifying our existence and activity is the spiritual welfare of souls. . . . We think that it is evident that at least a minimum of material security and well-being is required before the spiritual can flourish."[44] This stance, promoted in papal teaching and shared by several Catholic leaders during the bracero program, laid the groundwork for later Church-labor collaborations in the area of agricultural work.[45]

The doctrinal foundation of clergy-labor alliances that were articulated by the BCSS and the Spanish Mission Band directly informed César Chávez's own organizing of farmworkers. Father McDonnell not only introduced

Chávez to Fred Ross of the Community Service Organization, he also educated Chávez about the social encyclicals and gave him a copy of *Rerum Novarum*.[46] Chávez recalled, "I would do anything to get Father [McDonnell] to tell me more about labor history. I began going to bracero camps with him to help with the Mass, to the city jail with him to talk to the prisoners, anything to be with him."[47] One of the first actions that Chávez organized after the termination of the bracero program was the famous strike against grape growers in Delano, California. In September 1965, he called farmworkers to strike, saying:

> All men are brothers, sons of the same God; that is why we say to all men of good will, in the words of Pope Leo XIII: "Everyone's first duty is to protect the workers from the greed of speculators who use human beings as instruments to provide themselves with money. It is neither just nor human to oppress with excessive work to the point where their minds become enfeebled and their bodies worn out." God shall not abandon us![48]

While it would be a stretch to say that these comments cemented Catholic support for the nascent farmworkers union, several commentators have noted that Chávez's early commitment to religious rhetoric and images, followed up with the use of overt religious acts in UFW protests—fasting and pilgrimage—convinced Church leaders that the union took seriously Catholic social teachings.[49] Likewise, Chávez's use of *Rerum Novarum* and other Catholic doctrine in the UFW's campaigns meant that liberal Catholics could defend their support of the union with little threat of hierarchical displeasure. Indeed, Pope Paul VI gave Chávez and the farmworkers his personal blessing in a private audience.[50]

Catholic interaction with bracero and citizen migrant farmworkers was founded on Church doctrine. Namely, the pastoral activities, public statements, and ecclesiastical organizations that priests and bishops marshaled against the bracero program and in support of workers' rights found their basis in Catholic social teaching, especially in *Rerum Novarum*. The theological ideas articulated in the social encyclicals concerning human dignity, workers' rights to organize, a living wage, and the importance of family life made a positive and indelible impact on the lives of millions of Mexican and Mexican American farmworkers in the middle of the twentieth century. In effect, this means that Lucey, the BCSS, and the Spanish Mission Band came to the injustices of Mexican import labor with a language and a theological framework already in place with which to organize for dignity. And they, through their partnerships with labor organizers and Mexican American leaders, were able to bring these doctrinal structures to bear not only on the bracero program but also on the UFW and even on the movement for Mexican American civil rights. Catholic leaders and laypeople in the struggle against the bracero program found guidance and inspiration in the words of distant popes, thus confirming a central tenet of their faith: words can be incarnational.

Notes

1. Robert E. Lucey, "Report to the National Catholic Welfare Council," 18 November 1959, University of Notre Dame archives, cited in Stephen A. Privett, *The U.S. Catholic Church and Its Hispanic Members: The Pastoral Vision of Archbishop Robert E. Lucey* (San Antonio, TX: Trinity University Press, 1988), 115–16. The National Catholic Welfare Council is a predecessor of the US Conference of Catholic Bishops.

2. Leo XIII, "*Rerum Novarum*," in *Catholic Social Thought: The Documentary Heritage*, ed. David J. O'Brien and Thomas A. Shannon (Maryknoll, NJ: Orbis Books, 1992), 21.

3. For example, Marco Prouty, *César Chávez, the Catholic Bishops, and the Farm Workers' Struggle for Social Justice* (Tucson: University of Arizona Press, 2008); Mario T. García, ed., *The Gospel of César Chávez: My Faith in Action* (Lanham, MD: Sheed and Ward, 2007); Luis D. León, "César Chávez and Mexican American Civil Religion," in *Latino Religions and Civic Activism in the United States*, ed. Gastón Espinosa, Virgilio Elizondo, and Jesse Miranda (New York: Oxford University Press, 2005), 53–64; and Stephen R. Lloyd-Moffett, "The Mysticism and Social Action of César Chávez," in *Latino Religions and Civic Activism in the United States*, ed. Gastón Espinosa, Virgilio Elizondo, and Jesse Miranda (New York: Oxford University Press, 2005), 35–51.

4. Mae M. Ngai, *Impossible Subjects: Illegal Aliens and the Making of Modern America* (Princeton, NJ: Princeton University Press, 2004), 138–39; Rodolfo Acuña, *Occupied America: A History of Chicanos*, 3rd ed. (New York: Harper Collins, 1988), 261–66. See also Gilda L. Ochoa, *Becoming Neighbors in a Mexican American Community: Power, Conflict, and Solidarity* (Austin: University of Texas Press, 2004), 29–30; Kathleen Mapes, *Sweet Tyranny: Migrant Labor, Industrial Agriculture, and Imperial Politics* (Urbana: University of Illinois Press, 2009), 145–53; Jim Norris, *North for the Harvest: Mexican Workers, Growers, and the Sugar Beet Industry* (St. Paul: Minnesota Historical Society, 2009), 58–60, 73–74; and Deborah Cohen, *Braceros: Migrant Citizens and Transnational Subjects in the Postwar United States and Mexico* (Chapel Hill: University of North Carolina Press, 2011), 23.

5. Ngai, *Impossible Subjects*, 151–52.

6. Ibid., 153; Josephine Anne Kellogg, "The San Francisco Mission Band, 1948 to 1961" (master's thesis, Graduate Theological Union, 1974), 78.

7. Ngai, *Impossible Subjects*, 161. For more on the braceros' role in hurting unionization, see Ernesto Galarza, *Farm Workers and Agri-Business in California, 1947–1960* (Notre Dame, IN: Notre Dame University Press, 1977), 204–5.

8. Rosemary E. Smith, "The Work of the Bishops' Committee for the Spanish-Speaking on Behalf of the Migrant Worker" (master's thesis, Catholic University of America, 1958), 12.

9. Ernesto Galarza, *Strangers in Our Fields* (Washington, DC: Joint United States–Mexico Trade Union Committee, 1956), 75. It is important to note that some historians, especially those examining Mexican points of view, look on the bracero program, if not uncritically, in a less condemnatory tone. For example, Michael Snodgrass argues in several places that bracero contracts in Mexico were part of the PRI (Partido Revolucionario Institucional; Institutional Revolutionary Party) government's system of patronage and often resulted in greater prosperity and opportunity for the returned workers; see Snodgrass, "The Bracero Program, 1942–1964," in *Beyond La Frontera: The History of Mexico-U.S. Migration*, ed. Mark Overmeyer-Velázquez (New York: Oxford University Press, 2011), 79–102; and Snodgrass, "Patronage and Progress: The Bracero Program from the Perspective of Mexico," in *Workers across the Americas: The Transnational Turn in Labor History*, ed. Leon Fink (New York: Oxford University Press, 2011), 245–66. Likewise, in her fieldwork among older Mexicans who had once worked as braceros, Deborah Cohen finds that the memories men have of the program are relatively positive. She further argues that Catholic critiques of the program, which I treat here, betray the critics' commitment to modernity over and against the complex needs of the Mexican workers. Here I do not dispute her point but rather focus my arguments on the Catholic critics' religious ideation and framing of the bracero program in the United States; see Cohen, *Braceros*.

10. Acuña, *Occupied America*, 326.

11. Privett, *U.S. Catholic Church and Its Hispanic Members*, 96–97.

12. Alan J. Watt, *Farm Workers and the Churches: The Movement in California and Texas* (College Station: Texas A&M University Press, 2010), 51.

13. Smith, "Work of the Bishops' Committee for the Spanish-Speaking," 4–5; Saul E. Bronder, *Social Justice and Church Authority: The Public Life of Archbishop Robert E. Lucey* (Philadelphia: Temple University Press, 1982), 74–76.

14. "Report to the BCSS," 1950, University of Notre Dame archives, cited in Privett, *U.S. Catholic Church and Its Hispanic Members*, 101.

15. Indeed, Lucey was one of the first and most vocal opponents of the bracero program's continuation in the postwar era. Appointed by President Truman in 1950 to serve on a commission to investigate the conditions of migratory farm laborers, Lucey spoke out against the continued importation of Mexican labor. Despite Lucey's and others' condemnation of the program, Truman nonetheless prolonged the bracero program under Public Law 78 in 1951. See Bronder, *Social Justice*, 78–79.

16. Edward Marciniak, "The Catholic Church and Labor," in *The Catholic Church, U.S.A.*, ed. Louis J. Putz (Chicago: Fides, 1956), 268.

17. William Murphy, "*Rerum Novarum*," in *A Century of Catholic Social Thought: Essays on 'Rerum Novarum' and Nine Other Key Documents*, ed. George Weigel and Robert Royal (Washington, DC: Ethics and Public Policy Center, 1991), 8.

18. Leo XIII, "*Rerum Novarum*," in *Catholic Social Thought: The Documentary Heritage*, ed. David J. O'Brien and Thomas A. Shannon (Maryknoll, NY: Orbis Books, 1992),18.

19. Ibid., 31.

20. Ibid., 35.

21. Pius XI, "*Quadragesimo Anno*," in *Catholic Social Thought: The Documentary Heritage*, ed. David J. O'Brien and Thomas A. Shannon (Maryknoll, NY: Orbis Books, 1992), 50.

22. Thomas C. Kohler, commentary on "*Quadragesimo Anno*," in *A Century of Catholic Social Thought: Essays on 'Rerum Novarum' and Nine Other Key Documents*, ed. George Weigel and Robert Royal (Washington, DC: Ethics and Public Policy Center, 1991), 41.

23. Pius XI, "*Quadragesimo Anno*," 61.

24. Jesus M. Rendon, "Archbishop Robert E. Lucey and Organized Labor in San Antonio, Texas 1960–1968," *Journal of the Life and Culture of San Antonio*, http://www.uiw.edu/sanantonio/Lucey.html, accessed December 9, 2014.

25. *Proceedings of the Seventh Regional Conference, Catholic Council for the Spanish Speaking*, 19–21 April 1955, cited in Smith, "The Work of the Bishops' Committee for the Spanish-Speaking," 22. The Catholic Council for the Spanish Speaking was a lay and clergy organization that worked alongside the BCSS.

26. Ibid., 23.

27. Robert E. Lucey, "Migratory Workers," *Commonweal*, 15 January 1954, 371.

28. Remarks to the students of Assumption Seminary, San Antonio, 1960, Archdiocese of San Antonio archives, cited in Privett, *U.S. Catholic Church and Its Hispanic Members*, 112 (my emphasis, indicating quote from *Rerum Novarum*).

29. Letter to L. Avina, 1958, Archdiocese of San Antonio archives, cited in ibid., 115. With these statements, Lucey was likely playing to the Mexican Church's fears concerning the braceros. From the beginning of the program in the 1940s, Mexican Catholic officials had publicly worried that the workers would face Protestant proselytism, gambling, drink, prostitution, and general moral decay north of the border. In line with Catholic social teaching about the centrality of the family as the basic social unit, Mexican clergy also pointed out that the program had the unavoidable consequence of splitting apart families. In one example, the Mexican hierarchy made the astounding (and possibly exaggerated) claim that, of the two and a half million men who had left Mexico as braceros by the late 1950s, a full million never returned to their families; see Richard H. Hancock, *The Role of the Bracero in the Economic and Cultural Dynamics of Mexico: A Case Study of Chihuahua* (Stanford, CA: Hispanic American Society, 1959), 39.

30. Privett, *U.S. Catholic Church and Its Hispanic Members*, 129, 134, 143–44. Some Anglo Catholics in San Antonio were less laudatory. One businessman charged that Lucey cared "only for the poor Mexicans and the laboring person; he didn't care about the salvation of the souls of businessmen" (143).

31. Ernesto Galarza, *Merchants of Labor: The Mexican Bracero Story; an Account of the Managed Migration of Mexican Farm Workers in California, 1942–1960* (Charlotte, NC: McNally and Loftin, 1964), 94.

32. Jay P. Dolan and Gilberto M. Hinojosa, eds., *Mexican Americans and the Catholic Church, 1900–1965*, vol. 1 (Notre Dame, IN: University of Notre Dame Press, 1994), 214–15.

33. McNamara, "Bishops, Priests, and Prophecy: A Study in the Sociology of Religious Protest" (PhD diss., University of California, Los Angeles, 1968), 119; see also Kellogg, "San Francisco Mission Band," 178.

34. Kellogg, "San Francisco Mission Band," 94.

35. Wayne C. Hartmire, "The Plight of Seasonal Farm Workers," in *Witness to a Generation: Significant Writings from Christianity and Crisis, 1941–1966*, ed. Wayne H. Cowan (Indianiapolis, IN: Bobbs-Merrill, 1966), 175–76.

36. To be sure, many Catholic clergy and laypeople were quite publicly opposed to clergy support for worker organization among the farmworkers. One dramatic example of this sentiment is a pamphlet published in 1968 (a few years after the demise of the bracero program) that condemns Catholic collaboration with the nascent UFW; see Frank Bergon and Murray Norris, *Delano—Another Crisis for the Catholic Church!* (Fresno, CA: Rudell, 1968).

37. Dolan and Hinojosa, *Mexican Americans and the Catholic Church*, 219–20.

38. Ibid., 204, 219.

39. United Farm Workers, "The Rise of the UFW," http://uwww.ufw.org/_page.php p?menu=research&inc=history/03.html, accessed 9 December 2014.

40. Kellogg, "San Francisco Mission Band," 113–14.

41. Patrick J. Sullivan, *Blue Collar-Roman Collar-White Collar: U.S. Catholic Involvement in Labor Management Controversies, 1960–1980* (Lanham, MD: University Press of America, 1987), 11–12; Leo XIII, "*Rerum Novarum*," 21.

42. Ngai, *Impossible Subjects*, 165–66.

43. McNamara, *Bishops, Priests, and Prophecy*, 121–24. The Bishops' Committee for the Spanish Speaking, which in 1974 became the Secretariat for Hispanic Affairs within the US Conference of Catholic Bishops, continues its work on behalf of the growing numbers of Latinos/Latinas in the US Catholic Church.

44. James Vizzard, "Churches and Braceros," *America*, 25 March 1961, 811.

45. Of course, many Catholic "labor priests," by the time of the bracero program, had been advocating for decades for better conditions, wages, and protections for working people. Many of these prior efforts had likewise drawn on *Rerum Novarum* and other papal writings for doctrinal support. For one prominent example, see Father John A. Ryan, *A Living Wage: Its Ethical and Economic Aspects* (New York: Macmillan, 1906).

46. García, *Gospel of César Chávez*, 8; J. Craig Jenkins, *The Politics of Insurgency: The Farm Worker Movement in the 1960s* (New York: Columbia University Press, 1985), 131–33.

47. Quoted in George G. Higgins and William Bole, *Organized Labor and the Church: Reflections of a "Labor Priest"* (New York: Paulist Press, 1993), 87.

48. "Plan de Delano" in Gilberto López y Rivas, ed., *The Chicano: Life and Struggles of the Mexican Minority in the United States* (New York: Monthly Review Press, 1972), 109, quoted in García, *Gospel of César Chávez*, 37.

49. Randy Shaw, *Beyond the Fields: Cesar Chavez, the UFW, and the Struggle for Justice in the 21st Century* (Berkeley: University of California Press, 2008), 78; Joseph M. Palacios, *The Catholic Social Imagination: Activism and the Just Society in Mexico and the United States* (Chicago: University of Chicago Press, 2007), 83.

50. Higgins and Bole, *Organized Labor and the Church*, 96.

Black Freedom Struggles
and Ecumenical Activism in 1960s Chicago

ERIK S. GELLMAN

In April of 1969, the African American Reverend Archie J. Hargraves stepped up to the rostrum of the Riverside Church in New York City and asked, "Where is God speaking now?" His speech, delivered to a gathering on "The Church and the Urban Crisis," suggested that the Church should look for leadership beyond the pews of middle-class congregations to reach those far removed from and even cynical about Christianity. Ministers, he said, need to "humble ourselves" to "the new actors on the urban scene" whom he defined as "the Black, the poor and the young." To Hargraves, learning from these actors—whom others construed as social pariahs or even the underclasses responsible for urban disorder—would enable the Church to construct a "program for dealing with [the urban crisis]." By exhorting his fellow ministers to seek leadership from the people most forgotten by industrial "progress," Hargraves inverted the Church's mission programs that historically had sought to provide faith-based ethics to help unde-requipped people "adjust" to urban environments. While he admitted that having faith in inner-city people was "awfully frightening for most of us who have lived—as we have—in the leadership of American society," such faith was the pathway to locate the word of God and bring justice to the modern American metropolis.[1]

Hargraves came to this conclusion through his experiences at Chicago's Urban Training Center for Christian Mission (UTC), where he and others had experimented with new forms of "engagement and reflection" and "action training."[2] Begun in 1963 with the aim of channeling Christian energy toward the problems of American cities, the UTC was backed financially by more than a dozen denominations and a five-year, $400,000 grant from the Sealantic Fund of the Rockefeller Foundation. For the next decade, its staff conceived and ran a remarkably diverse series of training programs for seminarians, ministers, and laypeople.[3] The UTC's scope was national, but its students trained on the edge of the West Side "ghetto" in Chicago before returning to their "home situations." Although at first UTC staffers and trainees seemed to view the city as a social laboratory for their own religious education, they increasingly sought to contribute to local civil rights and economic justice networks on the West Side and across the Chicago metropolitan region.

The UTC represented an experimental response to some clergy members' fear that their relevance was declining. Most famously, an April 1966 *Time* magazine cover asked in bold red letters, "Is God Dead?" The cover's provocation was somewhat muted by the subsequent article estimating that 97 percent of Americans believed in God, but it fueled an ongoing debate over the quality of belief and the Church's significance in American society. "Secularization, science, urbanization," the article stated, "all have made it comparatively easy for the modern man to ask where God is, and hard for the man of faith to give a convincing answer, even to himself."[4] By studying the evolving dimensions of the UTC's staff, programs, and fieldwork, this chapter analyzes how a group of ministers and theologians sought to make the Church (and themselves) relevant through new forms of training and activism.

The UTC's innovative forms of urban mission speak to two interrelated but distinct threads of historical scholarship that have focused upon connections between religion and social movements. First, some labor historians have sought to understand the "lived religion" of working-class people in relation to the labor movement. As this volume's Introduction contends, scholars have only begun to investigate how people in social movements might have understood and applied theological ideas in resistance to the economic and social inequality generated by American capitalism. Analysis of the UTC's history reveals how one group of religiously inspired activists engaged with dominant social movements of the era—in particular, civil rights and Black Power—in a local context.

But the UTC activists were less steeped in the class-based politics of labor unions than in the race-based activism of civic protest organizations. Religion was essential to the 1960s civil rights movement, providing both an institutional base through African American churches and a wellspring of personal and collective faith.[5] And while scholars have recently illustrated how

Black Power activism represented a collection of social movements, they have largely elided Black Power's religious dimensions. Historian Ibram Rogers usefully refers to this significant yet marginalized aspect of Black Power as the "Black Religious Movement," whose adherents shared the desire to promote the growth of religious blackness, confront racist structures of American society, and liberate Christianity from Eurocentric theological assumptions.[6] Taking up this call for new religious studies, some historians have begun to reexamine the influence of the Nation of Islam, African American nationalist religious networks, and the black ministers who developed a theology of Black Power.[7] Analysis of the UTC, then, reveals how Christianity shaped both civil rights and Black Power activism among ministers, seminarians, and laypeople in the urban North.

In the case of the UTC, Christianity gave rise to cross-class and interracial activism. Although its leadership was largely white and middle class, the UTC sought bold remedies for the interrelated urban problems of racism and poverty. Throughout the 1960s, trainees and staff alike saw the UTC as a refuge or "perch" from which to plan for what their education director Richard Luecke called "faithful participation in perpetual rapid change."[8] This emphasis on participation led these urban missionaries to increasingly collaborate with local community organizations in pursuit of economic justice, welfare rights, and, eventually, black self-determination, which in turn changed the UTC itself from training white seminarians for urban mission to collaborating with African American community organizers and finally to hosting offshoot groups separated by race who amassed power among African Americans and combated institutional racism. However, in promoting dialogue and action between social-movement thinkers and actors, the UTC also provoked internal and external race and class tensions that ultimately circumscribed its impact and longevity.

The Early Days of the UTC

The UTC was founded in 1963 by a diverse group of Christian ministers to rethink the Church's role in Chicago's rapidly changing environment. During the previous decade, the second Great Migration doubled the size of the city's black population, and even though African Americans began to live in new neighborhoods on the South and West Sides, "white flight" intensified residential segregation.[9] As parishioners moved away, urban membership in several white denominations plummeted. The clergy who stayed behind found themselves at a difficult crossroads, wondering whether to follow many of their members to the suburbs or, instead, to recalibrate their work to deal with the urban poverty and racism their new neighbors faced. The UTC founders chose the latter. A key UTC staff member, Gibson Winter of the Divinity School at the University of Chicago, wrote in his 1962 book *The Suburban Captivity of the Churches* that clergy needed to adjust their efforts according to the needs of modern urban communities. Winter blamed a "narrow spirituality" of the past century by "the White church" for refusing to see the "metropolis [as] an interdependent community," and thereby contributing to "retaliation or mental withdrawal" by white parishioners. To Winter, scripture directed clergy to address new urban problems. He wrote that the "story of the Crucifixion demonstrates the cost of the torn web of human life" and "the Cross says *we are involved* here and now, whether we like it or not."[10] This book, remembered one UTC leader, "started the avalanche of movement," inspiring clergy to retrofit the Church for its new environment by forming the Urban Training Center.[11]

After a brief stint under a director who resigned, the UTC hired James Park Morton in 1964 to lead a board of denominational representatives and a handful of staff members. Morton was a thirty-three-year-old Episcopal priest who trained as an architect at Harvard University before entering the ministry. He attended Cambridge University in England for his theological training and then returned to minister to the poor along the waterfront in Newark, New Jersey. Similar to other UTC leaders who had backgrounds as elite intellectuals but chose to work for social change in urban contexts, Morton relished the opportunity to lead the UTC. As he had declared in one of his early speeches, "We are in the midst of a period of extraordinary creativity in theology." Such creativity should not merely be expressed from pulpits on Sunday mornings, Morton claimed, because "the secular world is the arena where God's acts are declared and demonstrated." For the rest of the 1960s, Morton helped foment such an "urban church strategy" by training clergy, seminarians, and laymen at the Urban Training Center.[12]

Described by its clergy and staff as perched "on the edge of the West Side ghetto," the UTC's headquarters at 40 North Ashland straddled a "historic barrier" between people of different races and classes.[13] The UTC leased its offices from the Chicago Missionary Society's Spanish-speaking mission. This site had once hosted the "stately" First Congregational Church that seated two thousand people but whose "worshipers, . . . feeling the tide of Negro and Spanish-speaking newcomers," had recently "moved to better neighborhoods."[14] The UTC set up shop in the adjacent Carpenter Chapel building. As a rare liminal space in hypersegregated Chicago, the chapel became, according to its director Morton, "an arena for open discussion with no holds barred except for a refusal to respect the integrity and freedom of the other." More specifically, as a 1966 UTC pamphlet called "The Now Thing" explained, "The scope and shape of human community are changing before our eyes," and "there is a lack of institutions by which people themselves participate in the decisions which affect their lives." The UTC sought to foster democratic dialogue among neighborhood people, engaging them in experiential field-work that crossed class and racial boundaries.[15]

This fieldwork began in the spring of 1964 when the UTC welcomed its first group of students, mostly young white seminarians, with the "rock bottom plunge." As an orientation to a ten-week training session, the plunge served to disorient trainees from their class privilege. "This amounts to three days and nights" on the streets of Chicago, one minister and early trainee explained, "with $3.00, a toothbrush, and . . . the shabbiest clothes they can muster."[16] The plunge forced trainees to "feel poverty in their guts," according to one *Newsweek* article, and Morton elaborated by calling it a "shock treatment" that "puts them in situations where they're forced to listen instead of spouting" so that the "scales fall from their eyes."[17] Plunge experiences were both profound and mundane, ranging from a white priest finding food and shelter in a black church, to a black minister finding more community with homeless people at the Pacific Garden Mission than with the clergy who "preached down to you," to the five women who took the plunge in 1965 and had to take extra precautions living on the streets.[18] Staff member Peggy Way remembered that some of the trainees required significant reflection to process the trauma of their temporary descent into poverty and homeless-ness. The plunge remained a mainstay of the UTC's training throughout the 1960s as the beginning of a ten-week "4–3–3" schedule: the first four weeks for orientation, reflection, and engagement; the next three weeks were "de-voted to the home situation" of their original community or parish; and a final three weeks of "specific project development."[19] In all, during its first five years, the center would train 1,280 clergy, seminarians, activists, and others, while thousands more used its space for meetings, "rap sessions," and press conferences.[20]

As director of mission development, Archie Hargraves supervised the trainings as well as all the early staff members. Hargraves stood out due to his being African American, his experience, and his charisma. After earning a bachelor's degree from the North Carolina A&T State University, he moved to New York City to further his education at Union Theological Seminary and Columbia University in the 1940s. Thereafter, he stayed in Harlem and, with two other Union graduates, founded the East Harlem Protestant Parish in 1948, where they pioneered a group ministry. Staffed by neighborhood volunteers and Union students, the parish provided devotional, economic, and political programs.[21] According to fellow East Harlem parish founder Don Benedict, "people were drawn to Archie by his intelligence" but also his "joyful shouting" style of preaching that included the chant of "I am somebody" (a refrain that Jesse Jackson would later make famous in Chicago). This experience in inner-city mission affirmed Hargraves's commitment to reforming the church to better serve the urban poor. In a 1963 United Church of Christ pamphlet titled "Stop Pussyfooting through a Revolution," Hargraves argued that because the city was "the doorway to human dignity in our time," the urban church's primary task was to keep "such counterforces as racial, class, and religious discrimination" from "trying to shut and lock that door." The pamphlet described a dozen examples of congregations whose members sought to "be a *mission* instead of a hospital." Hargraves thus seemed to seek his own opportunity to experiment with a mission model as a means to eliminate discrimination rather than treat its superficial symptoms.[22]

The UTC provided Hargraves with this opportunity. When he first arrived in Chicago in the early 1960s, Hargraves served as a pastor at the South Shore Community Church of Christ and taught at the Chicago Theological Seminary before Don Benedict, his old colleague in the Harlem parish, urged him to take on a leadership role at the nascent UTC. Hargraves came to have a significant impact on the UTC's relationship to its environment. The UTC was designed as a national training center, but its methods required clergy and laymen to think locally, applying the "social laboratory" concept pioneered by the University of Chicago to the city at large. The UTC's members and trainees thus sought to engage the city through both study and activism, a mission that was reflected by one humorous yet commanding poster hanging on the walls of the UTC's office: "For Christ's sake, what's the Church doing?"[23]

Hargraves sought to foster this sustained local and collaborative involvement. For example, in early 1965 staff member Carl Siegenthaler asked about the UTC's responsibility for "social change in Chicago" and then answered by saying, "My impression is we do not have that responsibility [because] Chicago is not our client." In rebuttal Hargraves explained that UTC had learned from its first trainees "to take a more collaborative approach" with local organizations. "We've been plunked in Chicago," he said, "and [are] therefore responsible for Chicago."[24] This approach won out, and UTC trainees and resources funded and inspired new organizations that became central to African Americans on the West Side, and thereafter, Chicago's freedom movement and Black Power Movement.

Congregating in UTC's Backyard:
The West Side Organization

The West Side Organization for Full Employment (WSO) represented one of the UTC's most prominent and controversial efforts to partner with a local constituency. It was created when four UTC trainees began to collaborate with West Side blacks to open a social-services office at 1527 West Roosevelt Road. Unlike the white ministers and seminarians who comprised the UTC's early trainees, the WSO leaders Chester Robinson, Bill Darden, and Bill Clark were working-class black men who lived in the neighborhood. The WSO brought together these neighborhood leaders, local volunteers, and even gang members of the Conservative Vice Lords and Egyptian Cobras who used the Roosevelt Road office as a "neighborhood hang out and community center." Yet, African Americans at the WSO office were not surprised to encounter the white UTC trainees who helped with day-to-day office tasks and editing and writing the WSO's newspaper, *The Torch*.[25] Aided by a two-year, $20,000 grant from the Stern Family Fund (secured by the UTC), the WSO became a viable five-hundred-member community organization within a matter of months.[26]

Comprised of working-class and jobless people, the WSO pressured neighborhood employers through labor-organizing tactics. Its first target was Centennial Laundry, located just down the street on Roosevelt Road. Centennial employed more than two hundred people, and its job advertisements called it a "good plant" with "top pay" and "fun at every unit," but the WSO knew that conditions were poor and wages were low.[27] Beginning in the fall of 1964, the WSO organized street rallies and pickets against the laundry, which yielded a series of negotiations and court battles, and eventually jobs, for people in the neighborhood. By the late 1960s, the WSO expanded its jobs division by participating in the West Side Development Corporation, training people for jobs in the health-care field and operating small businesses such as a Shell "freedom gas" station.[28] In total, the WSO helped local people complete 25,000 job applications and assisted more than one thousand neighborhood people in securing employment. While not a formal labor organization, the WSO's energetic organizing produced a class consciousness for neighborhood residents who desired access to living-wage jobs; as two UTC leaders concluded, "Permeating the whole struggle seemed to be a search for identity with black consciousness, for human dignity, for freedom from dependency."[29]

Parallel to its job-related engagement, the WSO also pioneered new forms of welfare activism. Members of the WSO, who were predominantly young black men, learned from the women in their community about welfare caseworkers' patronizing attitudes and arbitrary rules. With help from UTC resources and trainees, WSO organized a welfare union whose four branches spanned the West Side. In its first eighteen months, the WSO boasted that its union processed over 1,300 grievances against caseworkers' judgments without losing a single case. The WSO's union also won the right to represent welfare clients and won them 3 percent across-the-board increases as a result of a meeting with the Illinois Public Aid Division. As important as these victories, the WSO's organizing empowered women to see welfare as less a shameful handout than as a right. This activism predated and helped serve as a model for the founding of the National Welfare Rights Organization in 1967.[30]

Archie Hargraves believed that the WSO entered a "critical phase" for combating intimidation by 1965 because pressure on the welfare system, the administration of federal War on Poverty programs, and protests against police brutality provoked "increased political harassment," including against "UTC trainees who have volunteered their time in the evening." In April 1965, the police entered the WSO office without a warrant during a dance, beating and arresting those who did not manage to run away. Several months later, the press attacked Chester Robinson for his previous police record; the *Chicago American* called his lack of integrity "a crippling blow to the credibility of the whole program." These press attacks came at an inauspicious moment as Robinson prepared to lead a delegation of the Citizens Crusade Against Poverty to Washington. Some UTC board members fretted over this negative publicity, but residents of the West Side rejected the notion that a criminal record relegated someone to a permanent criminal underclass. West Siders rallied around Robinson by holding a testimonial dinner in his honor upon his return from Washington; more than one thousand people attended, including representatives from the UTC and civil rights groups.[31]

The UTC clearly took pride in its creation of and collaboration with the WSO, but the community organization largely rejected a religious ethos for its activism. As Don Benedict of the Chicago Missionary Society and UTC would later reflect, "the original cadre" in the WSO was "not openly 'religious.'" WSO participants balked at efforts by UTC ministers and trainees to discuss faith with them, including a plan to join in prayer on the picket line in front of Centennial Laundry. Chester Robinson responded, "I don't pray and never will," but he also admitted, "I fear God more than I do Mayor Daley or anybody else." John Crawford did express his religious convictions openly, earning the nicknames "Deacon" and "Preach," but more WSO members seemed to share Bill Clark's view. Clark claimed he had "too much respect for God to pray for myself," adding that "if this was a religious organization I never would have come in that door." While faith mattered to some WSO individuals, it was not a collective motive. This secularism must have disappointed some UTC board members, but its ministers "began to realize that while giving support they could not control [the WSO]."[32]

Openly faithful or not, the following summer's riot on the West Side tested the WSO's resolve as its office became a unique hub of neighborhood activity. When the initial incident of the closing of fire hydrants by city police on July 12, 1966, escalated into a neighborhood-wide riot, Martin Luther King Jr. and other Chicago Freedom Movement staff as well as the Chicago Police Department's Human Relations Department descended on the WSO office to consult its leaders. They all agreed that the WSO was the only group that had established a "rapport" with these "rampaging youths." During the violence, Chester Robinson and comedian and activist Dick Gregory patrolled the streets to "talk sense into people's heads," and in one remarkable incident, Archie Hargraves and Bill Clark acted as a human shield to protect a group of Puerto Ricans who had just been dragged from their cars at an impromptu roadblock on Ashland Avenue. Despite this heroic assistance, the police arrested several WSO members on trumped-up charges, taking special aim at those attempting to document the ongoing police brutality. The violence did not help the West Side neighborhood, but it did accentuate the crisis of racial inequality in Chicago and elevate the WSO as a bona fide community organization. Thereafter, the WSO would become a vital ally of the Coordinating Council of Community Organizations (CCCO), bringing West Siders into King's and the South Christian Leadership Conference's (SCLC) Chicago campaign, and then developing its own Black Power demonstrations and neighborhood commerce projects.[33]

Civil Rights and Wrongs

Meanwhile, the UTC unexpectedly got swept up in the civil rights movement, both in the South and in Chicago. Responding to an SCLC call for northern participation, UTC staff members and students caravanned to Selma, Alabama, in 1965 to help with the voting rights campaign there. As Andrew

Young of SCLC reflected at a UTC strategy session a few months later, "The reason that I'm here [is] that guys that came to Selma from UTC really functioned. They really bailed us out at a time when we were run down and needed people to fill the gap." Young attributed this effectiveness to the fact that they "were freer to function than most white people that came down. They had some understanding of what the revolution was all about" and while they might not have understood "the Negro community" there, they did not expect to "run things." These experiences convinced Young that white clergy could become radicalized for movement activity through the UTC, but also that black clergy and laypeople "could profit by a month of reading in revolutionary subjects" because, after all, "it's going to be a long revolution!"[34]

Director Morton explained to Young that the center was "on its maiden voyage." He hoped the preachers' galvanized sense of social justice would inflect their politics upon their return, wondering aloud whether the same preachers whose faith compelled them to "demonstrate in Selma and Washington" will "picket—and stay there—in front of City Hall?" Hargraves assured Morton as well as civil rights militants like Lawrence Landry and Nahaz Rogers of ACT that ministers could play an important role if the UTC ensured that its staff, ministers, and trainees acted as "servants of the civil rights movement." This mattered because the "Christian mission" of the UTC would not be missionary in the traditional sense of converting the unconverted but rather, following the WSO model, it would engage with activists and community residents on their own terms. Morton's question was partially answered that summer when more than thirty UTC ministers and trainees got arrested in Chicago Freedom Movement demonstrations led by the CCCO. They described their activism as "obedience to their consciences" due to the "current practices of deep inequalities to a large percentage of school children . . . making a mockery of the American principle of 'equal justice under law.'" According to one UTC trainee that summer, CCCO movement leader Al Raby "was doing a double-take on organized religion." Impressed by UTC participation in demonstrations, Raby visited the center to clasp hands, join in prayer, and sing spirituals. In response to Raby's visit and the newly politicized climate, that trainee hoped that this new activism would go "a long way to negate the attitude of 'Damn the churches,' and 'Damn the white liberals' that some of the more far out civil righters have been pushing."[35]

In addition to the UTC's endorsement of direct action in the civil rights movement, the staff called upon the famous architect of community organizing, Saul Alinsky, to advise and teach at its seminars. Alinsky's involvement in Chicago organizing stretched back to the 1930s. He was known for his collaboration with the Catholic Church in the Back of the Yards neighborhood, and his Industrial Areas Foundation by the 1960s had also helped launch protest organizations on Chicago's South Side (such as the Woodlawn Organization) and in other neighborhoods. As early as 1964, Alinsky had led dialogues in the UTC headquarters about how to build power through activism. Warning that community organizing was "hard work," Alinsky admonished some clergy and Chicago Freedom Movement participants for skipping ahead to the "dramatic moments" when real social change was built in "humdrum" and sustained day-to-day work. Alinsky praised the UTC program of fieldwork and reflection as "the kind of curriculum that can really open the doors [and] light the fire," and he continued to participate in discussions at the UTC over the next several years.[36]

Even as the UTC's emphasis on community organizing and engagement won accolades from civil rights leaders and liberal press outlets, several ministers amplified their long-standing reservations about the UTC experiment. The UTC was developed as a training laboratory, not as an active mission organization, they claimed. One prominent board member resigned because of this activist orientation and reliance on Alinsky's community-organizing techniques. Other UTC leaders, however, tolerated and welcomed Alinsky because UTC's strategy sessions rarely accepted a particular strategy wholesale. "What we meant by community organizing was, are you going to be with or against Alinsky," educational director Dr. Richard Luecke recalled, "and the Board had some feeling about that and they answered, 'yes.'" To UTC board member Don Benedict, Alinsky's activist ideology was based on "self-interest." The gospel "ought to lift above self-interest," Benedict concluded, and as such he felt "attracted but also repelled" by Industrial Areas Foundation's organizing tactics. But, as one evaluator noted, although disagreements often divided Alinsky and the trainees and staff during seminars, such dialogue proved productive and underscored his important role.[37]

Beyond the objection to Alinsky, other clergy critiqued the UTC's methods—in particular, its involvement in what they considered secular, political issues. A *Time* magazine article captured this national current in 1965: "Some church leaders are critical of what seems to be its blithe assumption that God endorses everything about the Negro Freedom movement." Dissident clergy wondered whether "the worldly, activist Christianity sacrifices the church's eschatological message for a goal that might be more efficiently accomplished by secular social workers." The UTC was one such religious group that took on secular issues, but its staff members argued that sacrificing a tighter focus on doctrine in favor of a more secular approach was the only way to make the Church relevant to contemporary urban problems. The UTC vowed to bridge the "relevance gap" between the Church and urban society but its leaders sparred over how much of that gap to accommodate while still remaining a religiously based (and funded) center.[38]

Black Power and Urban Mission

The major vehicle for bridging this "relevance gap" and gaining African American participation was the four-year Ford Foundation grant the UTC won in 1965. In its application, the UTC emphasized its recent participation in civil rights demonstrations "that make Chicago all the more important as a laboratory for Civil Rights" and that "special attention is devoted to working with churches of major Negro denominations, who are not yet members of the Board." The program would place trainees with civil rights organizations "to test projects which are unproven" and create "a body of knowledge with respect to Urban Church strategy."[39] The grant proposal sought to address racial discrimination in the North by training African American clergy and laymen to engage in community organizing and direct-action protests in their own communities.

Although most foundations would have dismissed such a proposal as too radical in August 1965, it arrived for review at the Ford Foundation at an opportune moment. By the mid-1960s, the Ford Foundation's $3.3 billion endowment was the largest of any foundation in the country. Thus, the Foundation "could afford to be ambitious and experimental." Moreover, the Foundation not only decided to fund activist-based projects but also increasingly supported separatist "social development" for blacks as a vehicle for social change. Historian Karen Ferguson's analysis of the Foundation has shown how this approach, rooted in modernization theory and the supposed cultural backwardness of African Americans, presented a way for white liberals to retreat from de facto integration. Yet the foundation nonetheless created a "conceptual convergence" that "would provide the Foundation with a link to the demand for self-determination voiced by black power advocates."[40]

The Ford Foundation grant accelerated the UTC's transformation to expand its leadership and training to African Americans. Upon receiving the Ford grant, the UTC hired C. T. Vivian as director of fellowships and internships. Vivian, a minister from western Illinois, had emerged as a civil rights leader during the Nashville sit-in campaign in 1960. He had faced off with sheriff Jim Clark in Selma, taken part in Alabama voting rights demonstrations in 1965, and helped to integrate the beaches in St. Augustine, Florida, before moving to Chicago to work with the UTC and the Chicago Freedom Movement.[41] The Ford Foundation grant allowed him to control a new program for African American clergy and community organizers, converting the UTC from an ecumenical space for progressive (and mostly white) clergy to one of training for concerted urban activism by African Americans. The first year's program for these Ford trainees focused on the civil rights movement in North Carolina, but by the following year, the black trainees and clergy at the center, including southern transplants A. I. Dunlap from the African Methodist Church and a young Jesse Jackson fresh out of seminary, became increasingly concentrated on Chicago. It was no coincidence, for example, that James Bevel, a key minister in the SCLC, convinced the organization to focus its attention on Chicago, then spent an entire year with UTC training and developing contacts on the West Side of Chicago.[42] As director Morton explained to the UTC board in 1966, "The Center has changed significantly in the past year. Where it was once predominantly a federation of white, Protestant denominations, it is now working in a meaningful way beyond the original limitations [with] the major Negro denominations. This has come about not by the efforts of the churches, but through a secular organization, the Ford Foundation."[43]

In addition to maintaining its close relationship with the WSO, the UTC collaborated through "local mission projects" with South Side community organizations such as Operation Breadbasket of SCLC and the Woodlawn Organization, and other West Side community-action organizations in East Garfield Park and Lawndale neighborhoods.[44] Meanwhile, inside the classroom, UTC hosted "Issue Seminars" including urban policy, civil rights, and poverty as well as unique subject areas such as an Alley Theater workshop by Oscar Brown Jr., "The New Revolution in Jazz" seminar by disc jockey and record producer Sid McCoy, and "The Youth Gang in Sociological Perspective" by teacher and activist Earl Doty.[45] The UTC was thus becoming a multifaceted organization led by African Americans in service to their own communities.

Doty's seminar on the "Systematic Review of Gang Theory from the Chicago School to the Present" fostered coordination between the UTC and Chicago's youth organizations, otherwise known as the Blackstone Rangers, Conservative Vice Lords, and Disciples street gangs. In June 1966, the UTC helped organize a gang summit at the Blackstone Hotel in Chicago's South Loop. This meeting, in which Hargraves presided, featured a speech by Dr. King to the gang representatives. He asked them to reorient themselves to fight Chicago's power structure rather than each other. "Power in Chicago," he said, "means getting the largest political machine in the nation to say yes when it wants to say no."[46] Although this concerted gang activity did not come to fruition during King's Chicago campaign, it would become essential to the Black Power Movement in the late 1960s as their representatives became a common sight at the UTC office on Ashland Avenue.

In a 1966 article called "The New Theology," the *Tribune* noted how the UTC trained "new style theologians" who seemed "intense" as strategists but also "reluctant to pull rank on the unchurched."[47] Stanley Hallett, a white Methodist UTC teacher, reflected, "There's a tendency in a movement to go with the flow and respond to problems—we were trying to think ahead" to build "in a discipline that's not externally imposed but that's in the nature of the work, because then everyone can see how the little piece they're doing is crucial."[48] But Archie Hargraves forewarned that the UTC had to craft new programming and act before the urban crisis exploded and history washed over them. Consulting with the board of the UTC, he said in the spring: "The community may erupt. The Rangers may shoot up the Disciples. And the police are going to pressure and somebody's going to get hurt. . . . Somebody's going to move into housing and you're going to have a ruckus around that" unless "we begin to conceptualize around the basis of happenings" in Chicago.[49]

In consultation with the UTC staff, Hargraves crafted a forward-looking proposal called the Chicago Action Training (CAT) to begin in 1968. Bringing together African American clergy and activists under the rubric of Black Power, the CAT departed from previous training methods. Yet Black Power was not a new concept at the UTC. Director James Morton recalled that Archie Hargraves had been emphasizing race-based power in debates over the curriculum from his first days at the UTC. Indeed, in one such exchange, Hargraves concluded: "We're talking about a particular organization of a community. . . . Power is what we are really talking about." Talk of power in terms of black unity accelerated in the fall of 1967 when the center had hosted Ron Karenga and a group of black nationalists from Los Angeles. Through a series of workshops, Karenga and other Black Power advocates debated black separatism with James Bevel of SCLC and other civil rights activists. "UTC was perhaps . . . unique . . . in America," one white minister surmised, because "the issues surrounding Black Power were debated in the open by such a diverse group."[50]

The design of CAT reflected these debates by taking Black Power's ideas and applying them to the UTC's mission to attack the urban crisis. CAT number one included black men "who are leaders of community organizations, black power groups, cultural organizations, and 'teen nations.'" The second CAT featured training specifically for black clergy. A third CAT, designed for white clergy in both black areas of Chicago and the suburbs, focused on neutralizing forms of "white power" that perpetuated institutional racism. Through these bold projects, CAT sought to bring black militants and clergy into a coalition, not for talk about integration or abstract notions of equality of opportunity, but, as Vivian explained, to get them "beyond a survival ethic" so they could wield power in their neighborhoods and across the Chicago metro area.[51]

The CAT programs brought a whole new cast of characters into the UTC. The involvement of black neighborhood leaders and gang members initially "scared-to-death" the secretarial staff (for example, a lit cigarette was placed in the mouth of a statue of Jesus on the cross), but after a while, their presence led to mutual respect and "brooked no opposition" to the rules of the office and library.[52] Through a rigorous schedule of meetings, training, and actions, participants worked to develop unity within black Chicago's communities that could serve as the first step toward claiming power citywide. The CAT sought transformation through Black Power on both a neighborhood and citywide level, which produced a new process for integration in American society.

The first CAT finished in March 1968, a tumultuous month in Chicago and nationwide. As an outgrowth of their three months of training, the participants created the Black Consortium to sustain a coalition between black community leaders, militants, youth, and clergy at the UTC. Yet just one week later, as the director of mission development explained, "Martin Luther King, Jr. was assassinated and Chicago's West Side went up in flames." UTC staff and trainees worked to quell the violence by taking to the streets of the West Side and calling for calm. When four UTC members were charged with arson during the riots, its ministers vigorously defended them as "political prisoners," which drew extra attention from Chicago's Red Squad police division. The events of April 1968 confirmed to the CAT activists that black unity was an urgent necessity to attack economic disfranchisement, which SCLC had tried to make visible with its national Poor People's Campaign—an effort that many at the UTC joined.[53] As important, the UTC staff envisioned new CATs through a specific definition of Black Power: the right of black people to "make decisions about their own community" and direct "public and private programs" through a "primary role in shaping the direction . . . of the larger society."[54] Thus, CAT leaders saw Black Power as emanating from organizing local neighborhoods but also in stitching neighborhood groups together to produce citywide results.

Independence and Interdependence

UTC leaders reasoned that black independence had to presage any attempt at meaningful integration or partnership between blacks and whites. Thus, they pursued racial separation.[55] White clergy and staff affirmed this approach but wondered what role it left them. In short order, CAT and the Black Consortium had transformed the trainers into the trainees, forcing them to relinquish their expertise and listen to their African American colleagues Vivian and Hargraves as well as the community activists who came from Chicago's poorest neighborhoods. As director Morton explained, the past year of CAT trainings had added "white racism" to our "working vocabulary."[56] New CATs for white clergy now emphasized neutralizing "white power" and training social workers, journalists, and lawyers to play key supporting roles. Out of these discussions, UTC leaders formed the Committee for One Society (COS), a new group premised on understanding that the "crisis" changed "the cry of the American Negro . . . from 'Freedom' to 'Power.'" The new committee, according to its founding documents, "will concentrate on the role of the White citizen who accepts the positive contribution of Black Power and does not know what to do." The committee condemned white-dominated institutions—including the UTC itself—as institutionally racist in response to charges levied by former UTC Ford Fellow Calvin Lockridge and other Black Power activists. Its members sought to understand how institutions consciously and unconsciously prevented racial equality and then to restructure them in concert with other Protestant, Catholic, and Jewish organizations as coalition partners.[57] In short, COS took seriously the call by Black Power advocates for white activists to stop thinking about the "Negro Problem" in favor of exposing and attacking their own institutional racism that they determined was the true cause of the urban crisis in Chicago.

Across the hall from the office of the COS at 40 North Ashland, another independent branch of the UTC emerged: A Black Strategy Center (ABC). This center would supplement the Black Consortium as a think tank and power broker between white political and business leaders and the West and South Side communities of Chicago. No longer would white liberals act as liaisons to these African American neighborhoods. Instead, the ABC would lead in consultation with the Committee for One Society and the UTC.[58] This move proved significant because ABC was designed to effectively provide more decision-making power for African American ministers, laypeople, and community activists.

Between the ABC proposal and its creation, the Coalition for United Community Action (CUCA) had emerged from the Black Consortium as an unprecedented and respected citywide representation of African American activist groups in Chicago. CUCA focused on economic power, and after an initial experiment in campaigning for employment at Red Rooster supermarkets in black neighborhoods, it expanded to take on the entire building-trades industry of contractors, unions, and political allies who had prevented African Americans from being employed in these lucrative construction jobs. In 1969, CUCA shut down millions of dollars of construction projects in Chicago, forced the federal government to form an ad hoc committee to investigate violations of affirmative action statutes, and brought the Democratic machine and all of the parties involved to the negotiating table for what became the "Chicago Plan."[59]

In 1969, ABC did not seem like a dream but a necessity if blacks were to continue to wield significant, unified power against the institutions that had for so long shut them out in Chicago.[60] In August, C. T. Vivian and Archie Hargraves joined Gaylord Freeman, the chairman of the First National Bank, and Arthur Wood, the president of Sears, Roebuck and Company at the downtown Chicago Club to persuade business leaders it was in their own best interest to support the new Strategy Center. "You, the leaders of Chicago business," Freeman explained, "have a very large corporate stake in the city of Chicago. You have offices, plants, stores, investments, and customers here." And statistics showed that the city would become majority black in the next few years, so putting financial resources into black Chicago was a healthy business investment, not charity. Hargraves followed by explaining that independence was a prerequisite for interdependence because "Black Power is the first item on the agenda [but] the long-range goal is not to withdraw or separate but to gain enough unified strength to inject new and needed black perspectives into the affairs and systems of this metropolis." Arthur Wood of Sears ended the meeting by asking these men to take out their checkbooks, saying this "isn't a big investment" considering the importance for the long-term stability of the city of Chicago. Five firms had already committed $25,000 each, he boasted, and he wanted Chicago Club members to fund the new ABC's $800,000 budget.[61] With this financial backing, the UTC's black-led coalition strove to open jobs and create pathways for upward mobility for African Americans.

The UTC's new emphasis on promoting Black Power while fighting institutional racism made great strides, but only for a short time. The Black Strategy Center made significant headway in 1968 and 1969 but ended abruptly in 1970. Paradoxically, its quick demise was a direct effect of the "good faith" that seemed to be the operating agenda for these programs. Parallel to the Chicago Plan that promised but did not deliver thousands of new jobs, the financial resources that were initially committed quickly evaporated. The ABC only received funding for one year as white corporate donors balked at fostering black radicalism. The Ford grant lost funding in 1971 when the Foundation concluded that the project should have become self-sustaining after five years through its own financial resources. The evaporation of funding forced the UTC to revert to its previous allegiance to major white Christian denominations and the programming changed as a result. These churches had less interest in sponsoring militant-activist training, especially under the Nixon administration's emphasis away from War on Poverty programs in favor of explanations of inner-city pathology and black capitalism. "I think it was a plan," UTC trainee and activist Sally Johnson reflected, "of getting gangs off the streets . . . to plan strategy." But, she concluded, "It was all a fake" because "we forgot one thing. [The white financiers] gave us no program money. . . . So you pay everybody a salary and your money is gone . . . so the support group didn't do us a favor, they did us harm." To Johnson and other blacks at the UTC, white church leaders encouraged the activists to expand their agenda, but then withdrew the resources they needed in order to carry it out.[62]

Meanwhile, some white activists within the UTC became overly deferential in the movement for racial justice. With their presence in black activist networks suspect, they began to see themselves as part of the problem as much as the solution to the urban crisis. The formation of the COS was a bold decision to expose and attack institutional racism, but this process sometimes hit too close to home when the battle stretched into the suburbs, or when "sent home to work on white racism, some of us no longer had homes," or when COS discovered institutional racism in the institutions of its allies, including its own parent institution, the UTC. By turning the lens on themselves, these UTC activists engaged in important work to root out institutional racism, but this process sometimes led to a level of racial deference that was problematic, both tactically and ethically. "I thought I was going crazy," Peggy Way remembered of these last days at the UTC and in the COS. "I sat and heard some of our paid speakers talk about killing and burning and watched us clap. I participated in paying street gang members to take our UTC students into ghettoes and 'understood' when they purposely lost them there and delighted in having ripped us off—again."[63] Certainly, the African American leadership in the UTC did not endorse these destructive tactics, and it only made their efforts more difficult when their white colleagues fell silent.

These internal racial tensions were then exacerbated when police surveillance turned into coordinated aggression. The Gang Intelligence Unit of the Chicago Red Squad increased it's harassment, CUCA leaders complained, against those activists and gang members who had become most involved in protest politics; some were arrested on trumped-up charges and tried in a special new "terrorist court." Others were shot by the police, signified most tragically with the murder of Black Panther leader Fred Hampton in December 1969.[64] By March 1970, the representatives of the Blackstone Rangers at the Black Strategy Center demanded money for attorneys and bail for its members, who had increasingly engaged in criminal activity to sustain themselves when other economic avenues never materialized.[65] The emphasis on police brutality shifted the movement away from economic justice and back to mere survival, and the UTC, absent Vivian and Hargraves by 1970, decided to refocus its attention on the important but less provocative issue of community health.[66]

Conclusion: Freed Spaces and Tested Faith

In the late 1960s, UTC director James Morton reflected on the UTC's campaigns against the intertwined urban crises of widespread racism and poverty. On the one hand, their accomplishments seemed modest. He said, "Each morning [when I] see the unchanged crumby block that surrounds us at 40 North Ashland . . . one voice insists: *show me any difference.*" But one aspect of the UTC's significance begins to come into focus when it is understood as what social-movement theorists have termed a "free space." In their 1986 book, Sara Evans and Harry Boyte explored how "under certain conditions communal associations become free spaces, breeding grounds for democratic change." These spaces, they concluded, "must . . . be relatively autonomous" places "between private life and large-scale institutions" where people "may broaden their sense of the possible, make alliances with others, develop practical skills and knowledge to maintain democratic organization."[67] In part, the UTC's lack of outward progress obscures the significant internal work UTC staffers first performed upon themselves. For many of the white clergy on staff, Morton concluded, "The beginning of wisdom" came from "the sober admission that *we have learned* what there was *to unlearn.*"[68]

The UTC's unique story undermines the assumption that northern cities had plenty of spaces for activists to congregate due to a lack of conspicuous

Jim Crow. Rather, the space for dialogue and congregation across race and religious denominations provided by the UTC was rare, even in Chicago. Chicago Freedom Movement leader Jesse Jackson, for example, noted with dismay the large number of ministers who closed their church doors when Martin Luther King Jr. and the national SCLC concentrated on Chicago in 1966 and 1967. Some of these reticent ministers feared retribution from the Democratic political machine famously controlled by Mayor Richard J. Daley since the mid-1950s. As African American activists observed, the machine's "plantation politics" stymied adequate political representation in black communities as its loyal political army—including aldermen, building inspectors, and the Chicago Red Squad and Gang Intelligence Unit of the police department as well as people who did business with the city—clamped down on activists and their spaces of congregation. As one prominent example, a mortgage broker suddenly revoked the loan for the construction of a new church at 45th and Princeton because its South Side black minister, the Reverend Clay Evans, supported the Chicago Freedom Movement. For seven years the unfinished foundation of his church remained as a symbol of city elites' stranglehold on even private spaces and served as a warning to those who sought to challenge the urban racial order.[69] Backed by denominational and grant support, the UTC did not suffer the same consequences. Yet, eventually, its funding also dried up as church leaders and foundations increasingly withdrew their support for its urban training in the early 1970s.

But during the vital and experimental years between 1964 and 1970, the UTC's freed space made it paradoxically more relevant and irrelevant. White UTC leaders learned from their experiences how to become servants to civil rights and put faith in Black Power, but in so doing, they had to downplay religion in their training and activism in order to attract black activists to their programs. Other ministers reproached the UTC members as nothing more than "community organizers in clerical collars" because "all they care about there is getting where the action is, not about the Christian sources."[70] Thus, while UTC leaders themselves drew inspiration from their theological backgrounds—especially that "identification with the poor is indeed a requirement of faith"—they also seemed to lose their collective identity as religious leaders in the process.

This paradox laid bare the ambiguous role of white ministers and laypeople in the black freedom struggle. The history of the UTC is in part a story of how white denominations funded a movement of sympathetic white progressive clergy to stay in the civil rights and Black Power Movements of the 1960s. But at the end of their workday, none of the white staff members lived on the West Side of Chicago, and some of the top leaders retreated to their vacation homes and left the programming to the junior staff members during the summer. As such, their lives sometimes seemed to contradict their own visions, and some expressed regret at fostering a solipsistic "subculture" that prevented them from moving "beyond them long enough to experience the pluralisms that we conceptualize."[71]

Other UTC ministers and trainees embraced the "pluralisms" to serve grassroots movements. They tried to leave their egos at the door in order to allow poor people to lead themselves. But this servant role could also become problematic if taken too far. Perhaps fueled by white liberal guilt, some UTC members sometimes marginalized themselves, especially in their reaction to Black Power in the late 1960s. As UTC leader Richard Luecke wrote, "Something more than 'joining' is required when participation is needed in many sectors of the society at once—as it seems the case in the modern city."[72] But extreme racial and class deference made them less trainers and strategists than joiners and bystanders. Their inability to participate based on the courage of their convictions actually compromised the very free space they had helped to create, which helps explain the disillusionment and trauma felt by some activists in trying to formulate new directions for social justice in the 1970s and beyond.

Even so, the UTC efforts resonated beyond its immediate community, and many participants became empowered by its training and engagement in social movements. More than one thousand official students and hundreds of other activists had passed through its doors. Further, twenty-two other training centers and many churches adopted the Chicago model of "engagement/involvement" that encompassed the transition from "rhetoric that proceeds from nitty gritty to RADICALIZATION" to "action."[73] Thus, UTC staff's concern that they fell short of their increasingly revolutionary goals in the late 1960s should not obscure the center's importance historically or today. As Stan Hallett of the UTC more recently recalled, "It's hard to remember that back in those days the church was a loud, articulate voice for justice. Our era now has very few sources of moral authority."[74] The UTC's history opens a window into the complex spaces and forms of interaction between religious activists and social movements of the 1960s—dynamics that are typically downplayed in postwar American urban history.

As a central space of protest formulation, action, and reflection, the UTC and its history suggests revisions to current narratives of Chicago's 1960s protest movements and the religious institutions and ideas that shaped them. Its programs provided critical support to organizations like the WSO, Operation Breadbasket, and other black community formations in the understudied West

Side as well as the South Side. The UTC also participated in the Chicago Freedom Movement of 1965 to 1967, and its white clergy remained active in the organization even *after* 1967 when they came to believe that a radical restructuring of society, through the application of Black Power, had become an urgent necessity. Thus, the UTC activism reached its culmination between 1968 and 1970, with its Black Power vision as an articulate and pragmatic challenge to Chicago's power structure as expressed through the Black Consortium, COS, ABC, and CUCA.

Overall, the UTC's history reveals how a network of religious leaders struggled to understand their changing context and to shape it into a hospitable urban climate for those most oppressed by it. While some UTC ministers and trainees may have surrendered their own religious and ethical direction by the end of the decade, this reflected the nature of their commitment. Their strategy of serving others provided opportunities for African Americans and other organic intellectuals to strategize and lead, which created a remarkable if temporary space where a diverse group of Chicagoans dared to imagine and work toward a more egalitarian metropolis.

Notes

Thanks to David Goldberg, Ibram X. Kendi (formerly Rogers), Calvin Morris, Kerry Pimblott, Katherine Turk, and Peggy Way for conversations about and scholarship on social movements and religion.

1. Archie Hargraves, "The Church and the Urban Crisis," *Renewal* 9, no. 6 (June 1969): 7–10.

2. Richard Luecke, *Perchings: Reflections on Society and Ministry* (Chicago: Urban Training Center Press, 1972), 18.

3. "Urban Mission Gets $415,000 5-Year Grant," *Chicago Tribune*, 15 July 1964; Kay Beldon Winterowd, "The Role of Para-Ecclesial Agencies in the Renewal of the Church and Society: An Analytical Study of the Mission Training Programs of Three Models" (PhD diss., Southern Baptist Theological Seminary, Louisville, KY, August 1971), 100–152.

4. "Is God Dead: Toward a Hidden God," *Time* 87, no. 14 (April 8, 1966).

5. See Aldon Morris, *The Origins of the Civil Rights Movement: Black Communities Organizing for Change* (New York: Free Press, 1984); and Charles Payne, *I've Got the Light of Freedom: The Organizing Tradition and the Mississippi Freedom Struggle* (Berkeley: University of California Press, 1999). Historian James Ralph noted the opposition of white Southwest Side churches and retaliation against ministers in Chicago who supported civil rights as well as how many black churches refused to support the movement. See Ralph, *Northern Protest: Martin Luther King, Jr., Chicago, and the Civil Rights Movement* (Cambridge, MA: Harvard University Press, 1993), 4, 67, 73–74, 128, 137, 204, and 264 n. 73.

6. See Ibram Rogers, "The Black Religious Movement: A Historic Mid-Twentieth-Century Synthesis of Black Religiosity, Nationalism, and Activism," *Journal of Gender and Cultural Critiques* 21, no. 1 (Spring 2009): 1–22.

7. See Mark L. Chapman, *Christianity on Trial: African-American Religious Thought before and after Black Power* (Maryknoll, NY: Orbis Books, 1996); C. Eric Lincoln and Lawrence H. Mamiya, *The Black Church in the African American Experience* (Durham, NC: Duke University Press, 1990); Angela Dillard, *Faith in the City: Preaching Radical Social Change in Detroit* (Ann Arbor: University of Michigan Press, 2007); James Forman, *The Making of Black Revolutionaries* (Seattle: University of Washington Press, 1972 [2000]); Robert S. Lecky and H. Elliott Wright, *Black Manifesto: Religion, Racism, and Reparations* (New York: Sheed and Ward, 1969); James H. Cone, *Back Theology and Black Power* (New York: Seabury Press, 1969); and Albert B. Cleage Jr., *The Black Messiah* (New York: Sheed and Ward, 1968).

8. Luecke, *Perchings*, 16.

9. Roger Shinn, United Church of Christ, "Mandate for the Churches," n.d. (early 1960s), folder 9, box 143, series 1, Institute on the Church in an Urban-Industrial Society records, Special Collections and University Archives, University of Illinois at Chicago (hereafter ICUIS). See also Beryl Satter, *Family Properties: How the Struggle over Race and Real Estate Transformed Chicago and Urban America* (New York: Metropolitan Books, 2009); and Amanda Seligman, *Block by Block: Neighborhoods and Public Policy on Chicago's West Side* (Chicago: University of Chicago Press, 2005).

10. Gibson Winter, *The Suburban Captivity of the Churches: An Analysis of Protestant Responsibility in the Expanding Metropolis* (New York: Macmillan, 1962), passim and quotes from 190–93.

11. "Report of the President to the Directors," appendix H to 26 May 1966 UTC board meeting minutes, folder 681, box 43, series 2, ICUIS.

12. "Clergy: School for a New Creation," *Time*, 19 November 1965; Serge Schmemann and Boris Nicoloff, interview with James Morton, "The Church in/and Society," *Concern* 3, no. 2 (Spring 1968), reprint in folder 1332, box 77, series 2, ICUIS; James Morton, "A Theological Basis for an Urban Church Strategy," address at the Meeting of Evangelical Executives, Harrisburg, PA, 20 September 1965, folder 393, box 28, series 1, ICUIS; and Richard Philbrick, "Religious News Notes," *Chicago Tribune*, 1 June 1972.

13. Interreligious Council on Urban Affairs, interim report on Community Organization of Englewood, 13 September 1968, folder 95, box 6, series 1, ICUIS.

14. Stephen Rose, "Our Stake in the City's Future," *United Church Herald*, 1965, copy in folder 1200, box 72, series 2, ICUIS; and Robert Friendly, "For Christ's Sake ... What Is the Church Doing?," *World Call*, July–August 1966, copy in folder 693, box 45, ICUIS.

15. UTC, "The Now Thing," pamphlet, 1966, copy in United Library, Northwestern University, Evanston, IL (hereafter NU).

16. Niles Carpenter, UTC trainee, to Betsey Carpenter, 1 July 1965, folder 766, box 51, series 2, ICUIS.

17. "The Plunge," *Newsweek* 65 (15 February 1965), and Morton quoted in "Clergy: School for a New Creation," *Time* 86, no. 21 (19 November 1965).

18. Kenan Hiese, "A Brutal Primer on Being Poor in Chicago," *National Catholic Reporter*, 2 June 1965, and "Inside the Inner City," *Episcopalian*, April 1965.

19. Peggy Way, telephone interview with author, 26 May 2014; UTC, "The Now Thing," pamphlet, 1966, NU.

20. UTC, "Five Years of UTC Students: 1964–1968," folder 1159, box 71, series 2, ICUIS.

21. Mel Reynolds, "Tribute to J. Archie Hargraves," *Congressional Record* 140, no. 66 (24 May 1994): E; Robert Handy, *A History of the Union Theological Seminary in New York* (New York: Columbia University Press, 1987), 252–53; Glenn T. Miller, *Piety and Profession: American Protestant Theological Education, 1870–1970* (Grand Rapids, MI: William B. Eerdmans, 2007), 610.

22. Don Benedict, *Born Again Radical* (New York: Pilgrim, 1982), 60, 68–69; Archie Hargraves, "Stop Pussyfooting through a Revolution: Some Churches That Did" (Philadelphia: United Church of Christ Stewardship Council, 1963), 2–3.

23. Robert Friendly, "For Christ's Sake . . . What Is the Church Doing?," *World Call*, July–August 1966, copy in folder 693, box 45, series 2, ICUIS.

24. Hargraves and Siegenthaler quoted in UTC, meeting minutes of the curriculum committee, 22–23 January 1965, folder 980, box 48B, series 2, ICUIS.

25. Lawrence Witmer and Gibson Winter, "Strategies of Power in Community Organizations," March 1968, manuscript in folder 661, box 42, series 2, ICUIS; William Elllis, *White Ethnics and Black Power: The Emergence of the West Side Organization* (Chicago: Aldine, 1969); and Jo Freeman, "On the Origins of the Women's Liberation Movement from a Strictly Personal Perspective," available at http://www.uic.edu/orgs/cwluherstory/CWLUMemoir/freeman.html, accessed January 2014.

26. David Hunter, Stern Family Fund, to James P. Morton, UTC, 3 August 1965, and UTC, Board of Directors Minutes, May 1965, both in folder 680, box 43, series 2, UCUIS. WSO information reports, flyers, and letters from 1964, file 147, Red Squad Papers, Chicago History Museum (hereafter CRS).

27. See "Female Help Wanted" section in *Chicago Defender*, daily edition, passim but, for example, see 8 April 1965, 36. Perhaps due to frequent advertisements in the *Defender*, the paper only made one passing mention to the Centennial strike; see Brenetta Howell, "West Side Round Up," 7, and "Pickets Air Truckers Bias," 11, *Chicago Defender*, national edition, 24 October 1964.

28. See "West Side Development Corporation" brochure, n.d. (1969), folder 139, box 9, series 1, ICUIS; and A. L. Lincoln and Eliot House, Harvard College, excerpts from "New Unionism: An Analysis of Militant Community Organizations in Chicago," folder 431, box 29, series 1, ICUIS.

29. Lawrence Witmer and Gibson Winter, "Strategies of Power in Community Organizations," 21 March 1968, folder 661, box 42, series 1, ICUIS papers.

30. UTC, Board Meeting Minutes and appendix B, 26 May 1966, folder 681, box 43, and Board Meeting Minutes, 28–29 June 1969, folder 664, box 44, series 2, ICUIS;

Lincoln and House, excerpts from "New Unionism: An Analysis of Militant Community Organizations in Chicago," folder 431, box 29, series 1, ICUIS; and Premilla Nadasen, *Welfare Warriors: The Welfare Rights Movement in the United States* (New York: Routledge, 2005), 3, 21.

31. Hargraves quoted in UTC, Board Meeting Minutes, 26 May 1966, and appendix B and H, all in folder 681, box 43, series 2, ICUIS; James Morton to UTC Board, 22 July 1966, folder 692, box 45, series 2, ICUIS; and quotes in Benedict, *Born Again Radical*, 143 and 138, 157.

32. Benedict, *Born Again Radical*, 156–57; Bernard Brown, *Ideology and Community Action: The West Side Organization of Chicago, 1964–1967* (Chicago: Center for the Scientific Study of Religion, 1978), 93–96.

33. Witmer and Winter, "Strategies of Power in Community Organizations"; CCCO delegates meeting agenda, 2 April 1966, folder 104, box 63, series 2, ICUIS. See also Ralph, *Northern Protest*, 109–13; Benedict, *Born Again Radical*, 177–82.

34. "100 from City to Be in Selma March Today," *Chicago Tribune*, 9 March 1965; UTC, Consultation on Training for Ministries in the Freedom Movement, 14 April 1965, folder 679, box 43, series 2, UCUIS.

35. UTC, Consultation on Training for Mass Community Organization Center, 15 April 1965, folder 679, box 43, series 2, UCUIS; Attorney Donald S. Frey, Motion to Consolidate Cases, First Municipal Court of Cook County, Summer 1965, folder 749, box 50, series 2, ICUIS; and Niles Carpenter, UTC trainee, to Betsey Carpenter, 1 July 1965, folder 766, box 51, series 2, ICUIS.

36. Saul Alinsky, *Reveille for Radicals* (Chicago: University of Chicago Press, 1946); Bob Hercules and Bruce Orenstein, "The Democratic Promise: Saul Alinsky and His Legacy," documentary film (Chicago: Berkeley Media, 1999); Sanford Horwitt, *Let Them Call Me Rebel: Saul Alinsky, His Life and Legacy* (New York: Knopf, 1989); Archie Hargraves, UTC curriculum, "Power and the American Negro," 23 November 1964, folder 749, box 50, series 2, ICUIS; and UTC, Consultation on Training for Mass Community Organization Center, 15 April 1965, folder 679, box 43, series 2, ICUIS.

37. Lutheran Minister Walter Kloetzli resigned from the UTC board over its organizing tactics. See Board Meeting Minutes, 13 December 1965, folder 680, box 43, series 2, ICUIS; UTC, Special Two-Day Consultation, 28–29 March 1969, folder 710, box 47, series 2, ICUIS; and Observations from Evaluation Session, 27 January 1967, folder 1334, box 78, series 2, ICUIS; Benedict, *Born Again Radical*, 160.

38. "Clergy: School for a New Creation," *Time*, 19 November 1965; Joseph Merchant, UTC board chairman, quoted in "The Plunge," *Newsweek*, 15 February 1965.

39. UTC, letter accompanying Ford Foundation application, 2 August 1965, and Ford Foundation to the UTC, 29 September 1965, both in folder 680, box 43, series 2, ICUIS.

40. Karen Ferguson, *Top Down: The Ford Foundation, Black Power, and the Reinvention of Racial Liberalism* (Philadelphia: University of Pennsylvania Press, 2013), 10–11 and 50–51.

41. Lydia Walker, *Challenge and Change: The Story of Civil Rights Activist C. T. Vivian* (Alpharetta, GA: Dreamkeeper Press, 1993); Tom Valentine, "Black Curfew Leader a Fighter," *Chicago Today*, 18 December 1969; and "Mission Given $600,000 for Fellowships," *Chicago Tribune*, 27 October 1965.

42. C. T. Vivian, "Mission Development," *UTC Newsletter*, Christmas 1965, 6, NU; UTC, "Report on the Ford Fellows," folder 681, box 43, "Report on Disbursement within Technical Assistant Program of Ford Grant," 1 January 1966 to 31 October 1967, folder 697, box 46, Board Meeting Minutes, 1 June 1967, folder 684, box 44, all series 2, ICUIS; "King's 'Action Team' Leads Tough Human Rights Drive," *Los Angeles Times*, 28 February 1968.

43. James Morton, *UTC Newsletter*, Summer 1966, 14, NU.

44. UTC, Board Meeting Minutes and appendix B, 26 May 1966, folder 681, box 43, series 2, ICUIS.

45. UTC, Board Meeting Minutes and appendices, 24 January 1967, folder 684, box 44, series 2, ICUIS. The UTC also hosted nine workshops on gangs through its Ford Program in 1967. See "Report on Disbursement within Technical Assistance Program of Ford Grant," 31 October 1967, folder 697, box 46, series 2, ICUIS.

46. Betty Washington, "SCLC Organizing Youth Gangs City Wide," *Chicago Daily Defender*, 13 June 1966, 3.

47. Martin Marty, "The New Theology: A Rocky Road to Relevance," *Chicago Tribune*, 17 July 1966, M16.

48. Hallett in William Wimsatt, "Anonymous Benefactor," *Chicago Reader*, 26 March 1998, available at http://www.chicagoreader.com/chicago/anonymous-benefactor/Content?oid=895912, accessed May 2015.

49. Archie Hargraves, "Comments on the Proposed Consultation," UTC meeting minutes, 18 May 1967, folder 752, box 52, series 2, ICUIS.

50. Hargraves, UTC curriculum, "Power and the American Negro," 23 November 1964, folder 749, box 50, series 2; UTC, Consultation on Training for Mass Community Organization Center, 15 April 1965, folder 679, box 43, series 2; Morton, UTC Board of Directors, 1 June 1967, folder 687, box 44, series 2; Morton, "Report of the Director," and Richard Luecke, "Comments on Curriculum, 1967–1968," January 1968, folder 971, box 47b, series 2, all ICUIS.

51. Board Meeting Minutes, 1 June 1967, folder 684, box 44; C. T. Vivian report, Board Meeting Minutes, 7–8 June 1968, folder 684, box 44, and trainee lists, folder 696, box 46, all series 2, ICUIS; and Winterowd, "Role of Para-Ecclesial Agencies," 116–17.

52. Elanie Bradpher, "The Bradpher Memoirs," *UTC Newsletter*, Fall 1968, 58.

53. Betty Washington, "Poor Marchers Get Big Sendoff," *Chicago Daily Defender*, 9 May 1968. See also Gordon Mantler, *Power to the Poor: Black-Brown Coalition and the Fight for Economic Justice* (Chapel Hill: University of North Carolina Press, 2013).

54. Report of the Director of Mission Development, n.d. (1968), folder 697, box 46, series 2, IUICS.

55. C. T. Vivian, "The New Model: Interdependence," *UTC Newsletter*, Fall 1968, 30–32.

56. James Morton, "Remarks of Director," *UTC Newsletter*, Fall 1968, 3.

57. UTC, "Committee for One Society" pamphlet, n.d. (Summer 1968), NU; Calvin Lockridge, "Letters," *Chicago Tribune*, 8 December 1968.

58. James Morton, "Remarks of Director," *UTC Newsletter*, Fall 1968, 6.

59. See Erik S. Gellman, "'The Stone Wall Behind': The Chicago Coalition for Community Action and Labor's Overseers, 1968–1973," in *Black Power at Work: Community Control, Affirmative Action, and the Construction Industry*, ed. Trevor Griffey and David Goldberg (Ithaca, NY: Cornell University Press, 2010), 112–33.

60. See "Beyond UTC," *UTC Newsletter*, Summer 1969, 27–29.

61. "A Black Center for Strategy, Training and Community Development," 25 August 1969 Chicago Club meeting, copy attached to information report, Black Center for Strategy, 29 August 1969, file 149, CRS.

62. Sally Johnson, interview with author, Chicago, 13 April 2005; Ferguson, *Top Down*, 13.

63. Peggy Way, "A Personal Essay: Public Ministries in Memory and Hope—Clarifying the Legacy," in *Belief in Ethics, Human Sciences and Ministry in Honor of W. Alvin Pitcher*, ed. W. Widick Schroeder and Gibson Winter (Chicago: Center for the Scientific Study of Religion, 1978), quotes from 377 and 379.

64. See Gellman, "'Stone Wall Behind.'"

65. See information report, 19 March 1970, folder 1158-C, box 238, CRS.

66. Winterowd, "Role of Para-Ecclesial Agencies," 125.

67. Sara Evans and Harry Boyte, *Free Spaces: The Sources of Democratic Change in America* (New York: Harper and Row, 1986), 187, 188, 202.

68. "Remarks of Director," *UTC Newsletter*, Fall 1968, NU, 4.

69. See William Grimshaw, *Bitter Fruit: Black Politics and the Chicago Machine, 1931–1991* (Chicago: University of Chicago Press, 1992); Frederick C. Harris, "Black Churches and Machine Politics in Chicago," in *Black Churches and Local Politics: Clergy Influence, Organizational Partnerships, and Civic Empowerment*, ed. R. Drew Smith and Fredrick C. Harris (Lanham, MD: Rowman and Littlefield, 2005), 124–26; and Benedict, *Born Again Radical*, 212.

70. Luecke, *Perchings*, 60, 132.

71. Way, "Personal Essay," 382.

72. Luecke, *Perchings*, 82.

73. Morton, "Remarks of Director," *UTC Newsletter*, Fall 1968, 2.

74. Wimsatt, "Anonymous Benefactor," *Chicago Reader*, 26 March 1998, available at http://www.chicagoreader.com/chicago/anonymous-benefactor/Content?oid=895912, accessed May 2015.

Contributors

CHRISTOPHER D. CANTWELL is an assistant professor of history and religious studies at the University of Missouri–Kansas City. He is currently completing a manuscript for publication titled "The Bible Class Teacher: Christianity and Capitalism in the Age of Fundamentalism."

HEATH W. CARTER is an assistant professor of history at Valparaiso University. He is the author of *Union Made: Working People and the Rise of Social Christianity in Chicago* (Oxford University Press, 2015).

JANINE GIORDANO DRAKE is an assistant professor of history at the University of Great Falls. She is currently completing a book manuscript titled "They Have Stolen Jesus From Us: Christian Socialism and the American Protestant Churches, 1880–1920."

KEN FONES-WOLF is the Stuart and Joyce Robbins Professor of History at West Virginia University. With Elizabeth Fones-Wolf he is the author of *Struggle for the Soul of the Postwar South,* published by the University of Illinois Press (2015).

ERIK S. GELLMAN is an associate professor of history at Roosevelt University in Chicago. He is the author of *Death Blow to Jim Crow: The National Negro Congress and the Rise of Militant Civil Rights* (2012) and, with coauthor Jarod Roll, *The Gospel of the Working Class: Labor's Southern Prophets in New Deal*

America (2011). His current manuscript focuses on social-protest networks in Chicago during the late 1960s.

ALISON COLLIS GREENE is an assistant professor of history at Mississippi State University. She is the author of *No Depression in Heaven: The Great Depression, the New Deal, and the Transformation of Religion in the Delta* (Oxford University Press, 2016).

BRETT HENDRICKSON is an assistant professor of religious studies at Lafayette College in Easton, Pennsylvania. He specializes in Mexican American religious history, religion and healing, and metaphysical religions. Hendrickson is the author of *Border Medicine: A Transcultural History of Mexican American Curanderismo* (New York University Press, 2014). He is currently at work on a history of the Santuario de Chimayó in New Mexico.

DAN MCKANAN is the Emerson Senior Lecturer at Harvard Divinity School, where he has taught since 2008. His most recent book is *Prophetic Encounters: Religion and the American Radical Tradition* (Beacon, 2011).

MATTHEW PEHL is an assistant professor of history at Augustana University in Sioux Falls, South Dakota. His first book, *The Making of Working-Class Religion*, is forthcoming from the University of Illinois Press.

KERRY L. PIMBLOTT is an assistant professor of African American and diaspora studies and history at the University of Wyoming. Her research interests include African American social movements, black nationalism and radicalism, and religious cultures and institutions. Pimblott is currently working on a book manuscript under contract with University Press of Kentucky, titled *Between the Bible and the Gun in Little Egypt: Black Power and Black Theology in Cairo, Illinois, 1969–74,* that chronicles the black church's overlooked contributions to the Black Power struggles of the late 1960s and early 1970s.

JAROD ROLL is an associate professor of history at the University of Mississippi. He is the author of *Spirit of Rebellion: Labor and Religion in the New Cotton South* and the coauthor, with Erik S. Gellman, of *The Gospel of the Working Class: Labor's Southern Prophets in New Deal America*, both published by the University of Illinois Press.

ARLENE SÁNCHEZ-WALSH is an associate professor of religious studies at Azusa Pacific University. She is the author of the award-winning book *Latino Pentecostal Identity: Evangelical Faith, Self, and Society.* She has authored more than a dozen articles and book chapters on the subject of Latino/Latina Pentecostalism, and has served as a media expert for outlets such as the *New York Times, Wall Street Journal,* and *On Being* with Krista Tippett, and has served as an expert on Latino/Latina religious history for the PBS series *God in America.* Sánchez-Walsh's current projects include a textbook on Pentecostalism in America and a monograph on race, ethnicity, and the prosperity gospel. Her current research is on deconversion and the growth of secular Latino/Latina millennials.

EVELYN STERNE is an associate professor and director of graduate studies in the Department of History at the University of Rhode Island. The author of *Ballots and Bibles: Ethnic Politics and the Catholic Church in Providence,* she currently is writing about evangelical Christians in twentieth-century New England.

Index

Stephens, Uriah, 29
St. Michael's Catholic Club, 57
Strangers in Our Fields (Galarza), 195
Streeby, Shelley, 35
Student Nonviolent Coordinating Committee (SNCC), 124, 125, 127
subsidiarity, 199
Sue, Eugene, 37, 44
suffrage, 51, 53; black, 30. *See also* voting

Tafolla, Carmen, 163, 164
Tenayuca, Emma, 145, 146, 148–150, 155–164; and Catholicism, 149–151, 155, 158, 160, 164; and Communism, 146, 150, 151, 155, 158, 160–162, 164
Tenayuca, Sharyll Sto, 162
"Ten Commandments for Labor," 63
Tentler, Leslie Woodcock, 57
theology, of working-class evangelicals, 101
Theosophical Society, 32
Theosophy, 26, 29–30
Thompson, E. P., vii; *The Making of the English Working Class*, vii
Trade Union Gospel (Fones-Wolf), 90
Trascendentalism, 26
Tyrrell County, N.C., 167–174, 178, 183, 184

unemployment, black, 119, 120, 125, 126, 134
Union of Catholic Parish Clubs, 57–58
unions, credit, 173, 174
Union Worker Magazine, 63
United Automobile Workers (UAW), 96, 99, 102, 104, 109
United Cannery, Agricultural, Packing, and Allied Workers of America (UCAPAWA), 148, 160
United Citizens for Community Action (UCCA), 131
United Farm Workers (UFW), 10, 193, 203, 205, 206
United Front, 115–116, 128–133
United Mine Workers, 10
United Nations Relief and Rehabilitation Administration (UNRRA), 177
United States, the, 43
Urban Training Center for Christian Mission (UTC), 211–214, 216–225, 227–232

Vargas, Zaragosa, 147, 150, 161, 164
Vicari, Fr. Vincenzo, 65–66
Vivian, C.T., 222–223, 226, 227, 229
Vizzard, James, 204
voting, 51, 53; black, 30; for immigrants vs. native-born citizens, 52–53; and land ownership requirements, 52. *See also* suffrage

WAAC (Women's Army Auxiliary Corps), 163
Wacker, Grant, 83
Waisbrooker, Lois, 44
Walsh, Rev. Richard, 56
Ward, Cyrenus Osborne, 37
Ward Chapel AME, 118, 122–125
Washington, George, 28
Washington, Joseph, 106
Way, Peggy, 228
Webb City, assembly of, 80
Weber, Max, 5
welfare, 218
Welks, Arthur, 122
Western Federation of Miners (WFM), 80, 89
West Side Organization for Full Employment (WSO), 217–220, 223
wetbacks, 194
White, Bouck, 37
White, Hugh, 98
White Citizen's Council, 131
Whitman, Walt, 33
Wiley, Efton, 87, 88, 89
Wiley, Everett, 87, 88, 89
Winter, Gibson, 214; *Suburban Captivity of the Churches, The*, 214
women, 56, 64, 67–68, 108, 109. *See also* gender
Wood, Arthur, 227
Woodhull, Victoria, 29
Workers Alliance, 156, 158, 161, 163
Workshop on Cooperative Living, 179
Works Progress Administration (WPA), 121
World War, First, 68

Young, Andrew, 220

THE WORKING CLASS IN AMERICAN HISTORY

The University of Illinois Press
is a founding member of the
Association of American University Presses.

University of Illinois Press
1325 South Oak Street
Champaign, IL 61820-6903
www.press.uillinois.edu